MANAGERIAL ECONOMICS

MANAGERIAL ECONOMICS

Bhavna Bahuguna

CENTRUM PRESS
NEW DELHI-110002 (INDIA)

CENTRUM PRESS

H.O.: 4360/4, Ansari Road, Daryaganj,
New Delhi-110002 (India)
Tel: 23278000, 23261597, 23255577, 23286875

B.O.: No. 1015, Ist Main Road, BSK IIIrd Stage,
IIIrd Phase, IIIrd Block, Bangalore-560085 (INDIA)
Tel: 080-41723429

Email: centrumpress@gmail.com
Visit us at: www.centrumpress.com

Managerial Economics

First Edition, 2011

ISBN 978-93-80921-00-6

PRINTED IN INDIA

Printed at Balaji Offset, Delhi.

Contents

Preface

'Managerial Economics' is designed to meet the needs of students who have to study some economics as part of their business course. It is a book about economics that focuses on those principles and analytic tools developed by economists that are important for an understanding of the business world.

This book describes the several functions that managers perform: planning, organizing, staffing, directing, motivating, controlling, decision-making, and measuring performance. In these usually lengthy descriptions of what management consists of the treatment of conceptual ideas is superficial and incomplete. Business management is both an art and a science; there are elements of both. In many areas of business, however, relatively few large enterprises command a disproportionately large share of trade and in these large enterprises management is collective, impersonal, and more dependent on applied science in most of its functions. This tendency has received reinforcement from the increasing maturity of management as an academic discipline. In the past quarter-century or so, the pace of new developments in management science, statistics, finance, and accounting, originating in the business schools, has considerably quickened.

Author

1

Introduction to Managerial Economics

MANAGERIAL ECONOMICS

Managerial economics is a branch of economics that applies microeconomic analysis to decision methods of businesses or other management units. As such, it bridges economic theory and economics in practice. It draws heavily from quantitative techniques such as regression analysis and correlation, Lagrangian calculus. If there is a unifying theme that runs through most of managerial economics it is the attempt to optimize business decisions given the firm's objectives and given constraints imposed by scarcity, *for example through the use of operations research and programming.*

Almost any business decision can be analysed with managerial economics techniques, but it is most commonly applied to:

- *Risk analysis*: Various models are used to quantify risk and asymmetric information and to employ them in decision rules to manage risk.
- *Production analysis*: Microeconomic techniques are used to analyse production efficiency, optimum factor allocation, costs, economies of scale and to estimate the firm's cost function.
- *Pricing analysis*: Microeconomic techniques are used to analyse various pricing decisions including transfer pricing, joint product pricing, price discrimination, price elasticity estimations, and choosing the optimum pricing method.

- *Capital budgeting*: Investment theory is used to examine a firm's capital purchasing decisions.

At universities, the subject is taught primarily to advanced undergraduates and graduate business schools. It is approached as an integration subject. That is, it integrates many concepts from a wide variety of prerequisite courses. In many countries it is possible to read for a degree in Business Economics which often covers managerial economics, financial economics, game theory, business forecasting and industrial economics.

THE MANAGERIAL DECISION-MAKING PROCESS

Managerial economics applies economic theory and methods to business and administrative decision making. Managerial economics prescribes rules for improving managerial decisions. Managerial economics also helps managers recognize how economic forces affect organizations and describes the economic consequences of managerial behaviour.

It links traditional economics with the decision sciences to develop vital tools for managerial decision making. This process is illustrated in Figure. Managerial economics identifies ways to efficiently achieve goals. *For example, suppose a small business seeks rapid growth to reach a size that permits efficient use of national media advertising*. Managerial economics can be used to identify pricing and production strategies to help meet this short-run objective quickly and effectively.

Similarly, managerial economics provides production and marketing rules that permit the company to maximize net profits once it has achieved growth objectives.

Managerial economics has applications in both profit and not-for-profit sectors. *For example, an administrator of a nonprofit hospital strives to provide the best medical care possible given limited medical staff, equipment, and related resources*. Using the tools and concepts of managerial economics, the administrator can determine the optimal allocation of these limited resources. In short, managerial economics helps managers arrive at a set of operating rules that aid in the efficient use of scarce human and capital resources.

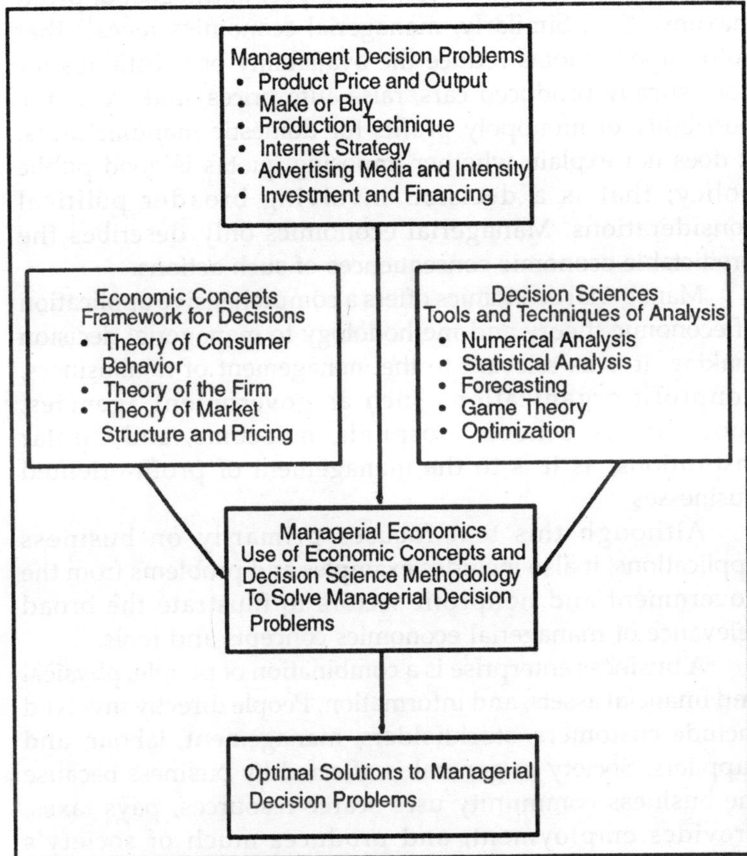

Fig. The Role of Managerial Economics in Managerial Decision-Making

By following these rules, businesses, nonprofit organizations, and government agencies are able to meet objectives efficiently. To establish appropriate decision rules, managers must understand the economic environment in which they operate. *For example, a grocery retailer may offer consumers a highly price-sensitive product, such as milk, at an extremely low markup over cost—1%or 2%—while offering less price-sensitive products, such as nonprescription drugs, at markups of as high as 40% over cost*. Managerial economics describes the logic of this pricing practice with respect to the goal of profit maximization. Similarly, managerial economics reveals that auto import quotas reduce the availability of substitutes for domestically produced cars, raise auto prices, and create the possibility of monopoly profits for domestic manufacturers. It does not explain whether imposing quotas is good public policy; that is a decision involving broader political considerations. Managerial economics only describes the predictable economic consequences of such actions.

Managerial economics offers a comprehensive application of economic theory and methodology to managerial decision making. It is as relevant to the management of nonbusiness, nonprofit organizations such as government agencies, cooperatives, schools, hospitals, museums, and similar institutions, as it is to the management of profit-oriented businesses.

Although this text focuses primarily on business applications, it also includes examples and problems from the government and nonprofit sectors to illustrate the broad relevance of managerial economics concepts and tools.

A business enterprise is a combination of people, physical and financial assets, and information. People directly involved include customers, stockholders, management, labour, and suppliers. Society in general is affected by business because the business community uses scarce resources, pays taxes, provides employment, and produces much of society's material and services output. Firms exist because they are useful for producing and distributing goods and services. They are economic entities and are best analysed in the context of an economic model. The model of business is called the theory of the firm. In its simplest version, the firm is thought to have profit maximization as its primary goal. The firm's ownermanager is assumed to be working to maximize the firm's short-run profits. Today, the emphasis on profits has been broadened to encompass uncertainty and the time value of money. In this more complete model, the primary goal of the firm is longterm expected value maximization.

SCOPE OF MANAGERIAL ECONOMICS

Managerial Economics deals with allocating the scarce resources in a manner that minimizes the cost. As we have already discussed, Managerial Economics is different from microeconomics and macro-economics. Managerial Economics has a more narrow scope - it is actually solving managerial issues using micro-economics. Wherever there are scarce resources, managerial economics ensures that managers make effective and efficient decisions concerning customers, suppliers, competitors as well as within an organization.

The fact of scarcity of resources gives rise to three fundamental questions:

1 What to produce?

2 How to produce?

3 For whom to produce?

The first question relates to what goods and services should be produced and in what amount/quantities. The managers use demand theory for deciding this. The demand theory examines consumer behaviour with respect to the kind of purchases they would like to make currently and in future; the factors influencing purchase and consumption of a specific good or service; the impact of change in these factors on the demand of that specific good or service; and the goods or services which consumers might not purchase and consume in future. In order to decide the amount of goods and services to be produced, the managers use methods of demand forecasting.

The second question relates to how to produce goods and services. The firm has now to choose among different alternative techniques of production. It has to make decision regarding purchase of raw materials, capital equipments, manpower, etc. The managers can use various managerial economics tools such as production and cost analysis, project appraisal methods, etc., for making these crucial decisions.

The third question is regarding who should consume and claim the goods and services produced by the firm. The firm, for instance, must decide which is it's niche market-domestic or foreign? It must segment the market. It must conduct a thorough analysis of market structure and thus take price and output decisions depending upon the type of market.

Managerial economics helps in decision-making as it involves logical thinking. Moreover, by studying simple models, managers can deal with more complex and practical situations. Also, a general approach is implemented. Managerial Economics take a wider picture of firm, i.e., it deals with questions such as what is a firm, what are the firm's objectives, and what forces push the firm towards profit and away from profit. In short, managerial economics emphasizes upon the firm, the decisions relating to individual firms and the environment in which the firm operates. It deals with key issues such as what conditions favour entry and exit of firms in market, why are people paid well in some jobs and not so well in other jobs, etc. Managerial Economics is a great rational and analytical tool. Managerial Economics is not only applicable to profit-making business organizations, but also to non- profit organizations such as hospitals, schools, government agencies, etc.

PRINCIPLES OF MANAGERIAL ECONOMICS

Economic principles assist in rational reasoning and defined thinking.

They develop logical ability and strength of a manager. Some important principles of managerial economics are:

- *Marginal and Incremental Principle*: This principle states that a decision is said to be rational and sound if given the firm's objective of profit maximization, it leads to increase in profit, which is in either of two scenarios:
  - If total revenue increases more than total cost.
  - If total revenue declines less than total cost.

  Marginal analysis implies judging the impact of a unit change in one variable on the other. Marginal generally refers to small changes. Marginal revenue is change in total revenue per unit change in output sold. Marginal cost refers to change in total costs per unit change in output produced.The decision of a firm to change the price would depend upon the resulting impact/change in marginal revenue and marginal cost. If the marginal revenue is greater than the marginal cost, then the firm should bring about the change in price.

- Incremental analysis differs from marginal analysis only in that it analysis the change in the firm's performance for a given managerial decision, whereas marginal analysis often is generated by a change in outputs or inputs. Incremental analysis is generalization of marginal concept. It refers to changes in cost and revenue due to a policy change. *For example, adding a new business, buying new inputs, processing products, etc.* Change in output due to change in process, product or investment is considered as incremental change. Incremental principle states that a decision is profitable if revenue increases more than costs; if costs reduce more than revenues; if increase in some revenues is more than decrease in others; and if decrease in some costs is greater than increase in others.
- *Equi-marginal Principle*: Marginal Utility is the utility derived from the additional unit of a commodity consumed. The laws of equi-marginal utility states that a consumer will reach the stage of equilibrium when the marginal utilities of various commodities he consumes are equal. The modern economists, this law has been formulated in form of law of proportional marginal utility. It states that the consumer will spend his money-income on different goods in such a way that the marginal utility of each good is proportional to its price, i.e.,

  $MUx/ Px = MUy/ Py = MUz/ Pz$

  Where, MU represents marginal utility and P is the price of good. Similarly, a producer who wants to maximize profit will use the technique of production which satisfies the following condition:

MRP1/ MC1 = MRP2/ MC2 = MRP3/ MC3

Where, MRP is marginal revenue product of inputs and MC represents marginal cost.

Thus, a manger can make rational decision by allocating/hiring resources in a manner which equalizes the ratio of marginal returns and marginal costs of varicus use of resources in a specific use.

- *Opportunity Cost Principle*: By opportunity cost of a decision is meant the sacrifice of alternatives required by that decision. If there are no sacrifices, there is no cost. Opportunity cost principle, a firm can hire a factor of production if and only if that factor earns a reward in that occupation/job equal or greater than it's opportunity cost. Opportunity cost is the minimum price that would be necessary to retain a factor-service in it's given use. It is also defined as the cost of sacrificed alternatives. For instance, a person chooses to forgo his present lucrative job which offers him Rs.50000 per month, and organizes his own business. The opportunity lost will be the opportunity cost of running his own business.
- *Time Perspective Principle*: This principle, a manger/ decision maker should give due emphasis, both to short-term and long-term impact of his decisions, giving apt significance to the different time periods before reaching any decision. Short-run refers to a time period in which some factors are fixed while others are variable. The production can be increased by increasing the quantity of variable factors. While long-run is a time period in which all factors of production can become variable. Entry and exit of seller firms can take place easily. From consumers point of view, short-run refers to a period in which they respond to the changes in price, given the taste and preferences of the consumers, while long-run is a time period in which the consumers have enough time to respond to price changes by varying their tastes and preferences.

- *Discounting Principle*: This principle, if a decision affects costs and revenues in long-run, all those costs and revenues must be discounted to present values before valid comparison of alternatives is possible. This is essential because a rupee worth of money at a future date is not worth a rupee today. Money actually has time value. Discounting can be defined as a process used to transform future dollars into an equivalent number of present dollars. For instance, $1 invested today at 10% interest is equivalent to $1.10 next year.

  $FV = PV^*(1+r)^t$

  Where, FV is the future value, PV is the present value (value at t0, r is the discount (interest) rate, and t is the time between the future value and present value.

ECONOMIC CONCEPTS

Scarcity: There exist only a finite amount of resources—human and non-human. Nature does not freely provide as much of everything as people want.

Resources: Are Scarce: Inputs used in the production of goods and services,

- *Land*: Original fertility and mineral deposits, topography, climate, water, and vegetation
- *Labour*: Contributions of humans who work
- *Capital*: All manufactured resources including buildings, equipment, machines, and improvements to land 4th factor? Entrepreneurship—human activity of raising capital, organizing, managing, assembling other factors of production, and making basic business policy decisions.

Economics: Social science studying how individuals make choices about the use of resources in order to satisfy needs. Scarcity requires Choice.

Economics is the study of how we make those choices:

- Use models or theories (simplified representations (abstraction) of the real world used to make predictions or to better understand the world)

- *Models are based on assumptions*: must decide on the usefulness of the model
  - *Microeconomics*: study of the economic behaviour of households and firms and how prices of goods and services are determined
  - *Macroeconomics*: is the study of economywide phenomena resulting from group decision making in entire markets. Deals with economy as a whole.
  - Positive versus Normative Economics
  - *Positive*: purely descriptive statements or scientific predictions
  - *Normative*: Value judgements about economic policies; relates to whether things are good or bad. What ought to be.
  - *Opportunity Cost*: The highest valued alternative that must be sacrificed to attain something or satisfy a want.
- Does not depend on who might use the resource but is the resource's highest value in any of the alternative uses not chosen
- *Production Possibilities Curve*: A curve representing all possible combinations of total output that could be produced assuming:
  - A fixed amount of productive resources
  - The efficient use of those resources

Assumptions:

- Referring to output possible over a specified time period
- Resources are fixed over the time period

DEMAND AND SUPPLY CONCEPTS

Demand

Law of demand: At higher prices, a lower quantity will be demanded than at lower prices, other things being equal. Alternatively, at lower prices, a higher quantity will be demanded, other things being equal.

Reasons why observe law of demand:

- *Substitution effect*: tendency of people to substitute in favour of cheaper commodities
- *Real-income effect*: change in purchasing power that occurs when the price of a good changes

Determinants of Demand

The major nonprice determinants of demand are:

- Income,
- Tastes and preferences,
- The price of related goods,
- Changes in expectations of future relative prices, and
- population (i.e., market size).

The major nonprice determinants of supply are:

- Input costs,
- Technology,
- Taxes and subsidies,
- Expectations of future relative prices, and
- The number of firms in the industry.

Substitutes: a change in the price of one causes a shift in demand for the other in the same direction

Complements:

- A change in the price of one good causes a shift in demand for the other in the opposite direction
- Distinguish between Changes in Demand and Changes in Quantity Demanded
- *Change in Demand*: Results from change in a non-price determinant of demand
- *Change in Quantity Demanded*: Results from change in price

Supply

Law of Supply: At higher prices, a larger quantity will generally be supplied than at lower prices, all other things being equal.

Reasons why observe supply law:

- Higher prices increase incentives for increasing production

- The law of increasing costs

Non-Price Determinants of Supply

- The prices of inputs used to produce the product
- Technology
- Taxes and subsidies
- Price Expectations
- Number of Firms

Distinguish between Changes in Supply and Changes in Quantity Supplied:

- *Change in Supply*: Results from change in a non-price determinant of supply
- *Change in Quantity Supplied*: Results from change in price

SUPPLY AND DEMAND TOGETHER

- *Equilibrium*: A situation in which the plans of the buyers and sellers coincide so that there is neither excess quantity supplied or demanded
- *Stable equilibrium*: A situation in which a shock disturbs the prevailing equilibrium between supply and demand, there will normally be self-corrective forces that automatically cause the disequilibrium to return eventually to equilibrium
- *Shortage*: Excess quantity demanded or insufficient quantity supplied. Difference between the quantity demanded and supplied at a specific price below the market clearing price.
- *Surplus*: Excess quantity supplied or insufficient quantity demanded. Difference between the quantity supplied and demanded at a price above the market clearing price.

THE MARKET OR PRICE SYSTEM AND EFFICIENCY

Scarcity requires that decisions be made about how resour*ces are to be allocated*

Resource allocation is solved by economic system:

- What and how much will be produced
- How will it be produced
- From whom will it be produced

Market—abstract concept concerning all the arrangements that individuals have exchanging with one another:

- *Transaction costs*: All the costs associated with exchanging, including the informational costs of finding out price and quality, service record, durability, etc. of a product, plus the cost of contracting and enforcing that contract

Concepts:

- Specialization results in higher outputs
- Individuals and nations specialize in their comparative advantages in order to reap benefits of specialization
- Comparative advantages are found by determining which activities have lowest opportunity cost or alternatively stated, the activities that yield the highest return for the time and resources used
- Individuals respond to changes in *relative* prices, not *absolute* prices, therefore, changes in the general price level must be purged from the analysis
- In a market economy, businesses seek profits. In seeking profits, businesses move resources out of declining industries into expanding industries
- *Consumers are sovereign*: They votes with their dollars

Efficiency concepts:

- *Technical*:The utilization of the cheapest production technique for any give output rate; no outputs are willfully wasted
- *Economic*: The use of resources that generate the highest possible value of output as determined in the market economy by consumers

What the market or price system does:

- Leads to technical and economic efficiency
- Maximizes individual or personal freedom
- Can lead to economic growth because the rewards

What the market or price systems CANNOT Do—(market failures):

- Capture all the costs and benefits external to an exchange
- Produce adequate public goods
- Equalize income distribution
- Ensure competition

Characteristics of Perfect Competition:

- The product that is sold by the firms is homogeneous
- Any firm can enter or exit the industry without serious impediments
- There must be large number of buyers and sellers—they act independently and no one buyer or seller has any influence on price
- Must be adequate information about prices, qualities, sources of supply

PRICE ELASTICITY OF DEMAND

The elasticity of demand is a measure of the price responsiveness to the quantity demanded and is equal to the percentage change in quantity demanded divided by the percentage change in price. Because the elasticity of demand can vary depending on whether one moves up or down the demand curve, elasticities of demand are often calculated by taking an average the prices and quantities given by the following formula: e_d = change in Q/ change in P

$$(Q_1 + Q_2)/2 \ (P_1 + P_2)/2$$

Determinants of price elasticity of demand:

- Existence of substitutes—the closer the substitutes for a particular commodity, the greater will be its price elasticity of demand
- Importance of the commodity in the consumers budget—the greater the percentage of a total budget spent on the commodity, the greater the person's price elasticity of demand for that commodity
- Time for adjustment in rate of purchase—the longer any price change persists, the greater the price elasticity of demand

Must distinguish between the short run and the long run. *For example, short run price elasticity of demand for airline travel is.6 whereas it is 2.4 in the long run.*

FUNDAMENTAL CONCEPTS OF ECONOMICS

Utility

In economics the words utility and value are given an exact definite meaning which must be clearly understood, since in everyday speech they are used in different senses.

Briefly, utility is want-satisfying power. Any-thing which men want is said to possess utility. If only one man desires it, then it possesses utility to him, but not to others. If a thing is intensely desired it is said to possess great utility; the less intense the desire, the less the utility. Potatoes, for example, are greatly desired for food and thus possess great utility. Diamonds are greatly desired because of their beauty and on that account possess utility.

Utility and usefulness are not synonyms. American Beauty roses can scarcely be said to be useful, yet they are greatly desired and therefore possess great utility. No one doubts that the potato is a useful vegetable. Yet a peck of comparatively use-less diamonds could possess greater utility than several million bushels of potatoes, since men are willing to give much more for a single diamond than they are for many bushels of potatoes.

The word usefulness implies the attainment of some practical and desired end. A crutch under the arm of a lame man is properly called useful; to him also it possesses utility. The slender canes which young men sometimes carry nobody would call useful, yet to the young man they may possess perhaps as much utility as the crutch does to the lame man.

Sometimes economists use the word utility in a substantive sense. For example, if a thing possesses utility they sometimes speak of it as being a utility, by which they merely mean that it is something desired by man, something capable of gratifying a human want. It is well to note at the outset that the economist sometimes thinks of commodities as being a mass of utilities.

Kinds of Utility

For convenience economists classify utilities in relation to time, form and place. Ice, for example, possesses greater value in summer than in winter. Hence we may say that an ice house serves to increase the time utility of ice. Cold storage houses preserve utilities from decay, besides keeping them until they possess greater time utility. Manufacturers in general increase the value of raw materials by increasing their form utility, wood being more valuable in the form of a chair than in the form of a board. Merchants of all classes increase the place utilities of the goods they handle, and hence are the joint producers of their value along with the farmers and manufacturers.

Value

Some objects possessing utility are sup-plied by nature so generously that man has to make no effort ordinarily to get all he wants. Air and water, except in cities; are utilities of this sort. So often in many country districts are apples and berries. Economists are not concerned about things of this kind. They are interested only in those substances which are not freely available for those who want them and for the production of which a certain amount of labour is necessary. Substances of this kind are said to possess value or exchange power because they combine utility and scarcity. Of course, utility is the first pre-requisite of value, for nobody will give anything in exchange for what nobody wants. An substance can possess value only on condition that it possesses utility and exists in a quantity insufficient to satisfy the de-sires of those who want it.

Value and income are probably the two most important words in political economy. Men toil in order that they may get things possessing value, for from the possession of such things they derive the psychic income or mental satisfaction which each regards as most desirable.

Popularly the word value is used in many different senses. Men speak of the value of a good name, for example. A business concern values its reputation and good will. A fine singer will think of'his voice as having great value. If

Paderewski thru the negligence of a corporation should lose one of his fingers a court would be called on to pass on its value, yet he could not sell one of his fingers. Most economists use the word in the sense of purchasing power, ex-change power.

Economic Goods, or Wealth

In. order to escape from the confusion of thought into which the English classical economists fell thru the use of the word"wealth," modern economists employ it sparingly and use in its stead the phrase"economic goods," meaning thereby any commodity or material thing which possesses value. Desirable things that possess no value are called"free goods," because they are supplied by nature gratuitously. The great mass of goods which are bought and sold in the market are economic goods and these are the things in which the economist is especially interested. He wants to know why they differ in value, why they fluctuate in value, what are their costs of production, how they are marketed, and why they are wanted.

In the English classical school of political economy all these economic goods were called wealth, that word being defined as including every-thing that has value or exchange power. But the word"wealth" is very broadly used in common speech, and hence the ceases of the economists with regard to wealth are often misunderstood by the public. For example, Mr. Carnegie is known to be a man of great"wealth," owning as he does a large number of the bonds of the United States Steel Corporation. These bonds give him a claim upon a certain portion of the earnings of the corporation, but they are not wealth in the economic sense. The economist would not call them economic goods. They are merely legal claims on the income produced by certain economic goods owned by the stockholders of the United States Steel Corporation. To be technically correct, these bonds should be called property, not wealth. In the same way a share of Pennsylvania Railroad stock is property, not wealth; it is the holder's legal evidence that he has an ownership interest in the railroad and is entitled to share in the distribution of its earnings.

Welfare

Again the word wealth is often used as if it were related to, if not synonymous with, welfare. A man of wealth is often spoken of as"well-to-do," yet wealth and welfare are independent of each other. The word welfare implies happiness and contentment. Great wealth may bring neither of these to a man or to a nation. Indeed, it is quite possible that a social census, if one could be taken, would find more misery and discontent among the rich than among those people who are obliged to work every day for their living.

The Producer

The economist thinks of the human family as producers and consumers. All are consumers, for otherwise they would perish, and the vast majority of them are also producers, for by their daily labour they must earn their income. Since the problems of production and consumption are entirely different, the economist studies them separately, sometimes to such an extent that the unwary reader gets an idea that in economics certain classes of society are consumers and others are almost exclusively producers. This is of course an erroneous conception.

In a civilized country, like the United States or Canada, there are very few people who are not both producers and consumers. The so-called idle rich are numerically almost negligible. So are the other non-producing classes, such as the sick, the defectives, the aged and such criminals as are not given employment.

A producer is a person who creates utility or helps bring it into existence. The earliest producers known in the history of the human race were herders and farmers, and in the popular mind the farmer is still thought of as being the greatest of all producers, for he coaxes from the soil the grains and fruits and vegetables which support human life. He also supplies us with most of the meat we eat. The earth is, of course, the real producer. The farmer by his labour merely manipulates and directs natural forces. Economically he is in no greater degree a producer than the conductor of the freight train who hauls his crop to market, or any one of the wholesalers and retailers who pass it on to consumers.

Let us trace a bushel of wheat from Dakota until it appears in New York City in loaves of bread. The railroad hauls it to Minneapolis, where it possesses greater utility than in Dakota and therefore greater value, because the millers want it. The miller, who is a manufacturer, converts the wheat into flour, thus adding to its utility and value.

The railroad hauls it to New York, where it possesses more utility than in Minneapolis, being more in demand. The baker turns it into bread, adding thereby both to its utility and value, for it is now in the form demanded by the so-called ultimate consumers.

Some of the loaves may be sold to consumers by grocers who have, like the railroad, merely increased their place utility, for they have saved the consumer the labour of going to the more distant bakery.

Intangible Utilities

We have been considering thus far only the producers of tangible goods, that is, economic goods. How about the producers of intangible utility Is there such a thing as an intangible utility, one not embodied in a material commodity? If not, we certainly cannot call lawyers, doctors, teachers, preachers, actors and artists producers unless we can show that their services are somehow helpful in the production of material goods.

` This can easily be done in the case of bankers, teachers and physicians, and a pretty strong argument could be made in the preachers' favour, but as suggested, not stop now to discuss this phase of the question.

From the economic point of view all these classes of men are producers of utility, for their services give positive satisfaction to the persons from whom they get their income. When you are sick the services of a physician possess greater utility to you than almost any material good. When you are well and have the means and necessary leisure, you may wish to hear Caruso sing. One artist thru the ear, the other thru the eye as well, appeals to your esthetic sense and gives you greater satisfaction than you could possibly get from a farmer's potatoes and cabbages. To many devout people the services of the clergyman possess greater utility than the services of any other single class of workers; they would gladly turn farmers and produce their own food and clothing.

We may sum up, then, as follows: In an economic sense every man or woman is a producer whose labour tends to the gratification of human wants or to the increase of utilities, whether thru a service which increases the supply of economic goods or thru a service which in itself gives pleasure to the consumer.

The Consumer

We consume a utility when we get pleasure or gratification from it. In many cases the consumption Of a utility means the destruction of the commodity in which it is embodied. This is true of all kinds of food and beverages, as is illustrated in the old adage,"We cannot eat our cake and have it too." In the ease of clothing the period of consumption is much longer, depending upon the habits and occupation of the wearer. Many people consume a straw hat in one summer, yet a certain city editor in Chicago was distinguished, among other things, be-cause of his attachment to an old straw hat, which he wore for twenty summers and constantly in the office during the winter months.

A period of consumption is popularly known as the"life" of the commodity. In New York City, for instance, the life of a house is commonly estimated at twenty years, it being assumed that its utility in its existing form will disappear at the end of that period and that a new house will be wanted on the site. The life of a steel rail depends upon the amount of traffic hauled over it. The life of a book depends upon the care given it and the charm of its content. We consume an oil painting when we get pleasure from contemplating it. The life of the canvas depends upon the care given it. Marbles and bronzes, humanly speaking, last forever. They may be daily consumed but never destroyed.

Exchange

No exposition is necessary to make the reader understand the necessity for the exchange of economic goods. Nothing in business is more obvious than the fact that few people produce the goods which they consume. At the present time nearly every man is a specialist.

In the production of some substances the labour of thousands of men is employed; each receives his compensation in the form of money and then buys the substances which he desires to consume.

Thus exchange has become the most conspicuous feature of our modern civilization. Nearly all producers expect to market their product.

Barter

It is fair to assume that in prehistoric times, as is the case today in some savage tribes, there was little division of labour, each family being able to produce enough to satisfy its own needs.

The first exchange was doubtless in the form of barter, a fortunate fisherman being perhaps glad to give up part of his catch in return for berries and goat's milk. This exchange of goods for goods is known as barter and is obviously awkward and inconvenient.

Money

Not until money appeared was it possible for men to specialize in their labour and to begin the development of an exchange civilization, each man devoting himself to the task which gave him the greatest pleasure or in which he was most proficient. Money is the medium which made this advance possible. It is a thing wanted not for itself but because with it one can buy what one wants. In a sense it may be called a third commodity, standing between the thing we have and wish to sell and the thing we wish to get in exchange.

Money may be defined as an economic good which is universally desired in any community and which is universally acceptable as a means of payment for goods or services.

Credit

As modern business is conducted in most civilized countries, actual money is very little used. Men are satisfied to accept in lieu of it a mere promise to pay money. This promise is known as credit and it is founded on the rock of confidence.

If business men of the United States should lose confidence in one another, or in the government, or in the courts of law, the great credit system by which gigantic totals of wealth are daily exchanged would collapse, business would be at a standstill and great distress would ensue, the rich suffering as well as the poor..

Price

The universal use of money and credit in modern business gives great importance to the word price. Popularly this word is confused with value. Yet they have different meanings. The price of a thing is the amount of money it exchanges for or that is asked for it. The price of wheat shows the value of a bushel of wheat with respect to money. It gives us no idea of the value of wheat unless we know the prices of many other substances and thus can make comparison.

Distribution of Income

The subject matter to be touched on in this part is usually called "distribution of wealth," but that phrase is misleading, for the problem before us relates, not to the distribution of all of the country's wealth, but solely to the distribution or sharing of the new wealth daily created.

Into a nation's markets there is constantly pouring a stream of new commodities and out of the proceeds of their sale various people who have aided in their production must get their compensation, the labour his wage, the landlord his rent, the capitalist his interest, the business man or entrepreneur his profit. Roughly speaking the total of new wealth produced in the country in any year, sometimes called the national income, is divided among those four classes of society.

DISTINCTION BETWEEN MICRO-MACROECONOMICS

MICROECONOMICS

Microeconomics is a branch of economics that studies how the individual parts of the economy, the household and the firms, make decisions to allocate limited resources, typically in markets where goods or services are being bought and sold. Microeconomics examines how these decisions and behaviours affect the supply and demand for goods and services, which determines prices, and how prices, in turn, determine the supply and demand of goods and services.

This is a contrast to macroeconomics, which involves the"sum total of economic activity, dealing with the issues of growth, inflation, and unemployment. Microeconomics also deals with the effects of national economic policies on the before aspects of the economy. Particularly in the wake of the Lucas critique, much of modern macroeconomic theory has been built upon'microfoundations' - i.e. based upon basic assumptions about micro-level behaviour.

One of the goals of microeconomics is to analyse market mechanisms that establish relative prices amongst goods and services and allocation of limited resources amongst many alternative uses. Microeconomics analyses market failure, where markets fail to produce efficient results, and describes the theoretical conditions needed for perfect competition. Significant fields of study in microeconomics include general equilibrium, markets under asymmetric information, choice under uncertainty and economic applications of game theory. Also considered is the elasticity of products within the market system.

Assumptions and Definitions

The theory of supply and demand usually assumes that markets are perfectly competitive. This implies that there are many buyers and sellers in the market and none of them has the capacity to significantly influence prices of goods and services. In many real-life transactions, the assumption fails because some individual buyers or sellers have the ability to influence prices. Quite often a sophisticated analysis is required to understand the demand-supply equation of a good model. However, the theory works well in simple situations.

Mainstream economics does not assume a priori that markets are preferable to other forms of social organization. In fact, much analysis is devoted to cases where so-called market failures lead to resource allocation that is suboptimal by some standard. In such cases, economists may attempt to find policies that will avoid waste directly by government control, indirectly by regulation that induces market participants to act in a manner consistent with optimal welfare, or by creating"missing markets" to enable efficient trading where none had previously existed. This is studied in the field of collective action. It also must be noted that"optimal welfare" usually takes on a Paretian norm, which in its mathematical application of Kaldor-Hicks Method, does not stay consistent with the Utilitarian norm within the normative side of economics which studies collective action, namely public choice. Market failure in positive economics is limited in implications without mixing the belief of the economist and his or her theory.

The demand for various commodities by individuals is generally thought of as the outcome of a utility-maximizing process. The interpretation of this relationship between price and quantity demanded of a given good is that, given all the other goods and constraints, this set of choices is that one which makes the consumer happiest.

Modes of Operation

It is assumed that all firms are following rational decision-making, and will produce at the profit-maximizing output. Given this assumption, there are four categories in which a firm's profit may be considered.

- A firm is said to be making an economic profit when its average total cost is less than the price of each additional product at the profit-maximizing output. The economic profit is equal to the quantity output multiplied by the difference between the average total cost and the price.

- A firm is said to be making a normal profit when its economic profit equals zero. This occurs where average total cost equals price at the profit-maximizing output.
- If the price is between average total cost and average variable cost at the profit-maximizing output, then the firm is said to be in a loss-minimizing condition. The firm should still continue to produce, however, since its loss would be larger if it were to stop producing. By continuing production, the firm can offset its variable cost and at least part of its fixed cost, but by stopping completely it would lose the entirety of its fixed cost.
- If the price is below average variable cost at the profit-maximizing output, the firm should go into shutdown. Losses are minimized by not producing at all, since any production would not generate returns significant enough to offset any fixed cost and part of the variable cost. By not producing, the firm loses only its fixed cost. By losing this fixed cost the company faces a challenge. It must either exit the market or remain in the market and risk a complete loss.

Market Failure

In microeconomics, the term "market failure" does not mean that a given market has ceased functioning. Instead, a market failure is a situation in which a given market does not efficiently organize production or allocate goods and services to consumers.

Economists normally apply the term to situations where the assumptions of the First Welfare Theorem fail leading to the market outcome no longer being on the Pareto frontier. On the other hand, in a political context, stakeholders may use the term market failure to refer to situations where market forces do not serve the public interest.

The four main types or causes of market failure are:

- Monopolies or other cases of abuse of market power where a "single buyer or seller can exert significant influence over prices or output". Abuse of market power can be reduced by using antitrust regulations.
- Externalities, which occur in cases where the "market does not take into account the impact of an economic activity on outsiders." There are positive externalities and negative externalities. Positive externalities occur in cases such as when a television programme on family health improves the public's health. Negative externalities occur in cases such as when a company's processes pollutes air or waterways. Negative externalities can be reduced by using government regulations, taxes, or subsidies, or by using property rights to incentivize companies and individuals to take the impacts of their economic activity into account.
- Public goods are goods that have the characteristics that they are non-excludable and non-rivalrous and include national defence, public transportation, federal highways, and public health initiatives such as draining mosquito-breeding marshes. For example, if draining mosquito-breeding marshes was left to the private market, far fewer marshes would probably be drained. To provide a good supply of public goods, nations typically use taxes that compel all residents to pay for these public goods. This usually results in a government-run or sponsored monopoly to service the public good as a solution - though government monopolies often have the same social costs as private monopolies.
- Cases where there is asymmetric information or uncertainty. Information asymmetry occurs when one party to a transaction has more or better information than the other party. For example, used-car salespeople may know whether a used car has been used as a delivery vehicle or taxi, information that

may not be available to buyers. Typically it is the seller that knows more about the product than the buyer, but this is not always the case. An example of a situation where the buyer may have better information than the seller would be an estate sale of a house, as required by a last will and testament. A real estate broker buying this house may have more knowledge about the house than the family members of the deceased.

This situation was first described by Kenneth J. Arrow in a seminal substance on health care in 1963 entitled "Uncertainty and the Welfare Economics of Medical Care," in the *American Economic Review*. George Akerlof later used the term asymmetric information in his 1970 work *The Market for Lemons*. Akerlof noticed that, in such a market, the average value of the commodity tends to go down, even for those of perfectly good quality, because the buyer has no way of knowing whether the product they are buying will turn out to be a "lemon".

Opportunity Cost

Opportunity cost of an activity is equal to the best next alternative foregone. Although opportunity cost can be hard to quantify, the effect of opportunity cost is universal and very real on the individual level. In fact, this principle applies to all decisions, not just economic ones. Since the work of the Austrian economist Friedrich von Wieser, opportunity cost has been seen as the foundation of the marginal theory of value.

Opportunity cost is one way to measure the cost of something. Rather than merely identifying and adding the costs of a project, one may also identify the next best alternative way to spend the same amount of money. The forgone profit of this next best alternative is the opportunity cost of the original choice. A common example is a farmer that chooses to farm her or his land rather than rent it to neighbours, wherein the opportunity cost is the forgone profit from renting. In this case, the farmer may expect to generate more profit alone. Similarly, the opportunity cost of attending university is the lost wages a student could have earned in the workforce, rather than the cost of tuition, books, and other requisite items. The opportunity cost of a vacation in the Bahamas might be the down payment money for a house.

Note that opportunity cost is not the sum of the available alternatives, but rather the benefit of the single, best alternative. Possible opportunity costs of the city's decision to build the hospital on its vacant land are the loss of the land for a sporting centre, or the inability to use the land for a parking lot, or the money that could have been made from selling the land, or the loss of any of the various other possible uses—but not all of these in aggregate. The true opportunity cost would be the forgone profit of the most lucrative of those listed.

One question that arises here is how to assess the benefit of disse must determine a dollar value associated with each alternative to facilitate comparison and assess opportunity cost, which may be more or less difficult depending on the things we are trying to compare. For example, many decisions involve environmental impacts whose dollar value is difficult to assess because of scientific uncertainty. Valuing a human life or the economic impact of an Arctic oil spill involves making subjective choices with ethical implications.

It is imperative to understand that nothing is free. No matter what one chooses to do, he or she is always giving something up in return. An example of opportunity cost is deciding between going to a concert and doing homework. If one decides to go the concert, then he or she is giving up valuable time to study, but if he or she chooses to do homework then the cost is giving up the concert. Opportunity Cost is vital in understanding microeconomics and decisions that are made.

Applied Microeconomics

Applied microeconomics includes a range of specialized areas of study, many of which draw on methods from other fields. Applied work often uses little more than the basics of price theory, supply and demand. Industrial organization and regulation examines topics such as the entry and exit of firms, innovation, role of trademarks. Law and economics applies microeconomic principles to the selection and enforcement of competing legal regimes and their relative efficiencies. Labour economics examines wages, employment, and labour market dynamics.

Public finance examines the design of government tax and expenditure policies and economic effects of these policies. Political economy examines the role of political institutions in determining policy outcomes. Health economics examines the organization of health care systems, including the role of the health care workforce and health insurance programmes. Urban economics, which examines the challenges faced by cities, such as sprawl, air and water pollution, traffic congestion, and poverty, draws on the fields of urban geography and sociology. The field of financial economics examines topics such as the structure of optimal portfolios, the rate of return to capital, econometric analysis of security returns, and corporate financial behaviour. The field of economic history examines the evolution of the economy and economic institutions, using methods and techniques from the fields of economics, history, geography, sociology, psychology, and political science.

MACROECONOMICS

Macroeconomics is a branch of economics that deals with the performance, structure, behaviour and decision-making of the entire economy, be that a national, regional, or the global economy. Along with microeconomics, macroeconomics is one of the two most general fields in economics.

Macroeconomists study aggregated indicators such as GDP, unemployment rates, and price indices to understand how the whole economy functions. Macroeconomists develop models that explain the relationship between such factors as national income, output, consumption, unemployment, inflation, savings, investment, international trade and international finance. In contrast, microeconomics is primarily focused on the actions of individual agents, such as firms and consumers, and how their behaviour determines prices and quantities in specific markets. While macroeconomics is a broad field of study, there are two areas of research that are emblematic of the discipline: the attempt to understand the causes and consequences of short-run fluctuations in national income and the attempt to understand the determinants of long-run economic growth. Macroeconomic models and their forecasts are used by both governments and large corporations to assist in the development and evaluation of economic policy and business strategy.

Development of Macroeconomic Theory

The term"macroeconomics" stems from a similar usage of the term"macrosystem" by the Norwegian economist Ragnar Frisch in 1933. and there was a long existing effort to understand many of the broad elements of the field. It fused and extended the earlier study of business fluctuations and monetary economics.

Mark Blaug, a notable historian of economic thought, proclaimed in his"Great Economists before Keynes: 1986" that Swedish economist Knut Wicksell"more or less founded modern macroeconomics".

Macroeconomic Schools of Thought

The traditional distinction is between three different approaches to economics: Keynesian economics, focusing on demand; neoclassical economics based on rational expectations and efficient markets, and innovation economics focused on long-run growth through innovation. Keynesian thinkers challenge the ability of markets to be completely efficient generally arguing that prices and wages do not adjust well to economic shocks. None of the views are typically endorsed to the complete exclusion of the others, but most schools do emphasize one or the other approach as a theoretical foundation.

Keynesian Tradition

Keynesian economics was an academic theory heavily

influenced by the economist John Maynard Keynes. This period focused on aggregate demand to explain levels of unemployment and the business cycle. That is, business cycle fluctuations should be reduced through fiscal policy and monetary policy. Early Keynesian macroeconomics was "activist," calling for regular use of policy to stabilize the capitalist economy, while some Keynesians called for the use of incomes policies.

Neo-Keynesians combined Keynes thought with some neoclassical elements in the neoclassical synthesis. Neo-Keynesianism waned and was replaced by a new generation of models that made up New Keynesian economics, which developed partly in response to new classical economics. New Keynesianism strives to provide microeconomic foundations to Keynesian economics by showing how imperfect markets can justify demand management.

Post-Keynesian economics represents a dissent from mainstream Keynesian economics, emphasizing the importance of demand in the long run as well as the short, and the role of uncertainty, liquidity preference and the historical process in macroeconomics.

Neoclassical Tradition

For decades Keynesians and classical economists split in to autonomous areas, the former studying macroeconomics and the latter studying microeconomics. In the 1970s new classical macroeconomics challenged Keynesians to ground their macroeconomic theory in microeconomics. The main policy difference in this second stage of macroeconomics is an increased focus on monetary policy, such as interest rates and money supply. This school emerged during the 1970s with the Lucas critique. New classical macroeconomics based on rational expectations, which means that choices are made optimally considering time and uncertainty, and all markets are clearing. New classical macroeconomics is generally based on real business cycle models.

Monetarism, led by Milton Friedman, holds that inflation is always and everywhere a monetary phenomenon. It rejects fiscal policy because it leads to "crowding out" of the private sector. Further, it does not wish to combat inflation or deflation by means of active demand management as in Keynesian economics, but by means of monetary policy rules, such as keeping the rate of growth of the money supply constant over time.

Macroeconomic Policies

To try to avoid major economic shocks, such as The Great Depression, governments make adjustments through policy changes they hope will stabilize the economy. Governments believe the success of these adjustments is necessary to maintain stability and continue growth.

This economic management is achieved through two types of strategies:

- Fiscal policy
- Monetary policy

2

Demand Analysis

AN OVERVIEW

DEMAND

A market exists when buyers and sellers interact to exchange products. You might think that the easiest market to explore would be the interaction between one buyer and one seller. For example, suppose Crusoe has coconuts and would really like some fish, and Friday has fish and would really like some coconuts. There is the possibility for a mutually beneficial trade here, but we cannot predict what the price or quantity will be even if we know their preferences because the outcome depends on their relative bargaining skills. Hence, economic theory has little to tell us about this most simple of markets.

It is easier to analyse a market in which there are many buyers and sellers, each small relative to the overall market. It helps also if both buyers and sellers are well informed, and buyers and sellers form distinct and separate groups. To explain a market with these qualities, economists use supply and demand analysis. You should be aware that supply and demand analysis does not work in all markets. If buyers are a group distinct from the sellers, we can analyse how they act separately from how sellers act. Only after we have looked at these two groups separately will we combine them and see how they interact. As suggested, begin by looking at the buyers. What determines the amount of a product that people are willing and ready to buy during some period of time? For example, what determines the amount of hamburger purchased in Chicago during a week? Economists answer such questions by examining the costs and benefits of buying the product. When any of the costs or benefits changes, the amount of the product that people will buy should also change. The benefits a person gets from a product depend on his goals. These goals are referred to in many ways in discussions of demand. The words "tastes," "wants," "needs," "preferences," and "usefulness" all refer to goals.

When people's goals change, the amount of benefit they get from the good changes, and this will cause them to change the amount of the good they want to buy. Goals depend on many factors, such as the age of people and the amount of education they have. Social custom is an important determinant of preferences and can account for many differences in demand among groups. One can explain the large differences in squid sales in Japan and the United States, or the large differences in consumption of horse meat in Europe and the United States, almost entirely in terms of differences in preferences caused by differences in social custom.

The most obvious cost a person bears in buying a product is the price of the product. Price reflects cost because people have a limited amount of funds that they can spend, and if they spend their money on one thing, they cannot spend it on another. When the price of a product goes up, the amount of other things that a person must give up in order to buy the product rises. As a result, we expect people to buy more hamburger if the price is $1.00 per pound than if it is $2.00 per pound. The amount of income a person receives affects the cost of buying an item because it determines which options a person must give up when buying a product. If a person with a low income spends $5000 for a trip around the world, he will have to cut back on food, clothing, or shelter. The same trip will cause a person with a high income to cut back on a very different set of options.

Increases in people's incomes raise consumption of most products. These products are called normal goods. There are some products, however, that people use less of as their income increases; these products are called inferior goods. Public transportation is an example—as people's incomes rise, they stop riding the bus and drive their own cars. Blue jeans were once another example—people with higher incomes bought them less frequently than people with lower incomes. It was because they were a symbol of "working-class" clothes that they were adopted by the radical left in the 1960s, and from there they moved into high fashion.

Prices of related goods also influence how much of a product people buy. Goods that are substitutes satisfy the same set of goals or preferences. An example of a substitute for hamburger is pork. If pork prices are high, people are tempted to shift away from pork to hamburger, and if pork prices are low, people are tempted to shift from hamburger to pork. The opposite of a substitute is a complement, a good that helps complete another in some way. Catsup and hamburger buns are complements to hamburger, and if they are priced low enough, consumption of hamburger may rise. Sometimes goods are such good complements that they are sold together and we think of them as a single item. Left shoes and right shoes are an example.

There are other factors that influence the amount of a particular product that people are willing to buy, such as the number of consumers in the market and their expectations about future prices, incomes, and quality changes. To get a complete list for any product might be time consuming and difficult, but it is not necessary because we want to focus on the relationship between price and the quantity of a product that people are willing to buy during some interval of time. To do this, as suggested, assume that all other factors are held constant.

THE DEMAND CURVE

The relationship between price and the amount of a product people want to buy is what economists call the demand curve. This relationship is inverse or indirect because as price gets higher, people want less of a particular product.

This inverse relationship is almost always found in studies of particular products, and its very widespread occurrence has given it a special name: the law of demand. The word "law" in this case does not refer to a bill that the government has passed but to an observed regularity.[1]There are various ways to express the relationship between price and the quantity that people will buy. Mathematically, one can say that quantity demanded is a function of price, with other factors held constant, or:

$$Qd = f$$

A more elementary way to capture the relationship is in the form of a table. The numbers in the table are what one expects in a demand curve: as price goes up, the amount people are willing to buy decreases.

Table. A Demand Curve

Price ofWidgets	Number of WidgetsPeople Want to Buy
$1.00	100
$2.00	90
$3.00	70
$4.00	40

The same information can also be plotted on a graph, where it will look like the graph.

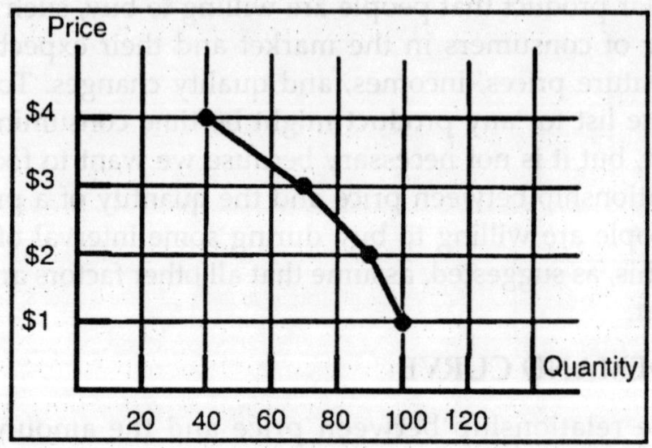

Fig. A Demand Curve Show How Price Influences the Amount People Want to Buy

If one of the factors being held constant becomes unstuck, changes, and then is held constant again, the relationship between price and quantity will change. For example, suppose the price of getwids, a substitute for widgets, falls. Then, people who previously were buying widgets will reconsider their choices, and some may decide to switch to getwids. This would be true at all possible prices for widgets. These changes in the way people will behave at each price will change the demand curve to look like the table.

Table. A Demand Curve Can Shift

Price ofWidgets	Number of WidgetsPeople Want to Buy
$1.00	[100] becomes 80
$2.00	[90] becomes 70
$3.00	[70] becomes 50
$4.00	[40] becomes 10

These are the same changes shown in a graph.

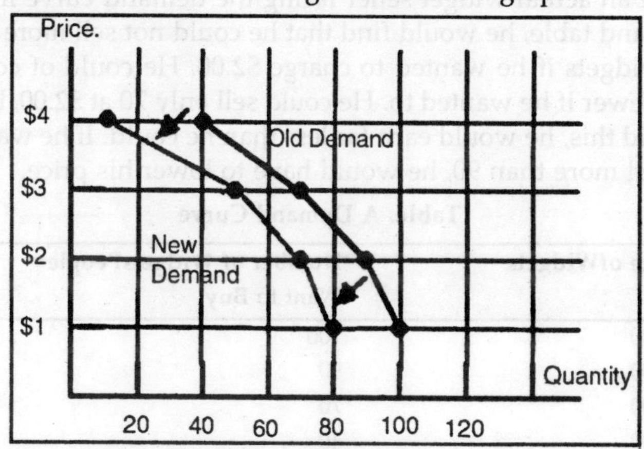

Fig. A Shift in Demand

DEMAND TERMINOLOGY

If the price of widgets is originally $1.00 and people are buying 100, they may change to 90 for two reasons. One reason is that the price may rise to $2.00. The other reason is that one of the factors that is assumed to be constant may change, so that even though the price has not changed, quantity will. Economists distinguish these two cases. In the first case the demand relationship or schedule has not changed, but there has been movement within the relationship. Economists call a change of this sort a change in quantity demanded. The second sort of change is an alteration of the relationship. The original pairing of price and quantity is destroyed and replaced by a new pairing. Economists call this sort of change a change in demand.

It is important to realise that though the demand relationship looks concrete when it is illustrated with a table or graph, in everyday life demand curves are hidden. A demand curve refers to what people would do if various prices were charged, and very rarely are enough prices charged so a clear demand curve can be seen. This is not to say that the concept is of no importance to people who sell. They may not be interested in the demand curve as a relationship, but they do find it a boundary or constraint on their behaviour. If there were an actual widget seller facing the demand curve in our demand table, he would find that he could not sell more than 90 widgets if he wanted to charge $2.00. He could of course sell fewer if he wanted to. He could sell only 70 at $2.00, but if he did this, he would earn far less than he could. If he wanted to sell more than 90, he would have to lower his price.

Table. A Demand Curve

Price ofWidgets	Number of WidgetsPeople Want to Buy
$1.00	100
$2.00	90
$3.00	70
$4.00	40

Thus, to an actual businessman the demand curve is important as a limitation on what he can do. A businessman may not know exactly where the demand curve is, and he may not think of it as fixed. Advertising—either informing or persuading people—can move the boundary. As we proceed further, as suggested, see that there are still other ways to view the demand curve in addition to seeing it as a mathematical relationship and as a boundary that limits sellers.

SUPPLY: BENEFITS AND COSTS

What determines the amount of a good or service that people are willing and ready to sell during some period of time? A discussion of exchange suggested that people sell things because it is a way, indirect but effective, of obtaining other things that they prefer.

Sellers intend to make a profit from their sales, and economists assume that they want their profits to be as large as possible. Because profit is the difference between benefits in the form of revenues and costs, anything that influences revenues or costs can influence the amounts sellers want to sell.

Revenue, the benefit that sellers get from producing and selling, is found by multiplying the price of the product by the amount sold.

A change in price changes revenues and hence profits, so it is a major determinant of the amount sellers will want to sell. Because a higher price leads to higher profit, and a higher profit leads to a larger amount that sellers will want to sell, one expects that a greater quantity should be supplied when the price is higher. Thus, the relationship between quantity that sellers will sell and price should be direct or positive.

Though the positive relationship is almost always the case, there are a few exceptions. An example is labour; as wages go up, people may decide to enjoy their higher wages and work less. As a result, there is no law of supply that matches the law of demand.

The cost of something is what must be given up in order to get it. When costs are only monetary, they are easy to see. If the price of an input increases, the cost of the output will increase, and, other things held constant, profits will decrease. The seller will then have to decide if shifting part of his resources and effort to other products will improve his well-being. Production costs are determined not only by the prices of inputs, but also by technology. Technology represents the knowledge of how inputs can be combined to produce the product.

If this knowledge increases so that people find cheaper ways to make the same output, then, other things held constant, profit increases and we expect sellers to respond by producing more.

Costs may be nonmonetary as well as monetary. For example, a farmer takes the expected price of soybeans into account in deciding how much corn to plant. If soybeans are expected to sell for a high price, then the farmer may find that shifting some of his land from corn production to soybean production will increase profit.

The decision to plant corn means that the farmer gives up the opportunity to plant soybeans. Because we have defined cost as what must be given up to get something, the prices of other goods that sellers could otherwise produce and sell must be part of the calculation of the cost of production.

There are other factors that can influence the amount of a product that sellers will sell, such as the number of sellers, expectations about the future, and whether or not there are by-products in production that are valuable. But as in the discussion of demand, the emphasis in the discussion of supply is on the relationship between quantity and price. To focus on this relationship, all other factors must be assumed to be constant.

THE SUPPLY CURVE

The relationship between the quantity sellers want to sell during some time period and price is what economists call the supply curve.

Though usually the relationship is positive, so that when price increases so does quantity supplied, there are exceptions. Hence there is no law of supply that parallels the law of demand.

The supply curve can be expressed mathematically in functional form as,

$$Qs = f.$$

It can also be illustrated in the form of a table or a graph.

Table. A Supply Curve

Price ofWidgets	Number of WidgetsSellers Want to Sell
$1.00	10
$2.00	40
$3.00	70
$4.00	140

The graph shown has a positive slope, which is the slope one normally expects from a supply curve.

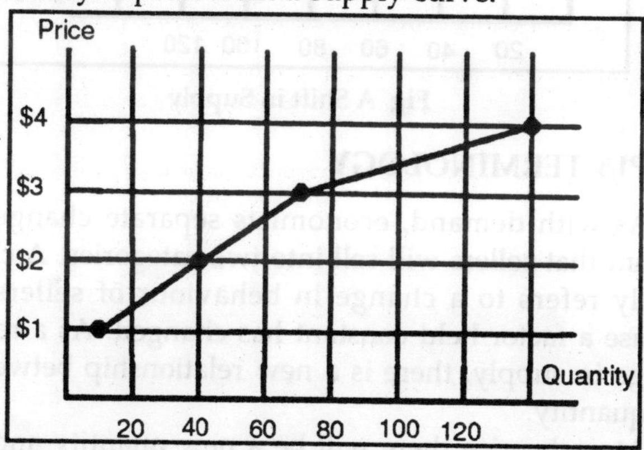

Fig. A Supply Curve Shows How Price Influences Sellers

If one of the factors that is held constant changes, the relationship between price and quantity, will change. If the price of an input falls, for example, the supply relationship may change, as in the following table.

Table. A Supply Curve Can Shift

Price ofWidgets	Number of WidgetsSellers Want to Sell
$1.00	[10] becomes 20
$2.00	[40] becomes 60
$3.00	[70] becomes 100
$4.00	[140] becomes 180

The same changes can be shown with a graph that shows the supply curve shifting to the right. Notice each price has a larger quantity associated with it.

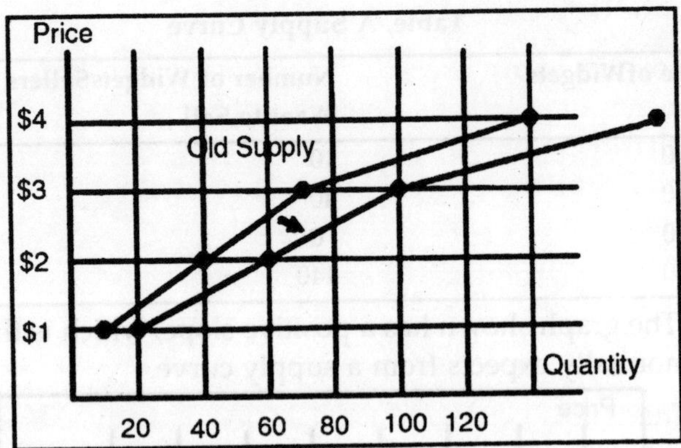

Fig. A Shift in Supply

SUPPLY TERMINOLOGY

As with demand, economists separate changes in the amount that sellers will sell into two categories. A change in supply refers to a change in behaviour of sellers caused because a factor held constant has changed. As a result of a change in supply, there is a new relationship between price and quantity.

At each price there will be a new quantity and at each quantity there will be a new price. A change in quantity supplied refers to a change in behaviour of sellers caused because price has changed. In this case, the relationship between price and quantity remains unchanged, but a new pair in the list of all possible pairs of price and quantity has been realised.

Supply curves as well as demand curves appear much more concrete on an economist's graph than they appear in real markets.

A supply curve is mostly potential—what will happen if certain prices are charged, most of which will never be charged. From the buyer's perspective, the supply curve has more meaning as a boundary than as a relationship.

The supply curve says that only certain price-quantity pairs will be available to buyers—those lying to the left of the supply curve.

THE MODEL OF SUPPLY AND DEMAND

To this point, we have developed two behavioural statements, or assertions, about how people will act. The first says that the amount buyers are willing and ready to buy depends on price and other factors that are assumed constant.

The second says that the amount sellers are willing and ready to sell depends on price and other factors that are assumed constant. In mathematical terms our model is,

$$Qd = f$$
$$Qs = g$$

This is not a complete model. Mathematically, the problem is that we have three variables and only two equations, and this system will not have a solution.

To complete the system, we add a simple equation containing the equilibrium condition:

$$Qd = Qs.$$

In words, equilibrium exists if the amount sellers are willing to sell is equal to the amount buyers are willing to buy.

If we combine the supply and demand tables in earlier parts, we get the table.

It should be obvious that the price of $3.00 is the equilibrium price and the quantity of 70 is the equilibrium quantity.

At any other price, sellers would want to sell a different amount than buyers want to buy.

Table. Supply and Demand Together at Last

Price of Widgets	Number of Widgets People Want to Buy	Number of Widgets Sellers Want to Sell
$1.00	100	10
$2.00	90	40
$3.00	70	70
$4.00	40	140

The same information can be shown with a graph. On the graph, the equilibrium price and quantity are indicated by the intersection of the supply and demand curves.

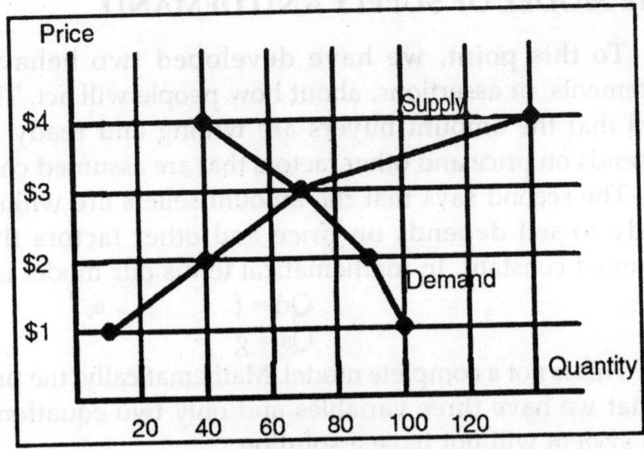

Fig. Supply and Demand

If one of the many factors that is being held constant changes, then equilibrium price and quantity will change. Further, if we know which factor changes, we can often predict the direction of changes, though rarely the exact magnitude. For example, the market for wheat fits the requirements of the supply and demand model quite well. Suppose there is a drought in the main wheat-producing areas of the United States. How will we show this on a supply and demand graph? Should we move the demand curve, the supply curve, or both? What will happen to equilibrium price and quantity?

A dangerous way to answer these questions is to first try to decide what will happen to price and quantity and then decide what will happen to the supply and demand curves. This is a route to disaster. Rather, one must first decide how the curves will shift, and then from the shifts in the curves decide how price and quantity would change.

What should happen as the result of the drought? One begins by asking whether buyers would change the amount they purchased if price did not change and whether sellers would change the amount sold if price did not change. On reflection, one realises that this event will change seller behaviour at the given price, but is highly unlikely to change buyer behaviour. Further, at any price, the drought will reduce the amount sellers will sell. Thus, the supply curve will shift to the left and the demand curve will not change. There will be a change in supply and a change in quantity demanded. The new equilibrium will have a higher price and a lower quantity. These changes are shown.

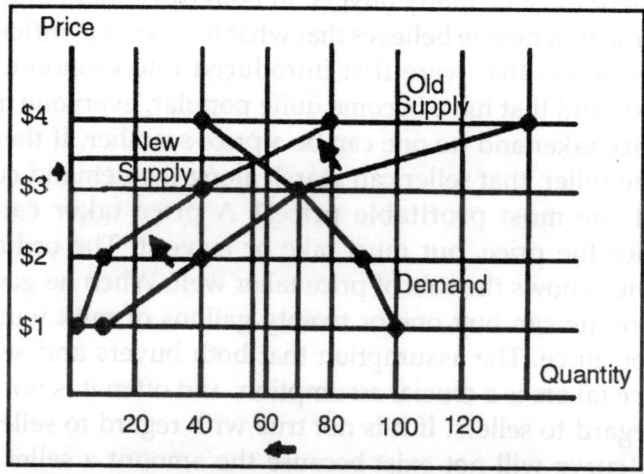

Fig. Shifting the Supply Curve Moves us along the Demand Curve

What should one predict if a new diet calling for the consumption of two loaves of whole wheat bread sweeps through the U.S.? Again one must ask whether the behaviour of buyers or sellers will change if price does not change. Reflection should tell you that it will be the behaviour of buyers that will change. Buyers would want more wheat at each possible price. The demand curve shifts to the right, which results in higher equilibrium price and quantity. Sellers would also change their behaviour, but only because price changed. Sellers would move along the supply curve.

ASSUMPTIONS

The supply and demand model does not describe all markets--there is too much diversity in the ways buyers and sellers interact for one simple model to explain everything. When we use the supply and demand model to explain a market, we are implicitly making a number of assumptions about that market.

Supply and demand analysis assumes competitive markets. For a supply curve to exist, there must be a large number of sellers in the market; and for a demand curve to exist, there must be many buyers. In both cases there must be enough so that no one believes that what he does will influence price. In terms that were first introduced into economics in the 1950s and that have become quite popular, everyone must be a price taker and no one can be a price searcher. If there is only one seller, that seller can search along the demand curve to find the most profitable price.1 A price taker cannot influence the price, but must take or leave it. The ordinary consumer knows the role of price taker well. When he goes to the store, he can buy one or twenty gallons of milk with no effect on price. The assumption that both buyers and sellers are price takers is a crucial assumption, and often it is not true with regard to sellers. If it is not true with regard to sellers, a supply curve will not exist because the amount a seller will want to sell will depend not on price but on marginal revenue.

The model of supply and demand also requires that buyers and sellers be clearly defined groups. Notice that in the list of factors that affected buyers and sellers, the only common factor was price. Few people who buy hamburger know or care about the price of cattle feed or the details of cattle breeding. Cattle raisers do not care what the income of the buyers is or what the prices of related goods are unless they affect the price of cattle. Thus, when one factor changes, it affects only one curve, not both. When buyers and sellers cannot be clearly distinguished, as on the New York Stock Exchange, where the people who are buyers one minute may be sellers the next, one cannot talk about distinct and separate supply and demand curves.

The model of supply and demand also assumes that both buyers and sellers have good information about the product's qualities and availability. If information is not good, the same product may sell for a variety of prices. Often, however, what seems to be the same product at different prices can be considered a variety of products. A pound of hamburger for which one has to wait 15 minutes in a check-out line can be considered a different product from identical meat that one can buy without waiting.

Finally, for some uses the supply and demand model needs well-defined private-property rights. Elsewhere, we discussed how private-property rights and markets provide one way of coordinating decisions. When property rights are not clearly defined, the seller may be able to ignore some of the costs of production, which will then be imposed on others. Alternatively, buyers may not get all the benefits from purchasing a product; others may get some of the benefits without payment.

Even if the assumptions underlying supply and demand are not met exactly, and they rarely are, the model often provides a fairly good approximation of a situation, good enough so that predictions based on the model are in the right direction. This ability of the model to predict even when some assumptions are not quite satisfied is one reason economists like the model so much.

BUYER AND SELLER EQUILIBRIUM

We have developed the model of supply and demand as an equilibrium model. We have said nothing about how adjustments from disequilibrium to equilibrium take place. To develop this idea, it is useful to take still another view of supply and demand curves, to view demand as points of buyer equilibrium and supply as points of seller equilibrium.

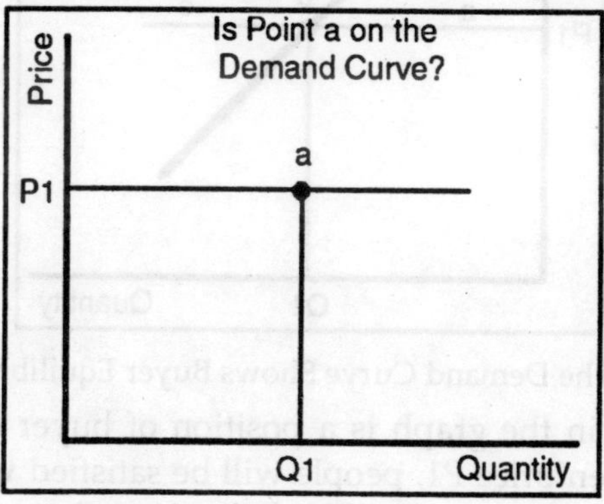

Fig. Is Point a on the Demand Curve?

Suppose that price is at P1 in the graph. Will point a be a point on the demand curve? If people would like to buy more than Q1 at price P1, point a must lie to the left of the demand curve. In this case, some consumers are unhappy with the amount they have purchased and will try to purchase more. If there is no more to purchase, some will attempt to offer more money for the product or they will increase the time they devote to getting the product.

The important idea is that if point a lies to the left of the demand curve, people will be unhappy with their situation and will change their behaviour. If point a lies to the right of the demand curve, people will decide that they are buying too much of the product and will cut purchases. In cease, if a position is not on the demand curve, people will change their behaviour, which indicates that only positions on the demand curve are positions of buyer equilibrium.

Similar reasoning explains why the demand curve can be considered a boundary. In the graph, buyers are not in equilibrium at point a, but they can be held there and made to adjust in ways that do not change the money price. They cannot be held at point c unless there is some way to force people to buy a product when they do not want it.

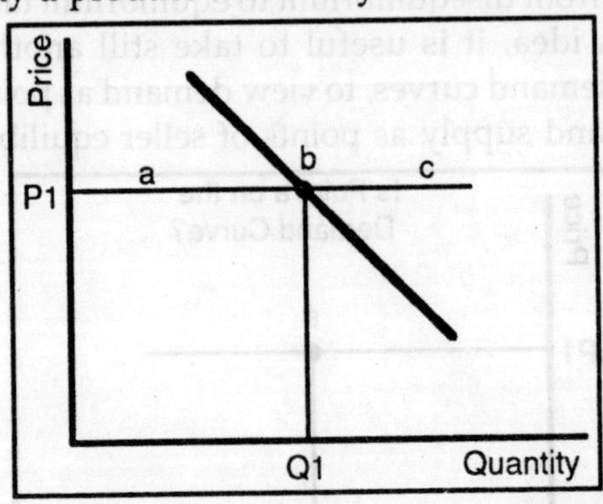

Fig. The Demand Curve Shows Buyer Equilibrium

Point b in the graph is a position of buyer equilibrium because, given price P1, people will be satisfied with Q1 and will do nothing to change their behaviour. Buyers would, of course, prefer a lower price than P1—they are always willing to move down the demand curve. However, this is not the issue here. Given P1, Q1 is the preferred quantity.

Just as the demand curve shows positions of buyer equilibrium, the supply curve shows positions of seller equilibrium. At point a in the picture, suppliers find that they could increase profits by moving to the right to a larger quantity. If they could not increase profits by moving towrds the right, they would stay at point a. Because they do not, they are not in equilibrium and on the supply curve but to the left of it. If they find that they could increase profits by cutting production, they are to the right of the supply curve and out of equilibrium. There is a quantity at the price P1 that maximizes profits and towrds which sellers will adjust. This point, shown as b in the picture, is on the supply curve.

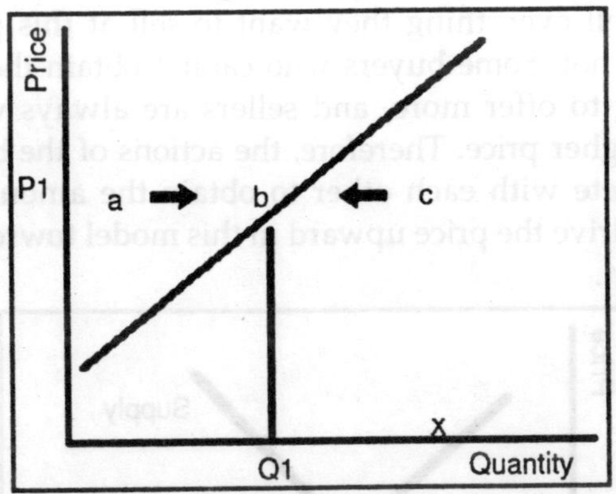

Fig. The Supply Curve Shows Seller Equilibrium

It is possible to force sellers to a position left of the supply curve. This is the case in which sellers would like to sell more at the given price, but for some reason can not. One reason might be that the buyers will not buy as much as the sellers would like to sell. It is virtually impossible—short of slavery—to force sellers to the right of the supply curve. If sellers are selling more than they want to at the given price, they can simply stop selling. Thus, the supply curve represents a boundary facing the buyers. If buyers could force sellers to the right of the supply curve, they would find it advantageous to force sellers to a position such as x in graph, which represents getting something for nothing. Sellers prefer higher prices to lower prices. Although all points on the supply curve represent points of equilibrium, not all are equally preferred by sellers. Sellers are always happy to move up along a supply curve.

SHORTAGES AND SURPLUSES

Viewing points on the demand curve as points of buyer equilibrium and points on the supply curve as points of seller equilibrium helps explain how an adjustment process takes place in the supply and demand model. If price is originally P1 in the graph, only Q1 will be sold even though buyers would like to buy Q2. The difference Q2 - Q1 represents a shortage. The sellers are in equilibrium in this situation because they can sell everything they want to sell at this price, but buyers are not. Some buyers who cannot obtain the product are willing to offer more, and sellers are always willing to accept a higher price. Therefore, the actions of the buyers, as they compete with each other to obtain the amount that is available, drive the price upward in this model towrds market equilibrium.

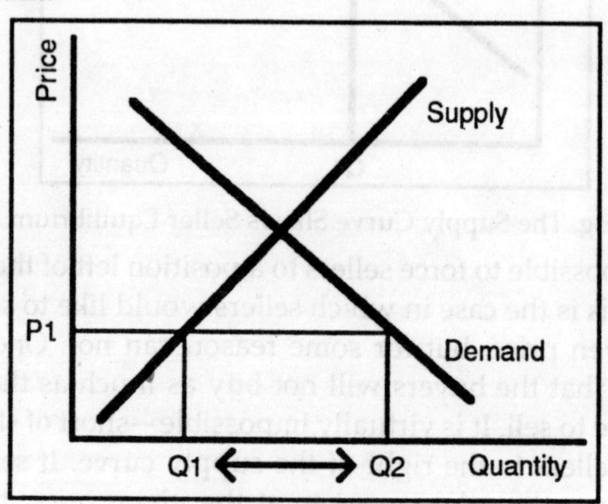

Fig. A Shortage

If price is originally at P1 in the picture, only Q1 will be sold because this is all that buyers will purchase, even though sellers are willing to sell more, Q2. The difference Q2 - Q1 is called a surplus. In this situation the buyers are in equilibrium because they can buy all they want to buy at the going price. However, the sellers are not in equilibrium and will compete among themselves to get rid of the surplus. Some sellers will be willing to offer their product at a lower price. Buyers are always willing to move down the demand curve, so there is a tendency to move downward towrds market equilibrium in the picture.

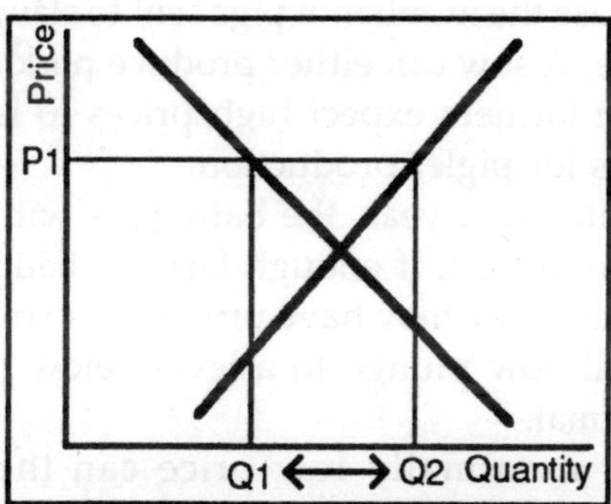

Fig. A Surplus

If left to itself, a supply-and-demand market tends to adjust to the point where the supply and demand curves cross. The price at this intersection is called the market-clearing price. There is, however, the possibility that the existence of lags in the adjustment process may make the adjustment more complex.

Suppose that the price of cattle feed rises sharply. This event should affect the supply curve of cattle by shifting it to the left. The profitability of cattle production is reduced at each possible price, and some producers will drop out of the industry while others will curtail production. Looking at the curves, we see that price should rise and quantity should drop. However, initially price might drop and quantity might rise, which is the exact opposite of the prediction from the supply and demand graph. The higher costs of feed will encourage farmers to raise fewer cattle, but as part of that cutback, they will temporarily send more cattle to the slaughterhouses. The prediction that supply-demand analysis gives will ultimately be correct, but it will not be correct in the process of adjustment. More complicated adjustment patterns are possible. Suppose, for example, that higher beef prices shift the demand for pork to the right. Supply and demand analysis says that this should increase pork prices, and at the higher prices, farmers should produce more hogs.

However, hog production takes time, and will only happen if farmers expect the higher prices to continue for a long time. If pork producers do expect the higher prices to last, they may decrease the number of pigs sent to slaughter, further increasing price. A sow can either produce pork or baby pigs, but not both. If farmers expect high prices to last, they will keep their sows for piglet production.

In six months to a year, the baby pigs will have grown enough to go to market. If enough farmers had expected the high prices to last, they may have produced so many pigs that pork prices will now plunge to a level below that which is considered normal.

The new, abnormally low price can then influence decisions that will not affect the price for many months. You should see that, once disturbed, a market with long time lags in production may bounce around for years before it finally finds its way back to equilibrium. If such a market is disturbed often enough, its prices and quantities will never come to rest at equilibrium levels.

Microeconomic discussion generally ignores adjustment problems, at least at the introductory level. Microeconomics assumes that markets clear, that is, they are always in equilibrium.

Its analysis begins with the assumption that equilibrium has been reached and then asks questions about that equilibrium. However, adjustment problems are very important in macroeconomics.

Macroeconomics cannot assume there are no adjustment problems or else it assumes away one of the problems it wants to explain, unemployment. In fact, much of macroeconomics is about the forces that bump an economy away from equilibrium, and why, once it is away, it has problems reaching a new equilibrium.

DEMAND ANALYSIS

Transportation demand, simply stated, is the demand for trips that exist in any area. All of this demand, however, may or may not materialize into physical trips —and some of it generally remains latent and is referred to as hidden demand.

The importance of analyzing the transportation demand in order to be able to predict the expected number of trips in a given network cannot be overstated.

The demand for transportation forms the primary input in any decision related to creation and management of transportation and traffic facilities, such as roads, intersections, parking lots, transit system, and so on.

The lecture is divided into three parts. The first part describes the nature of transportation demand and how it can be analysed.

Then it presents the sequential demand analysis technique — the most frequently used method of determining transportation demand. Finally it briefly describes some of the data collection mechanisms employed in travel demand analysis.

Transportation demand, unlike demand for other commodities, such as wheat, coffee, housing, clothing, etc., is a derived demand.

That is, one demands to be transported not because he/she just wants to move but because he/she wants to achieve some other purpose such as reaching school, or office or a movie theater.

In other words, the need for achieving some goal creates the need to travel. Hence, travel demand is primarily generated by the population's need to work, entertain, socialize, study, etc. Therefore, it is not surprising that two of the major aspects in travel demand analysis are land use and trip purpose.

Land use refers to the pattern of land usage in an area. Land use affects transportation demand through generation and distribution of trips.

The effect of land use on transportation demand is not necessarily a one-way effect but rather a part of cycle in which land use changes transportation needs which in turn change land use. Figure shows a simple schematic of how land use and transportation demand are related.

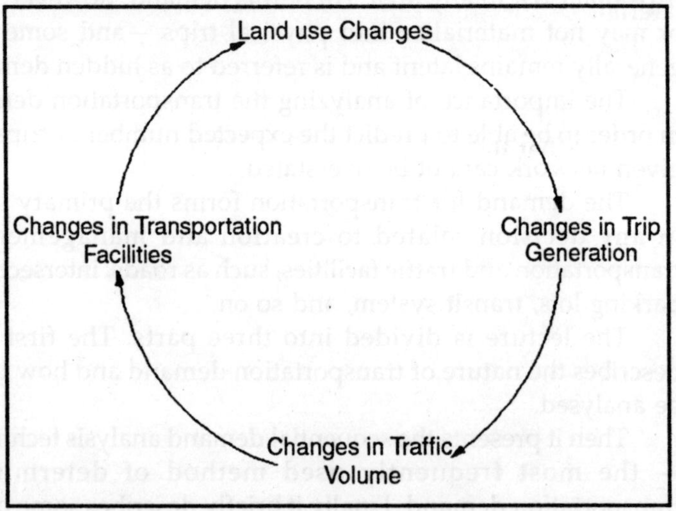

Fig. Relationship Between Land use and Transportation Demand.

Trip purpose refers to the purpose for which the trip is being undertaken. Travel demand behaviour changes with the trip purpose. For example, a person hardly exercises any choice for work trips; i.e. does not necessarily decide every time whether to go to work or not.

A person obviously does not decide where to go to work, even the choice of route and mode are not daily decisions. On the other hand, for recreational trips, an individual makes a large number of decisions, such as whether to go or not, where to go, how to go.

Consequently, the travel demand behaviour for work trips varies considerably from that of recreational trips. This example, can obviously be extended to other types of trips such as shopping trips, etc. Given the effect of trip purpose on travel demand behaviour, the analysis of travel demand is done separately for different trip-purposes.

Although, the discussion throws light on some of the factors which affect travel demand, some more understanding of travel demand is necessary before one can analyse the demand and can, with some degree of confidence, predict the volume on various links of a network. Generally, a trip materializes after the trip-maker makes certain decisions.

These decisions can be broadly classified as follows:

- The decision to travel. The trip-maker, given his/her requirements, makes a conscious decision to travel so that the requirements can be met.
- The decision on the choice of destination. The trip maker also makes a decision as to where he/she wants to go; for certain kinds of trip purpose, such as work trips, this decision may not exist; yet for other kinds of trips, such as shopping trips, there may be certain alternative locations to choose from.
- The decision on the choice of mode. The trip-maker also takes a decision as to what mode of transport to use for a given trip. This decision, however, is only available to those who have access to different modes and are not captive users of any particular mode.
- The decision on the choice of route. The trip-maker on any given trip takes a definite decision on which route to take so as to reach the destination. Again, this decision is available to only those trip -makers who have access to modes which can use different routes as per the wishes of the trip maker. Such modes would generally include personal automobiles or two wheelers.

Although, there is unanimity on the fact that the decisions can aptly capture the entire trip-making behaviour of an individual and hence can be used to analyse travel demand pattern of an area, it is difficult to ascertain whether there exists any definite sequence in which these decisions are made.

Generally it is assumed, primarily for the ease of analysis rather than anything else, that the decisions are made in a strict sequence as shown in Figure Analysis techniques which assume that such a sequence exists are referred to as sequential demand analysis techniques.

Although, even today transportation demand is analysed sequentially, the assumption that the four major decisions of a trip-maker follow a strict sequence is possibly not the most appealing.

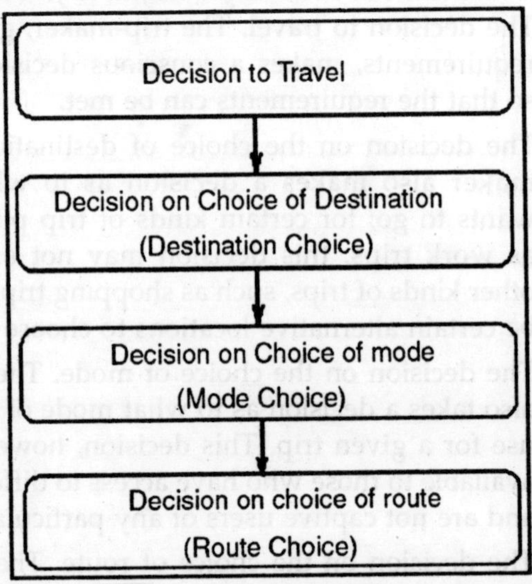

Fig. Schematic Representation of the Assumption of Sequential Decision Making.

Quite often, the *decision to travel* is changed because an appropriate destination does not exist; or an *initial choice of destination* is changed because it cannot be reached by the desirable mode of transport.

It is possibly a truer picture of reality if the decision making framework is assumed to have feedback loops. One such possible structure is shown in Figure.

In this structure, unlike in Figure, there are feedback loops indicating that decisions taken earlier can be changed based on a latter decision.

For example, the decision to travel may be aborted because at the *mode choice* stage if it is realised that none of the available modes suit the requirements.

As stated earlier, even though the assumption of the existence of a strict sequence in the decision-making process of a potential trip-maker may be debatable, generally sequential demand analysis is used to determine the travel demand. As will be seen throughout this lecture, even with this simplifying assumption of sequential decision making, the analysis of transportation demand remains sufficiently complex.

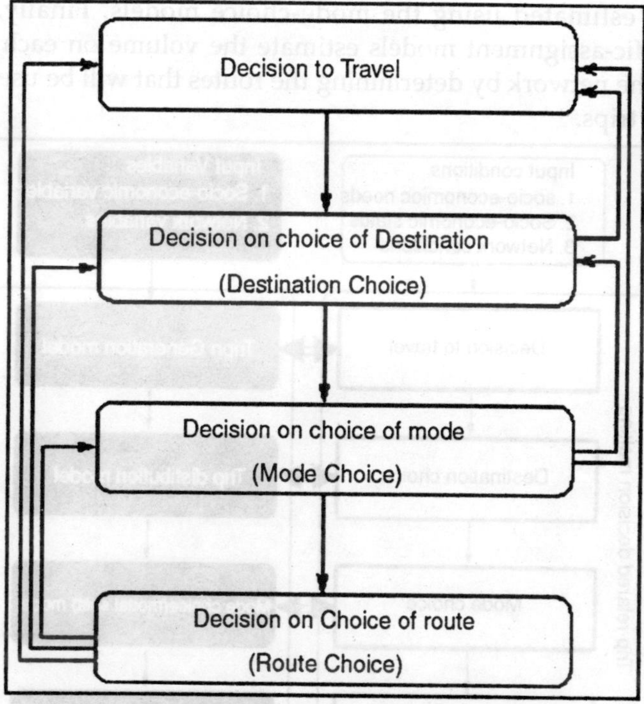

Fig. An Example of the Assumption of Non-sequential Decision Making

Figure shows a schematic of the sequential demand analysis procedure. The figure attempts to not only illustrate the logic of the analysis procedure but also gives the names of the different classes of models used to mathematically describe each decision-making phase of the analysis procedure.

Before presenting the models, a general overview of the entire process is provided. In this analysis procedure, first the entire study area is divided into various zones. These zones are generally obtained from the land-use pattern of the area.

Next, for each zone the total number of trips generated in that zone are estimated using the trip-generation models. The outputs of the trip-generation models are then used to determine the number of trips between all zone pairs using the trip-distribution models. Given the trip-distribution pattern, the relative shares of these trips for the different modes are estimated using the mode-choice models. Finally, the traffic-assignment models estimate the volume on each link of the network by determining the routes that will be used by the trips.

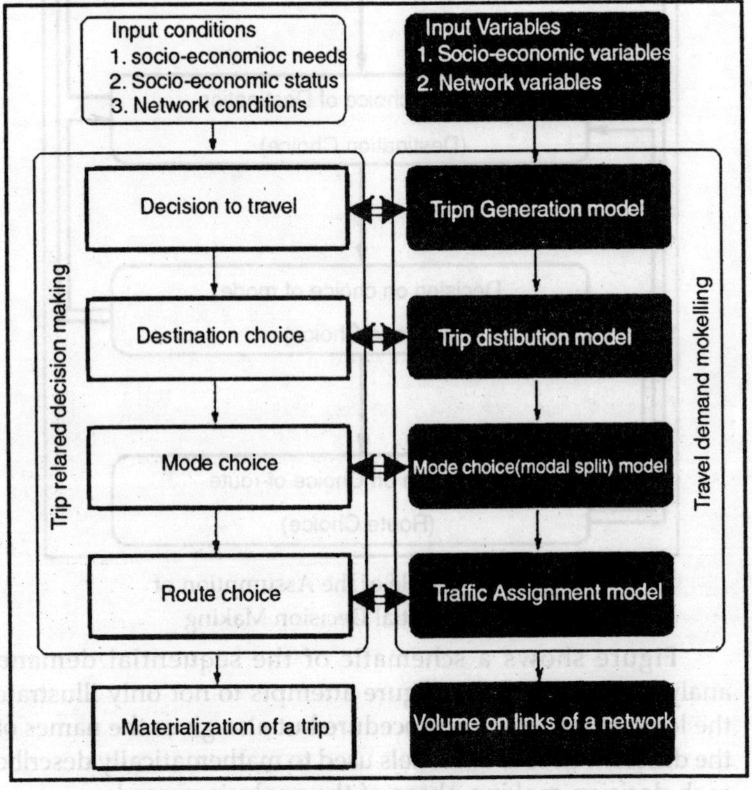

Fig. Sequential Demand Analysis Procedure

TYPES OF DEMAND

- Individual demand and Market Demand

- Demand for capital goods and demand for consumer goods
- Autonomous demand and derived demand direct and indirect demand
- Demand for durable and non-durable goods
- Short term demand and long term demand

DETERMINANTS OF DEMAND ANALYSIS

Economic analysis has recognized the role of key variables in determining demand and consumption. In practice, the distinction between demand and consumption as an equilibrium quantity at a given price, is frequently ignored. The development of "gap" type models illustrate the common approach of projecting 'demand' as a fixed quantity independent of price.

Demand, as the relationship between price and quantity, is subject to change over time due to changes in the underlying factors held constant by the static notion of demand. Changes in demand "shifters" are often included in economic estimation of demand representing anticipated dynamics in these determinants.

LEVELS OF INCOME

A key determinant of demand is the level of income evident in the appropriate country or region under analysis. As a generality, the higher the level of aggregate and/or personal income the higher the demand for a typical commodity, including forest products. More of a good or service will be chosen at a given price where income is higher. Thus determinants of demand normally utilize some form of income measure, including Gross Domestic Product.

POPULATION

Population is of course a key determinant of demand. Although all forest products do not necessarily enter final consumer markets, the actual markets are largely presumed to be functionally related to population. Growing populations are positively correlated to timber demands in the aggregate, as well as specifically to individual forest products. Frequently, population and income estimators are combined, as in the case of the use of Gross Domestic Product per capita.

END MARKET INDICATORS

The use of end market indicators as determinants of demand is frequently incorporated into demand analysis. For example, much of the final use of forest products is linked to construction. Indicators and trends related to construction activities, or which are determinants of construction, provide indirect estimates of the influence of these activities as the source of derived demand for wood. Housing starts, public investments, interest rates, etc. can be highly correlated to timber demand.

AVAILABILITY AND PRICE OF SUBSTITUTE GOODS

Consumption choices related to timber are also influenced by the alternative options facing users in the relevant marketplace. The availability of potential substitute products, and their prices, weigh heavily in determining the elasticity of demand, both in the short run sense and over time. Fuelwood, as a dominant use of timber in the Asia Pacific Region, reflects conditions of very limited options for energy sources at 'reasonable' prices. Rural low income or subsistence populations simply do not have 'options' regarding energy - they use wood or go without. Demand, at this basic level, in almost perfectly inelastic. The cost does not materially affect consumption quantity.

Suitability of alternative goods and services is, in part, a question of knowledge as well as availability. Market information regarding alternative products, quality, convenience, and dependability all influence choices. Under conditions of increased scarcity and rising prices for tropical hardwood panels, for example, users have a positive incentive to search for and investigate the suitability of alternatives that were previously overlooked or ignored.

TASTES AND PREFERENCES

All markets are shaped by collective and individual tastes and preferences. These patterns are partly shaped by culture and partly implanted by information and knowledge of products and services. Different societies use forest products differently because of these differences in taste and preferences. For example, markets for wood products in Japan are commonly recognized as requiring very high product quality standards, the importance of visual attributes of wood, and other preferences not commonly found in many other markets.

ELASTICITY

In economics, elasticity is the ratio of the per cent change in one variable to the per cent change in another variable. It is a tool for measuring the responsiveness of a function to changes in parametres in a unit-less way. Frequently used elasticities include price elasticity of demand, price elasticity of supply, income elasticity of demand, elasticity of substitution between factors of production and elasticity of intertemporal substitution.

Elasticity is one of the most important concepts in economic theory. It is useful in understanding the incidence of indirect taxation, marginal concepts as they relate to the theory of the firm, and distribution of wealth and different types of goods as they relate to the theory of consumer choice. Elasticity is also crucially important in any discussion of welfare distribution, in particular consumer surplus, producer surplus, or government surplus.

In empirical work an elasticity is the estimated coefficient in a linear regression equation where both the dependent variable and the independent variable are in natural logs. Elasticity is a popular tool among empiricists because it is independent of units and thus simplifies data analysis.

Generally, an "elastic" variable is one which responds "a lot" to small changes in other parametres. Similarly, an "inelastic" variable describes one which does not change much in response to changes in other parametres. A major study of the price elasticity of supply and the price elasticity of demand for US products was undertaken by Hendrik S. Houthakker and Lester D. Taylor.

MATHEMATICAL DEFINITION

The definition of elasticity is based on the mathematical notion of point elasticity.

In general, the "x-elasticity of y" is:

$$E_{y,x} = \left|\frac{\partial \ln y}{\partial \ln x}\right| = \left|\frac{\partial y}{\partial x} \cdot \frac{x}{y}\right| = \left|\frac{\%\Delta y}{\%\Delta x}\right|$$

The "x-elasticity of y" is also called "the elasticity of y with respect to x".

SPECIFIC ELASTICITIES

Elasticities of Demand

- *Price elasticity of deman*: Price elasticity of demand measures the percentage change in quantity demanded caused by a per cent change in price. As such, it measures the extent of movement along the demand curve. This elasticity is almost always negative and is usually expressed in terms of absolute value. If the elasticity is greater than 1 demand is said to be elastic; between zero and one demand is inelastic and if it equals one, demand is unit-elastic.
- *Income elasticity of demand*: Income elasticity of demand measures the percentage change in demand caused by a per cent change in income. A change in income causes the demand curve to shift reflecting the change in demand. YED is a measurement of how far the curve shifts horizontally along the X-axis. Income elasticity can be used to classify goods as normal or inferior. With a normal good demand varies in the same direction as income. With an inferior good demand and income move in opposite directions.
- *Cross price elasticity of demand*: Cross price elasticity of demand measures the percentage change in

demand for a particular good caused by a per cent change in the price of another good. Goods can be complements, substitutes or unrelated. A change in the price of a related good causes the demand curve to shift reflecting a change in demand for the original good. Cross price elasticity is a measurement of how far, and in which direction, the curve shifts horizontally along the x-axis. A positive cross-price elasticity means that the goods are substitute goods.

- *Cross elasticity of demand between firms*: Cross elasticity of demand for firms, sometimes referred to as conjectural variation, is a measure of the interdependence between firms. It captures the extent to which one firm reacts to changes in strategic variables made by other firms.

Elasticities of Supply

- *Price elasticity of supply*: The price elasticity of supply measures how the amount of a good firms wish to supply changes in response to a change in price. In a manner analogous to the price elasticity of demand, it captures the extent of movement along the supply curve. If the price elasticity of supply is zero the supply of a good supplied is "inelastic" and the quantity supplied is fixed.
- *Elasticities of scale*: Elasticity of scale or output elasticities measure the percentage change in output induced by a per cent change in inputs. A production function or process is said to exhibit constant returns to scale if a percentage change in inputs results in a equal percentage in outputs. It exhibits increasing returns to scale if a percentage change in inputs results in greater percentage change in output. The definition of decreasing returns to scale is analogous.

APPLICATIONS

The concept of elasticity has an extraordinarily wide range of applications in economics. In particular, an understanding of elasticity is fundamental in understanding the response of supply and demand in a market.

Some common uses of elasticity include:

- Effect of changing price on firm revenue.
- Analysis of incidence of the tax burden and other government policies.
- Income elasticity of demand can be used as an indicator of industry health and as a guide to firms investment decisions.
- Effect of international trade and terms of trade effects.
- Analysis of consumption and saving behaviour.
- Analysis of advertising on consumer demand for particular goods.

PRICE ELASTICITY OF DEMAND

Price elasticity of demand refers to the way prices change in relationship to the demand, or the way demand changes in relationship to pricing. Price elasticity can also reference the amount of money each individual consumer is willing to pay for something. People with lower incomes tend to have lower price elasticity, because they have less money to spend. A person with a higher income is thought to have higher price elasticity, since he can afford to spend more. In both cases, ability to pay is negotiated by the intrinsic value of what is being sold. If the thing being sold is in high demand, even a consumer with low price elasticity is usually willing to pay higher prices.

Elasticity implies stretch and flexibility. The flexibility or the price elasticity of demand will change based on each item. Changing nature of both price and demand are affected by a number of factors.

Generally, goods or services offered at a lower price lead to a demand for greater quantity. If you can get socks on sale you might buy several pairs or several packages, instead of just a pair. This means that though the seller offers the socks at a lower price, he usually ends up making more money, because demand for the product has increased. However if the price is set too low, the retailer may lose money by selling too many pairs of socks at a reduced rate. Price elasticity of demand evaluates how change in price influences demand. In certain circumstances, demand remains inelastic, despite higher prices. This is true of a number of medications that are available to treat certain conditions, where there is no substitute. Demand remains constant in spite of high prices.

It's also true of fuel consumption, where few substitutes exist. In 2006, when gasoline prices skyrocketed, demand for gasoline was only slightly affected.

Some people were able to use less gas for their cars, or to purchase cars that were hybrids, but these were in short supply. Since few alternatives existed, people continued to buy gasoline, and demand was thus considered inelastic. Price didn't significantly alter demand. Other utilities, like water, often are highly inelastic in price because they have no substitute to which a consumer can turn.

Price elasticity of demand also explains that price becomes more elastic, when higher prices may turn away most consumers who can choose to buy something else that is less expensive. When a good or service has numerous substitutes, prices are more elastic and will change with demand. In fact, availability of substitution is often a better predictor of price elasticity than is demand. Amount of competition, numerous companies offering the same items, can also affect price elasticity of demand. Usually, competition in the marketplace keeps prices lower and more flexible. Generic equivalents of certain items have lowered the demand for brand name items, thus lowering their price.

In economics, complex formulas show how the price elasticity of demand can be either profitable or detrimental to the seller. These formulas describe how good or bad price elasticity of demand functions. Examples of good price elasticity of demand include inelastic pricing. In this example, a small drop in demand is made up for by higher prices. A unit price elasticity that raises demand can also be profitable for a company. On the other hand, bad price elasticity occurs when quantity demand increases, but does not make up for discounted price, causing a drop in company profits.

A perfectly elastic price is equally detrimental. Raised price in the good eliminates demand completely. The most profitable arrangement in pricing is when demand is perfectly inelastic, as with the medicine. Despite rise in price, demand does not decrease, resulting in the highest profits for a company.

DEMAND FORECASTING

A demand forecast is the prediction of what will happen to your company's existing product sales. It would be best to determine the demand forecast using a multi-functional approach.

The inputs from sales and marketing, finance, and production should be considered. The final demand forecast is the consensus of all participating managers. You may also want to put up a Sales and Operations Planning group composed of representatives from the different departments that will be tasked to prepare the demand forecast.

Determination of the demand forecasts is done through the following steps:

- Determine the use of the forecast
- Select the items to be forecast
- Determine the time horizon of the forecast
- Select the forecasting model(s)
- Gather the data
- Make the forecast
- Validate and implement results

The time horizon of the forecast is classified as follows:

Description	Forecast Horizon		
Short-range	Medium-range	Long-range	
Duration	Usually less than 3 months, maximum of 1 year	3 months to 3 years	More than 3 years
Applicability	Job scheduling, worker assignments	Sales and production planning, budgeting	New product development, facilities planning

HOW IS DEMAND FORECAST DETERMINED?

There are two approaches to determine demand forecast:

- The qualitative approach,
- The quantitative approach.

The comparison of these two approaches is shown:

Description	Qualitative Approach	Quantitative Approach
Applicability	Used when situation is vague & little data exist	Used when situation is stable & historical data exist
Considerations	Involves intuition and experience	Involves mathematical techniques
Techniques	Jury of executive opinion Sales force composite Delphi method Consumer market survey	Time series models Causal models

QUALITATIVE FORECASTING METHODS

Your company may wish to try any of the qualitative forecasting methods if you do not have historical data on your products' sales.

Qualitative Method	Description
Jury of executive opinion	The opinions of a small group of high-level managers are pooled and together they estimate demand. The group uses their managerial experience, and in some cases, combines the results of statistical models.
Sales force composite	Each salesperson is asked to project their sales. Since the salesperson is the one closest to the marketplace, he has the capacity to know what the customer wants. These projections are then combined at the municipal, provincial and regional levels.
Delphi method	A panel of experts is identified where an expert could be a decision maker, an ordinary employee, or an industry expert. Each of them will be asked individually for their estimate of the demand. An iterative process is conducted until the experts have reached a consensus.
Consumer market survey	The customers are asked about their purchasing plans and their projected buying behavior. A large number of respondents is needed here to be able to generalize certain results.

Quantitative Forecasting Methods

There are two forecasting models here:

(1) The time series model and

(2) The causal model.

A time series is a s et of evenly spaced numerical data and is o btained by observing responses at regular time periods. In the time series model, the forecast is based only on past values and assumes that factors that influence the past, the present and the future sales of your products will continue.

On the other hand, t he causal model uses a mathematical technique known as the regression analysis that relates a dependent variable to an independent variable in the form of a linear equation.

The time series forecasting methods are:

Time Series Forecasting Method	Description
Naïve Approach	Assumes that demand in the next period is the same as demand in most recent period; demand pattern may not always be that stable For example: If July sales were 50, then Augusts sales will also be 50
Moving Averages	MA is a series of arithmetic means and is used if little or no trend is present in the data; provides an overall impression of data over time. A simple moving average uses average demand for a fixed sequence of periods and is good for stable demand with no pronounced behavioral patterns. *Equation*: F 4 = [D 1 + D2 + D3] / 4 F - forecast, D - Demand, No. - Period A weighted moving average adjusts the moving average method to reflect fluctuations more closely by assigning weights to the most recent data, meaning, that the older data is usually less

	important. The weights are based on intuition and lie between 0 and 1 for a total of 1.0. *Equation*: WMA 4 = (W) (D3) + (W) (D2) + (W) (D1) WMA - Weighted moving average, W - Weight, D - Demand, No. - Period
Exponential Smoothing	The exponential smoothing is an averaging method that reacts more strongly to recent changes in demand by assigning a smoothing constant to the most recent data more strongly; useful if recent changes in data are the results of actual change instead of just random fluctuations, F t + 1 = a D t + (1 - a) F t Where, F t + 1 = the forecast for the next period D t = actual demand in the present period F t = the previously determined forecast for the present period, = a weighting factor referred to as the smoothing constant
Time Series Decomposition	The time series decomposition adjusts the seasonality by multiplying the normal forecast by a seasonal factor.

3

Cost Analysis

CONCEPT OF COST ANALYSIS

Studies of costs and related economic implications comprise a major group of methods used in HTA. These studies can involve attributes of either or both of primary data collection and integrative methods.

That is, cost data can be collected as part of RCTs and other clinical studies, as well as administrative databases used in health care payment.

Cost data from one or more such sources often are combined with data from primary clinical studies, epidemiological studies, and other sources to conduct cost-effectiveness analyses and other cost studies that involve weighing health and economic impacts of health technology.

Interest in cost analyses has accompanied concerns about rising health care costs, pressures on health care policymakers to allocate resources, and the need for health product makers and other technology advocates to demonstrate the economic benefits of their technologies. This interest is reflected in a considerable increase in the number of reports of cost analyses in the literature and further refinement of methods.

TYPES OF COST ANALYSIS

There is a variety of approaches to cost analysis, the suitability of any of which depends upon the purpose of an assessment and the availability of data and other resources. It is rarely possible or necessary to identify and quantify all costs and all benefits and the units used to quantify these may differ.

Main types of cost analysis include the following:

- *Cost-of-illness analysis*: a determination of the economic impact of an illness or condition e.g., of smoking, arthritis or bedsores, including associated treatment costs
- *Cost-minimization analysis*: a determination of the least costly among alternative interventions that are assumed to produce equivalent outcomes
- *Cost-effectiveness analysis*: a comparison of costs in monetary units with outcomes in quantitative non-monetary units, e.g., reduced mortality or morbidity
- *Cost-utility analysis*: a form of cost-effectiveness analysis that compares costs in monetary units with outcomes in terms of their utility, usually to the patient, measured, e.g., in QALYs
- *Cost-consequence analysis*: a form of cost-effectiveness analysis that presents costs and outcomes in discrete categories, without aggregating or weighting them
- *Cost-benefit analysis*: compares costs and benefits, both of which are quantified in common monetary units.

Contrasts the valuation of costs and outcomes among these alternative economic analyses.

Table. Different Types of Economic Analysis

	Valuation of costs		**Valuation of outcomes**
Cost of Illness	$	vs.	None
Cost Minimization	$	vs.	Assume same
Cost Effectiveness	$	÷	Natural units
Cost Utility	$	÷	Utiles
Cost Benefit	$	÷ or -	$

Cost-minimization analysis, CEA and CUA necessarily involve comparisons of alternative interventions. A technology cannot be simply cost effective, though it may be cost effective compared to something else. Although CBA typically involves comparisons of alternative technologies, this is not necessary.

Because it measures costs and outcomes in monetary terms, CBA enables comparison of disparate technologies, e.g., coronary artery bypass graft surgery and screening for breast cancer. A drawback of CBA is the difficulty of assigning monetary values to all pertinent outcomes, including changes in the length or quality of human life. CEA avoids this limitation by using more direct or natural units of outcomes such as lives saved or strokes averted. As such, CEA can only compare technologies whose outcomes are measured in the same units. In CUA, estimates of utility are assigned to health outcomes, enabling comparisons of disparate technologies.

Two basic approaches for cost-benefit analysis are ratio approach and the net benefit approach. The ratio approach indicates the amount of benefits that can be realised per unit expenditure on a technology vs. a comparator. In the ratio approach, a technology is cost beneficial vs. a comparator if the ratio of the change in costs to the change in benefits is less than one. The net benefits approach indicates the absolute amount of money saved or lost due to a use of a technology vs. a comparator. In the net benefits formulation, a technology is cost-beneficial vs. a comparator if the net change in benefits exceeds the net change in costs. The choice between a net benefits approach or a benefit/cost approach for a CBA can affect findings.

The approach selected may depend upon such factors as whether costs must be limited to a certain level, whether the intent is to maximize the absolute level of benefits, whether the intent is to minimize the cost/benefit ratio regardless of the absolute level of costs, etc. Indeed, under certain circumstances these two basic approaches may yield different preferences among alternative technologies.

Basic formulas for determining CEA, CUA, and CBA.

Basic Formulas for CEA, CUA, and CBA

Int: Intervention; *Comp*: Comparator

Cost-Effectiveness Ratio:

$$\text{CE Ratio} = \frac{\$\text{Cost}_{\text{Int}} - \$\text{Cost}_{\text{Comp}}}{\$\text{Effect}_{\text{Int}} - \$\text{Effect}_{\text{Comp}}}$$

For Example: "$45,000per life-year saved"or"$10,000per lung cancer averted"

Cost-Utility Ratio:

$$\text{CU Ratio} = \frac{\$\text{Cost}_{\text{Int}} - \$\text{Cost}_{\text{Comp}}}{\$\text{Utile}_{\text{Int}} - \$\text{Utile}_{\text{Comp}}}$$

Utiles, units of utility or preference, are often measured in QALYs. So, for example:

"$45,000 per life-year saved" or "$10,000 per lung cancer case averted"

Cost-Benefit, Ratio Approach:

$$\text{CE Ratio} = \frac{\$\text{Cost}_{\text{Int}} - \$\text{Cost}_{\text{Comp}}}{\$\text{Benefit}_{\text{Int}} - \$\text{Benefit}_{\text{Comp}}}$$

For example: "Cost-benfit ratio of 1.5"

Cost-Benfit, Net Benefit Approach:

$$\text{CB Net} = (\$\text{Cost}_{\text{Int}} - \$\text{Cost}_{\text{Comp}}) - (\$\text{Benfit}_{\text{Int}} - \$\text{Benefit}_{\text{Comp}})$$

For example: "Net cost of $5,000."

QUADRANTS OF COST-EFFECTIVENESS

A basic approach to portraying a cost-effectiveness comparison of a new intervention to a standard of care is to consider the cost and effectiveness of a new intervention in the space of four fields as shown in Box 20, starting with the upper figure. The level of costs and the level of effectiveness for the standard of care are indicated by the"X" in the middle of the figure. A new intervention may have higher or lower costs, and higher or lower effectiveness, such that its plot may fall into one of the four quadrants surrounding the costs and effectiveness of the standard of care. If it is known that the plot of the new intervention falls into either of two of the quadrants, i.e., where the new intervention has higher costs and lower effectiveness or it has lower costs and higher effectiveness then no further analysis may be required.

If it is known that the plot of the new intervention falls into either of the other two quadrants, i.e., where the new intervention has higher costs and higher effectiveness, or it has lower costs and lower effectiveness, then further analysis weighing the marginal costs and effectiveness of the new intervention compared to the standard of care may be required. Within either of the two quadrants that entail weighing tradeoffs of costs and effectiveness, it may be apparent that the marginal tradeoff of costs and outcomes is so high or low as to suggest rejection or adoption. This arises when the new intervention yields only very low marginal gain in effectiveness at a very high marginal cost or yields very high marginal improvements in effectiveness at a very low marginal cost.

KEY ATTRIBUTES OF COST ANALYSES

The approaches to accounting for costs and outcomes in cost analyses can vary in a number of important respects. These should be carefully considered by assessors, as well as the policymakers who intend to make use of assessment findings. Given the different ways in which costs and outcomes may be determined, all studies should make clear their methodology in these respects.

Comparator. Any cost analysis of one intervention versus another must be specific about the comparator. This may be standard of care, minimum practice, or no intervention. Some analyses that declare the superiority of a new intervention may have used a comparator that is no longer in practice or is considered sub-standard care or that is not appropriate for the patient population of interest.

Perspective. The perspective of a cost analysis refers to the standpoint at which costs and outcomes are realised. For instance, the perspective of an analysis may be that of society overall, a third-party payer, a physician, a hospital, or a patient. Clearly, costs and outcomes are not realised in the same way from each of these perspectives. Many analysts favour using the broad perspective of society and identifying all costs and all outcomes accordingly. However,"society" as such may not be the decisionmaker, and what is cost effective from that perspective may not be what is cost effective from the standpoint of a ministry of health, third-party payer, hospital manager, patient, or other decisionmaker. It is possible that this perspective may resemble that of a national or regional government, if indeed that government experiences all of the costs and outcomes that are included in a societal perspective.

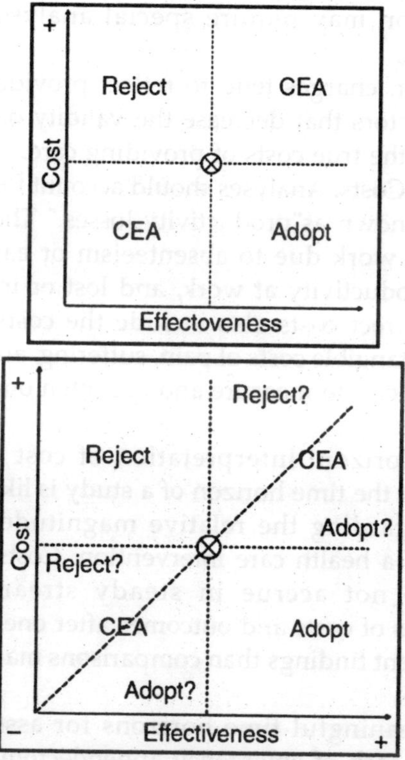

Fig. Quadrants of Cost-Effectiveness

Direct Costs. Depending upon the perspective taken, cost analyses should identify two types of direct costs. Direct costs represent the value of all goods, services, and other resources consumed in providing health care or dealing with side effects or other current and future consequences of health care. Two types of direct costs are direct health care costs and direct non-health care costs.

Direct health care costs include costs of physician services, hospital services, drugs, etc. involved in delivery of health care. Direct non-health care costs are incurred in connection with health care, such as for care provided by family members and transportation to and from the site of care. In quantifying direct health care costs, many analyses use readily available hospital or physician charges rather than true costs, whose determination may require special analyses of resource consumption.

However, charges tend to reflect provider cost shifting and other factors that decrease the validity of using charges to represent the true costs of providing care.

Indirect Costs. Analyses should account for indirect costs, sometimes known as"productivity losses." These include the costs of lost work due to absenteeism or early retirement, impaired productivity at work, and lost or impaired leisure activity. Indirect costs also include the costs of premature mortality. Intangible costs of pain, suffering, and grief are real, yet very difficult to measure and are often omitted from cost analyses.

Time Horizon. Interpretation of cost analyses must consider that the time horizon of a study is likely to affect the findings regarding the relative magnitudes of costs and outcomes of a health care intervention. Costs and outcomes usually do not accrue in steady streams over time. Comparisons of costs and outcomes after one year may yield much different findings than comparisons made after 5, 10, or 25 years.

The meaningful time horizons for assessing the cost horizons of each of emergency appendectomies, cholesterol-lowering in high-risk adults, and smoking cessation in teenagers are likely to be quite different.

For example, an analysis conducted for the Medicare programme in the US to determine cost and time tradeoffs of hemodialysis and kidney transplantation showed that the annualized expenditure by the Medicare End-Stage Renal Disease Programme for a dialysis patient was $32,000. Although patients with functioning transplanted kidneys required a first-year expenditure of $56,000, they cost Medicare only an average of $6,400 in succeeding years.

On average, estimated cumulative dialysis and transplantation costs reach a break-even point in about three years, after which transplantation provides a net financial gain compared to dialysis.

Time horizons should be long enough to capture streams of health and economic outcomes. These could encompass a disease episode, patient life, or even multiple generations of life.

Quantitative modeling approaches may be needed to estimate costs and outcomes that are beyond those of available data. Of course, the higher the discount rate used in an analysis, the less important are future outcomes and costs.

Average Costs vs. Marginal Costs. Assessments should make clear whether average costs or marginal costs are being used in the analysis.

Whereas average cost analysis considers the total costs and outcomes of an intervention, marginal cost analysis considers how outcomes change with changes in costs, which may provide more information about how to use resources efficiently. Marginal cost analysis may reveal that, beyond a certain level of spending, the additional benefits are no longer worth the additional costs.

For example, as shown in Box 21, the average cost per desired outcome of an iterative screening test may appear to be quite acceptable whereas marginal cost analysis demonstrates that the cost of adding the last test to detect another case of cancer would be astronomical.

AVERAGE COST ANALYSIS VS. MARGINAL COST ANALYSIS

The importance of determining marginal costs is apparent in the analysis by Neuhauser and Lewicki of a proposed protocol of sequential stool guaiac testing for colon cancer.

Here, average cost figures obscure a steep rise in marginal costs of testing because the high detection rate from the initial tests is averaged over subsequent tests that contribute little to the detection rate.

This type of analysis helps to demonstrate how it is possible to spend steeply increasing health care resources for diminishing returns in health benefits.

Table. Cancer Screening and Detection Costs with Sequential Guaiac Tests

No. of cancers detected	Additional cancers detected	Total cost ($) of diagnosis	Additional ($) cost of diagnosis	Average cost ($) per cancer detected	Marginal cost ($) per cancer detected
65.9469	65.9469	77,511	77,511	1,175	1,175
71.4424	5.4956	107,690	30,179	1,507	5,492
71.9004	0.4580	130,199	22,509	1,810	49,150
71.9385	0.0382	148,116	17,917	2,059	469,534
71.9417	0.0032	163,141	15,024	2,268	4,724,695
71.9420	0.0003	176,331	13,190	2,451	47,107,214

This analysis assumed that there were 72 true cancer cases per 10,000 population. The testing protocol provided six stool guaiac tests per person to detect colon cancer. If any one of the six tests was positive, a barium-enema test was performed, which was assumed to yield no falsepositive and no false-negative results. Other assumptions: the true-positive cancer detection rate of any single guaiac test was 91.667%; the false-positive rate of any single guaiac test was 36.508%; the cost of the first stool guaiac test was $4 and each subsequent guaiac test was $1; the cost of a barium-enema was $100. The marginal cost per case detected depends on the population screened and the sensitivity of the test used.

Discounting. Cost analyses should account for the effect of the passage of time on the value of costs and outcomes. Costs and outcomes that occur in the future usually have less present value than costs and outcomes realised today. Discounting reflects the time preference for benefits earlier rather than later; it also reflects the opportunity costs of capital, i.e., whatever returns on investment that could have been gained if resources had been invested elsewhere. Thus, costs and outcomes should be discounted relative to their present value.

Discounting allows comparisons involving costs and benefits that flow differently over time. It is less relevant for"pay as you go" benefits, such as if all costs and benefits are realised together within one year. It is more relevant in instances where these do not occur in parallel, such as when most costs are realised early and most benefits are realised in later years. Discount rates used in cost analyses are typically based on interest rates of government bonds or the market interest rates for the cost of capital whose maturity is about the same as the duration of the effective time horizon of the health care intervention of programme being evaluated. Box 22 shows the basic formula for calculating present values for a given discount rate, as well as how the present value of a cost or benefit that is discounted at selected rates is affected over time.

Cost analyses should also correct for the effects of inflation, such as when costs or cost-effectiveness for one year are compared to another year.

Sensitivity Analysis. Any estimate of costs, outcomes, and other variables used in a cost analysis is subject to some uncertainty.

Therefore, sensitivity analysis should be performed to determine if plausible variations in the estimates of certain variables thought to be subject to significant uncertainty affect the results of the cost analysis. A sensitivity analysis may reveal, for example, that including indirect costs, or assuming the use of generic as opposed to brand name drugs in a medical therapy, or using a plausible higher discount rate in an analysis changes the cost-effectiveness of one intervention compared to another.

COLLECTING COST DATA ALONGSIDE CLINICAL STUDIES

The validity of a cost-related study depends upon the sources of the data for costs and outcomes. Increased attention is being given to collection of cost data in more rigorous, prospective studies, particularly RCTs. The closer integration of economic and clinical studies raises important methodological issues.

In order to promote more rational diffusion of new technologies, it would be desirable to generate reliable cost and outcomes data during the early part of a technology's lifecycle, such as during RCTs required prior to marketing approval. An RCT would be expected to yield the most reliable data concerning efficacy of an intervention; however, the care given in an RCT and the costs of providing it may be atypical compared to more general settings. For example, RCTs may involve more extensive and frequent laboratory tests and other patient monitoring, and may occur more often in academic medical centres whose costs tend to be higher than in community health care institutions.

Other aspects of trial design, sample size, choice of outcome measures, identification and tabulation of costs, burden on investigators of data collection and related matters affect the usefulness of clinical trial data for meaningful economic studies.

Also, the growth of multinational clinical trials of drugs and other technologies raises challenges of estimating country-specific treatment effects and cost-effectiveness, given differences in epidemiological factors, health care delivery models, resource use, and other factors.

Discount Rate Calculation and Use in Determining Present Value of Future Costs and Benefits.

Discount rate calculation: Compling the discounted stream of costs (or benefits) over time

$$P = \sum_{n=1}^{n} \frac{Fn}{(1+r)^n}$$

P = present value

F = future cost (or benefits) at year n

r = annual discount rate

Present valuem (P) of future cost (F) occurring at year n at selected annual discount rate (r)

Table. Discount Rate

year	3%	5%	10%
1	0.97	0.95	0.91
5	0.86	0.78	0.62
25	0.48	0.30	0.09
50	0.23	0.09	0.009

For example, the present value of a cost (or benfit) of $1,000 occurring:

- 1 year in the future, using 10% discount rate, is $910

- 5 years in the future, using 3% discount rate, is $860
- 50 yrs in the future, using 5% discount rate, is $90

In practice, there is wide variation in economic study methodologies. Although some variation is unavoidable, many differences in perspective, accounting for direct and indirect costs, time frames, discounting and other aspects are often arbitrary, result from lack of expertise, and may reflect biases on the part of investigators or sponsors.

This diminishes comparability and transferability of study results as well as credibility of findings. National and international groups have developed and revised voluntary standards for conducting and reporting economic studies of health care technologies.

A recent review of 25 guidelines from North America, Europe, and Australia found a general trend towrds harmonization in most methodological aspects, although there were more differences in such dimensions as choice of economic perspective, resources, and costs to be included in analysis.

RELATIONSHIP BETWEEN SHORT RUN AND LONG RUN COST FUNCTIONS

- The SRTC can be tangent to the LRTC at only one point. The SRTC cannot intersect the curve. The SRTC can lie wholly"above" the curve with no tangency point.
- The SRTC curve is tangent to LRTC at long run cost minimizing level of production. At the point of tangency LRTC = SRTC. At all other levels of production SRTC will exceed LRTC.
- Average cost functions are the total cost function divided by the level of output. Therefore the LRATC is also tangent to the SRATC at cost minimizing level of output. At the point of tangency LRATC = SRATC. At all other levels of production SRATC > LRATC
- The slope of the total cost curves equals marginal cost. Therefore when LRTC is tangent to SRTC, SRMC = LRMC.

- At the long run cost minimizing level of output LRTC = SRTC; SRATC = LRATC and SRMC = LRMC.
- The long run cost minimizing level of output may be different from minimum SRATC.
- If constant returns to scale then (min) SRATC = LRATC = SRMC = LRMC.
- If increasing returns to scale (min) SRATC will occur at higher level of production than long run cost minimizing level of production. While LRTC = SRTC; SRATC = LRATC and SRMC = LRMC. SRMC does not equal LRMC and LRMC does not equal LRAC.
- With decreasing returns (min) SRATC will be tangent to the LRAC curve at a lower level of production lower than long run cost minimizing level of production. While LRTC = SRTC; SRATC = LRATC and SRMC = LRMC. SRMC does not equal LRMC and LRMC does not equal LRAC
- A firm that is experiencing increasing returns to scale and is producing at min SRAC can always reduce average cost by expanding the use of the fixed input.
- LRATC will always equal or be less than SRATC.

THE SUPPLY CURVE

Price usually is a major determinant in the quantity supplied. For a particular good with all other factors held constant, a table can be constructed of price and quantity supplied based on observed data. Such a table is called a supply schedule, as shown in the following example:

Table. Supply Schedule

Price	QuantitySupplied
1	12
2	28
3	42
4	52
5	60

By graphing this data, one obtains the supply curve:

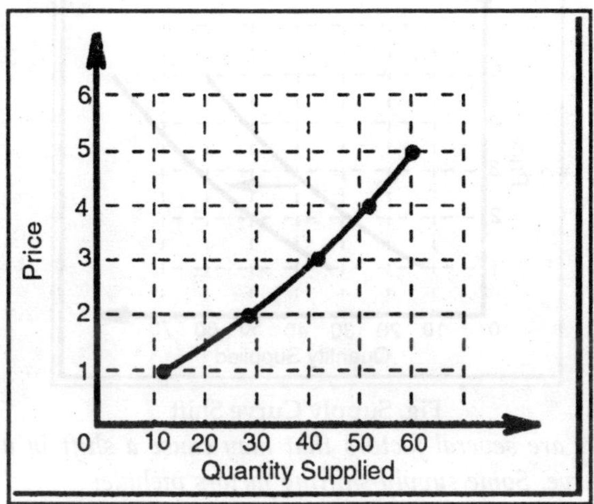

Fig. Supply Curve

As with the demand curve, the convention of the supply curve is to display quantity supplied on the x-axis as the independent variable and price on the y-axis as the dependent variable. The law of supply states that the higher the price, the larger the quantity supplied, all other things constant. The law of supply is demonstrated by the upward slope of the supply curve. As with the demand curve, the supply curve often is approximated as a straight line to simplify analysis. A straight-line supply function would have the following structure:

Quantity = a + (b x Price)

where a and b are constant for each supply curve.

A change in price results in a change in quantity supplied and represents movement along the supply curve.

SHIFTS IN THE SUPPLY CURVE

While changes in price result in movement along the supply curve, changes in other relevant factors cause a shift in supply, that is, a shift of the supply curve to the left or right. Such a shift results in a change in quantity supplied for a given price level. If the change causes an increase in the quantity supplied at each price, the supply curve would shift to the right:

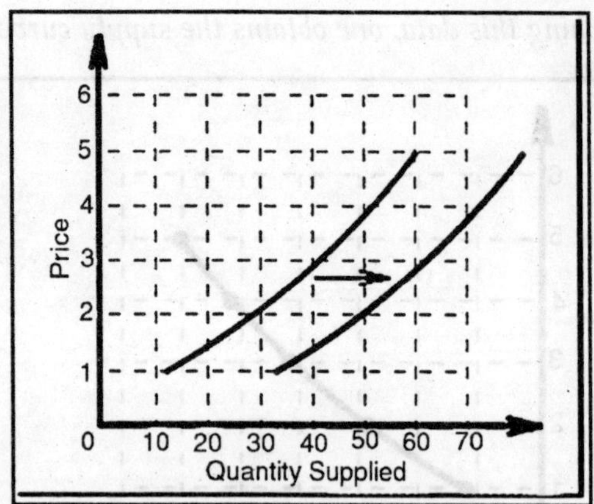

Fig. Supply Curve Shift

There are several factors that may cause a shift in a good's supply curve. Some supply-shifting factors include:

- *Prices of other goods*: The supply of one good may decrease if the price of another good increases, causing producers to reallocate resources to produce larger quantities of the more profitable good.
- *Number of sellers*: More sellers result in more supply, shifting the supply curve to the right.
- *Prices of relevant inputs*: If the cost of resources used to produce a good increases, sellers will be less inclined to supply the same quantity at a given price, and the supply curve will shift to the left.
- *Technology*: Technological advances that increase production efficiency shift the supply curve to the right.
- *Expectations*: If sellers expect prices to increase, they may decrease the quantity currently supplied at a given price in order to be able to supply more when the price increases, resulting in a supply curve shift to the left.

ISOQUANT CURVE

The term"isoquant" has been derived from the Greek word"iso" meaning equal and Latin word"quantus" meaning"quantity". The"isoquant curve" is,therefore, also known as"Equal product curve" or"Production Intelligence

Curve". An isoquant curve is locus of point representing various combinations of two inputs - capital and labour - yielding the same output. *Isoquant curves are drawn on the basis of the following assumptions*:

- There are only two inputs, v12, labour (L) and capital (K) tom produce a commodity X.
- The two inputs - L and K - can substitute each other but at diminishing rate.
- The technology of production is given.

Given these assumptions, it is always possible to produce given quantity of commodity X with various combination of labour and capital. The factor combinations are so formed that the substitution of one factor for the other leaves the output unaffected.The technology is presented through are isoquant curve (IQ1 = 100). The curve IQ1 all along its length represents a fixed quantity, 100 units of product X. This quantity of output can be produced with a number of labour-capital combination.

For example: Points A, B, C and D on the isoquant curve IQ1 shows four different combinations of inputs, K and L, all yielding the same output - 100 units. The movement from A to B indicates decreasing Quantity Of K and increasing number of L.This implies substi- -tution Of labour for capital such that all the input combinations yield the same quantity of commodity X i.e.. IQ1 = 100.

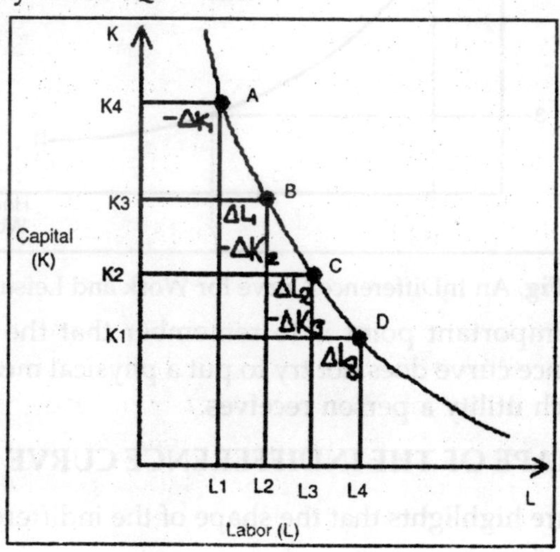

INDIFFERENCE CURVE ANALYSIS

The aim of indifference curve analysis is to analyse how a rational consumer chooses between two goods. In other words, how the change in the wage rate will affect the choice between leisure time and work time. Indifference analysis combines two concepts; indifference curves and budget lines (constraints)

THE INDIFFERENCE CURVE

An indifference curve is a line that shows all the possible combinations of two goods between which a person is indifferent. In other words, it is a line that shows the consumption of different combinations of two goods that will give the same utility to the person. For instance, in Figure the indifference curve is I1. A person would receive the same utility from consuming 4 hours of work and 6 hours of leisure, as they would if they consumed 7 hours of work and 3 hours of leisure.

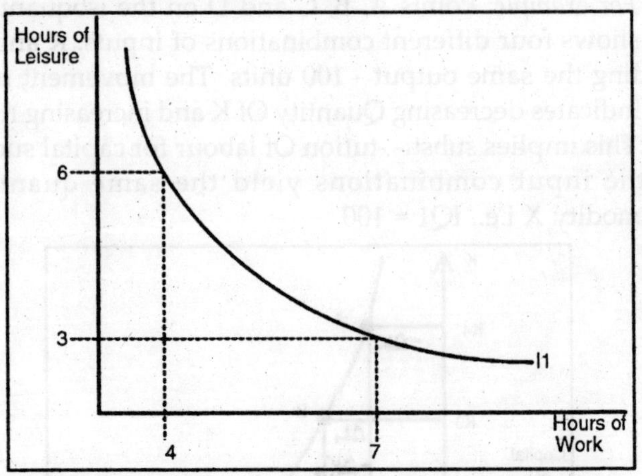

Fig. An InDifference Curve for Work and Leisure

An important point is to remember that the use of an indifference curve does not try to put a physical measure onto how much utility a person receives.

THE SHAPE OF THE INDIFFERENCE CURVE

Figure highlights that the shape of the indifference curve

is not a straight line. It is conventional to draw the curve as bowed. This is due to the concept of the diminishing marginal rate of substitution between the two goods. The marginal rate of substitution is the amount of one good that has to be given up if the consumer is to obtain one extra unit of the other good.

The equation is: The marginal rate of substitution (MRS) = change in good X/ change in good Y. Using Figure, the marginal rate of substitution between point A and Point B is;

$$MRS = -3/3 = -1 = 1$$

Note, the convention is to ignore the sign.

The reason why the marginal rate of substitution diminishes is due to the principle of diminishing marginal utility. Where this principle states that the more units of a good are consumed, then additional units will provide less additional satisfaction. Therefore, as a person consumes more of one good then they will receive diminishing utility for that extra unit, hence, they will be willing to give up less of their leisure to obtain one more unit of work. The relationship between marginal utility and the marginal rate of substitution is often summarised with the following equation;

$$MRS = Mu_x / Mu_y$$

It is possible to draw more than one indifference curve on the same diagram. If this occurs then it is termed an indifference curve map.

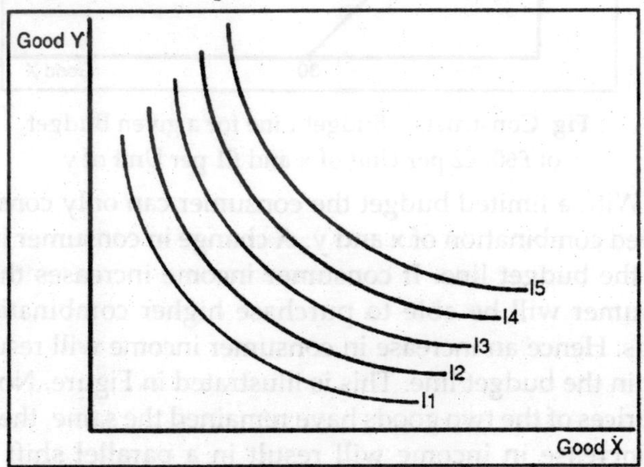

Fig. An Indifference Map

The general rule is that indifference curves further too the right show combinations of the two goods that yield a higher utility, while curves to the left show combinations that yield lower levels of utility.

A BUDGET LINE

The budget line is an important component when analysing consumer behaviour. The budget line illustrates all the possible combinations of two goods that can be purchased at given prices and for a given consumer budget. Remember, that the amount of a good that a person can buy will depend upon their income and the price of the good. This discussion outlines the construction of a budget line and how the change in the determinants will affect the budget line.

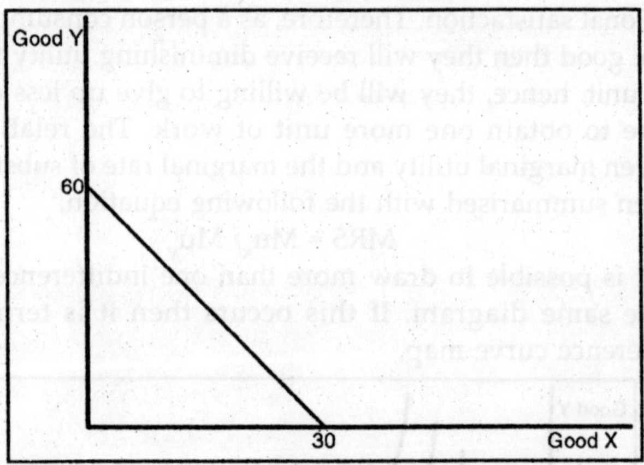

Fig. Constructs a Budget Line for a given Budget of £60, £2 per Unit of x and £1 per Unit of y.

With a limited budget the consumer can only consume a limited combination of x and y. A change in consumer income and the budget line. If consumer income increases then the consumer will be able to purchase higher combinations of goods. Hence an increase in consumer income will result in a shift in the budget line. This is illustrated in Figure. Note that the prices of the two goods have remained the same, therefore, the increase in income will result in a parallel shift in the budget line.

Assume consumer income increased to £90.

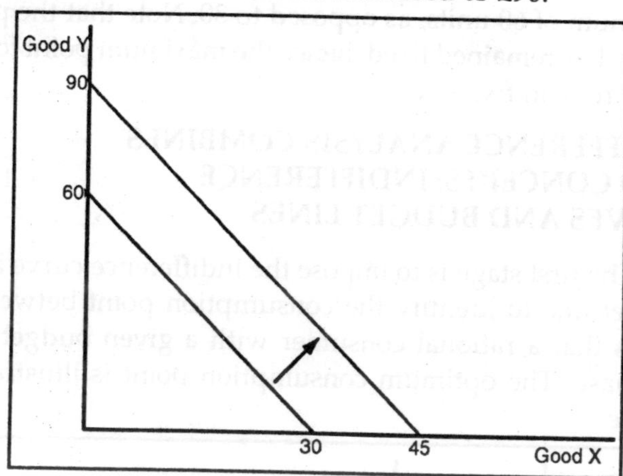

Fig. An Increase in Consumer Income

If consumer income fell then there would be a corresponding parallel shift to the left to represent a fall in the potential combinations of the two goods that can be purchased. A change in the price of a good and the budget line. If income is held constant, and the price of one of the goods changes then the slope of the curve will change. In other words, the curve will pivot. This is illustrated in Figure.

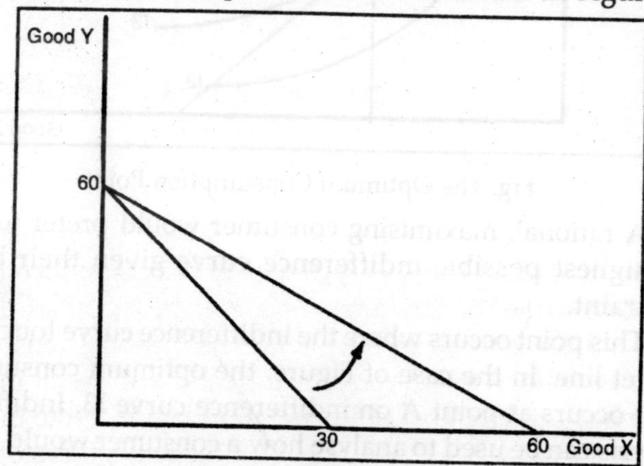

Fig. A Change in Price

The reduction of the price of good x from £2 to £1 means

that on a fixed budget of £60, the consumer could purchase a maximum of 60 units, as opposed to 30. Note that the price of good y has remained fixed, hence the maximum point for good y will remain fixed.

INDIFFERENCE ANALYSIS COMBINES TWO CONCEPTS; INDIFFERENCE CURVES AND BUDGET LINES

The first stage is to impose the indifference curve and the budget line to identify the consumption point between two goods that a rational consumer with a given budget would purchase. The optimum consumption point is illustrated on Figure.

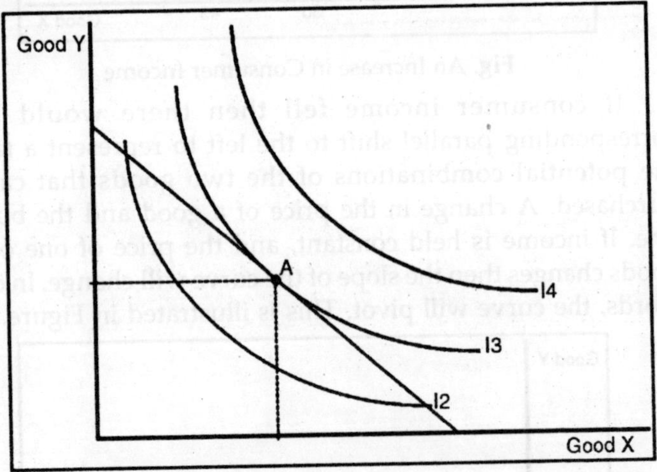

Fig. The Optimum Consumption Point

A rational, maximising consumer would prefer to be on the highest possible indifference curve given their budget constraint.

This point occurs where the indifference curve touches the budget line. In the case of Figure, the optimum consumption point occurs at point A on indifference curve I3. Indifference analysis can be used to analyse how a consumer would change the combination of two goods for a given change in their income or the price of the good.

The next part looks at the income and substitution effects

of a change in price. If we assume that the good is normal, then the increase in price will result in a fall in the quantity demanded. This is for two reasons; the income effect and the substitution effect. These two processes can be visualised using indifference analysis.

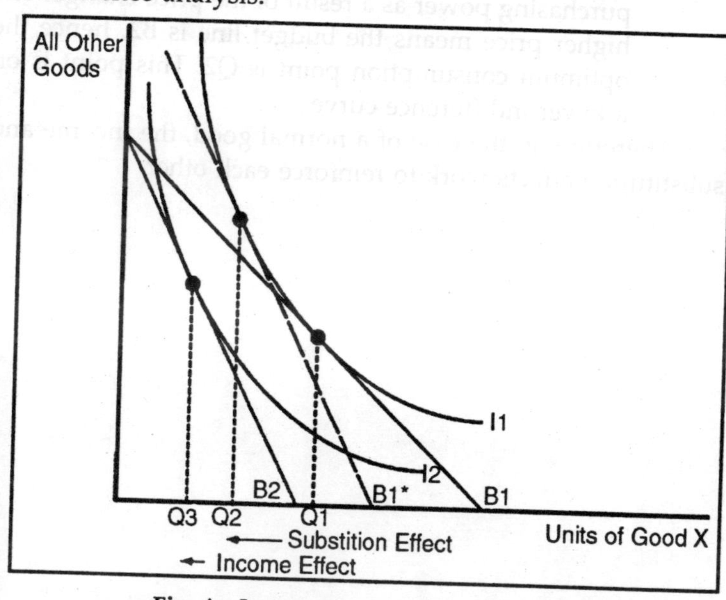

Fig. An Increase in the Price of Good x

Due to the price of good x increasing, the budget line has pivoted from B1 to B2 and the consumption point has moved.

The decrease in the quantity demanded can be divided into two effects;

The Substitution Effect

- The substitution effect is when the consumer switches consumption patterns due to the price change alone but remains on the same indifference curve. To identify the substitution effect a new budget line needs to be constructed. The budget line B1* is added, this budget line needs to be parallel with the budget line B2 and tangential to I1.

Therefore, the movement from Q1 to Q2 is purely due to the substitution effect.

The Income Effect

- The income effect highlights how consumption will change due to the consumer having a change in purchasing power as a result of the price change. The higher price means the budget line is B2, hence the optimum consumption point is Q2. This point is on a lower indifference curve.

Therefore, in the case of a normal good, the income and substitution effects work to reinforce each other.

4

Pricing Analysis

INTRODUCTION

In marketing Price Analysis refers to the analysis of consumer response to theoretical prices in survey research. In general business Price Analysis is the process of examining and evaluating a proposed price without evaluating its separate cost elements and proposed profit/fee.

Price analysis may also refer to the breakdown of a price to a unit figure.

Usually per square metre or square foot of accommodation or per hectare or even square metre of land. The price with suitable adjustment for various differences, is then applied to the valuation problem.

MARKET STRUCTURE

Market structure is best defined as the organisational and other characteristics of a market. We focus on those characteristics which affect the nature of competition and pricing - but it is important not to place too much emphasis simply on the market share of the existing firms in an industry.

Traditionally, the most important features of market structure are:

- The number of firms
- The market share of the largest firms
- The nature of costs
- The degree to which the industry is vertically integrated - vertical integration explains the process by which different stages in production and

distribution of a product are under the ownership and control of a single enterprise.

A good example of vertical integration is the oil industry, where the major oil companies own the rights to extract from oilfields, they run a fleet of tankers, operate refineries and have control of sales at their own filling stations.

- The extent of product differentiation
- The structure of buyers in the industry
- The turnover of customers, i.e., how many customers are prepared to switch their supplier over a given time period when market conditions change.

The rate of customer churn is affected by the degree of consumer or brand loyalty and the influence of persuasive advertising and marketing

Table. Market Structures

Characteristic	Perfect Competition	Oligopoly	Monopoly
Number of firms	Many	Few	One
Type of product	Homogenous	Differentiated	Limited
Barriers to entry	None	High	High
Supernormal short run profit	ü	ü	ü
Supernormal long run profit	û	ü	ü
Pricing	Price taker	Price maker	Price maker
Profit maximization?	ü	Not always	Usually, but not always
Non price competition	û	ü	ü
Economic efficiency	High	Low	Low
Innovative behaviour	Weak	Very Strong	Potentially strong

MARKET STRUCTURE AND INNOVATION

Which market conditions are optimal for effective and sustained innovation to occur? This is a question that has vexed economists and business academics for many years.

High levels of research and development spending are frequently observed in oligopolistic markets, although this does not always translate itself into a fast pace of innovation.

The recent work of William Baumol provides support for oligopoly as market structure best suited for innovative behaviour. Innovation is perceived as being"mandatory" for businesses that need to establish a cost-advantage or a significant lead in product quality over their rivals.

"As soon as quality competition and sales effort are admitted into the sacred precincts of theory, the price variable is ousted from its dominant position.....But in capitalist reality as distinguished from its textbook picture, it is not that kind of competition which counts but the competition which commands a decisive cost or quality advantage and which strikes not at the margins of profits and the outputs of the existing firms but at their foundations and their very lives. This kind of competition is as much more effective than the other as a bombardment is in comparison with forcing a door"

Supernormal profits persist in the long-run in an oligopoly and these can be used to finance R&D

GOVERNMENT POLICY AND INNOVATION IN THE ECONOMY

The current government places a huge emphasis on the potential value from more innovation across all sectors of the British economy.

This is because of the economic gains that follow:
For example:

- Improvements in the competitiveness of UK producers in home and overseas markets.
- Innovation helps to protect and develop comparative advantage.
- Higher productivity will keep down unit labour costs against the challenge of low-cost competition from emerging market economies.
- Innovation is a potential source of higher long-term trend growth - indeed supply creates its own demand and can give businesses much higher rates of return on their investment than an expansion of their existing capacity and product range.
- Innovation can also create many thousands of new jobs even though some jobs may be lost because of the adoption of labour-saving technology. The new

jobs emerge in training and other services together with the demand for labour that comes from expanding output to supply an expansion to new markets.

- There might also be significant social benefits from innovative behaviour - for example the delivery of new health treatments or innovations that provide safer forms of transport.

GOVERNMENT POLICY AND INNOVATION

Supply-side strategies are usually linked directly with attempts to promote more innovative behaviour. Indeed the focus of government policy is firmly focused on improvements in the microeconomics of markets. Consider this extract from a recent speech by Gordon Brown

"If the past century of economic policymaking has taught us anything, it is that achieving strong long term growth often has less to do with macroeconomic policies that with good microeconomics, including fostering competitive markets that reward innovation and restricting government to only a limited role."

Which policies might encourage more innovation?

- Tax credits/investment allowances
- Policies to encouragement small business creation and entrepreneurship
- Toughening up of competition policy to expose cartel behaviour, but to allow and promote joint ventures to fund research and development
- Lower corporation taxes to encourage innovative foreign companies to establish in Britain
- Increased funding for research in our universities

Important developments:

- Increasingly most innovation is done by smaller firms - indeed multinational corporations are now out-sourcing their research and development spending to small businesses at home and overseas - much is being shifted to cheaper locations"offshore"-in India and Russia

- Innovation is now a continuous process - in part because the length of the product cycle is getting shorter as innovations are rapidly copied by competitors, pushing down profit margins and"transforming today's consumer sensation into tomorrow's commonplace commodity" - a good example of this is the introduction of two major competitors to the anti-impotence drug Viagra
- Innovation is not something left to chance - the most successful firms are those that pursue innovation in a systematic fashion
- Demand innovation is becoming more important: In many markets, demand is either stable or in long-run decline. The response is to go for"demand innovation" - discovering new forms of demand from consumers and adapting an existing product to meet them - the toy industry is a classic example of this
- Globalisation is driving innovation and not just in manufactured goods but across a vast range of household and business services and in particular in high-value knowledge industries

Classic examples of innovation first achieved by smaller firms:

- Air-conditioning
- Hydraulic brakes
- Digital X-Rays
- Soft contact lenses
- Quick frozen food
- Zip fastener

PRICE DETERMINATION UNDER DIFFERENT MARKET SITUATIONS

PRICE DEFINED

Among the many responsibilities of the purchasing agent is that of determining the best price for goods and services. What is"price"? Price is the measure of value for a unit of a commodity or service that expresses its worth relative to other goods or services. Economists define price as the value of any item expressed in monetary terms, money. The function of obtaining the best price for the greatest value is an important element in the purchasing cycle.

The best price or correct price is not necessarily the lowest price, for price is only one of the variables a buyer must consider before making the decision to purchase. In the manufacturing industry, the purchasing agent spends up to 60 per cent of the company's income on incoming goods. The purchasing agent has the duty and responsibility to see that these funds are expended to obtain the full measure of value in what is received.

This responsibility is discharged when all prices are carefully reviewed, be they from the past, present, or potential suppliers. Don't become just a"price buyer" by separating price from the considerations of quality and service.

THAT"LOW" PRICE

There is a tendency to exaggerate the importance of a low price in the purchasing function. The experienced purchasing agent will always avoid quick decisions to buy simply because the seller is quoting a price below the prevailing price. It must be remembered that the quality of the goods and the service offered are as important as the price.

During any recession or depressed market conditions, many firms would be happy just to maintain continuous operation and offer low prices for that purpose. The short-term goal for these firms is survival, with the long-term goal that improved economic conditions will enable them to again operate at a profit. After all, the primary goal of all enterprises is to operate at a profit, thus ensuring continuing and expanding ventures.

If the profit is reasonable and fair for the seller, then the price would be reasonable and fair for the buyer. Good will and cooperation between the seller and buyer makes for a good relationship, which includes reasonable and fair prices for both.

There are situations where a supplier quotes a low price in order to unload excess inventory that is costing carrying charges and thus tying up capital and reducing cash flow. This can be caused by the cancellation of an order by another customer or can be caused by an overstock resulting from anticipation of increased sales that did not materialize. This may be a genuine good buy.

Then there is the low price quoted by a supplier who is financially insecure and just wants your order to get your money. Such low prices lose their attractiveness when deliveries become uncertain and are often late, quality is questionable and requires extensive inspection, and complaints are never promptly resolved. Such purchases are not in the best interest of the buyer's company. Then there is the new supplier who quotes a low price and is willing to take less of a profit at this time in order to become established with the buyer's company. In this type of situation, the purchase may represent a good buy.

When the buyer receives a low price quote from any supplier, that buyer should be alert to all possibilities for that quote and its effect on the operation within the company. Find out the reason for such low price. Reputable suppliers will not hesitate to give you an honest answer. Beware of high-pressure tactics to get you to place the order.

WHO SETS THE PRICE?

The primary aim of the supplier is not only to remain in business but to make a profit that will permit expansion and increase profits. It has been assumed that the seller has the"privilege" of establishing the price at which he is willing to shell his product or service.

In the economics of the business world, the price must be attractive to the buyer to result in any transaction. Otherwise, there is no market for the goods or services, no business transaction, and no one makes money.

Neither can the buyer establish the price at which he is willing to buy. There would not be a seller willing to sell at a price that does not include a reasonable profit. Thus, to have a business transaction, there must be a"meeting of the minds" to establish a price that is mutually agreeable to both parties.

ECONOMIC CONSIDERATIONS

Two types of economic considerations are involved in arriving at the price the seller offers to the buyer. There is the monopolistic approach, where there is only one supplier of the needed goods.

This could happen through ownership of the single source, such as a mine, or the exclusive legal protection of a patent or copyright.

Should the supplier's price be exceedingly high, there will be a tendency for the buyers to seek substitute goods or to ask engineering to make some modification in design or variation of the finished product so as not to require those specific goods. This can result in lessening the hold or even eliminating the need for the monopolistic supplier.

The other consideration is the competitive method whereby two or more suppliers make an effort to secure the purchase order by offering the most favourable terms. There are two forms of competition: the perfect competitive method and the imperfect competitive method.

The pure or perfect competitive method exists where there are a large number of independent suppliers and buyers competing for identical commodities, dealing with each other yet retaining the privilege of entering or exiting from the market at any time. The price is usually determined by the supply and demand forces.

The oligopoly form in the imperfect competitive market exists when each of the limited number of suppliers is strong enough to influence the market, but not strong enough to disregard the reaction from his competitors.

In the oligopolistic auto industry, no one auto maker can influence the market without equal or greater counter influences from competitors. When one of the auto makers offers a cash rebate, the others follow with a similar or greater rebate or some other counter influencing offer. We see that each alone cannot influence the market for its own gain without the counteraction of his competitors, resulting in a healthy economic market.

With the lifting of the voluntary import quotas for foreign

automobiles, more foreign cars became available to the American consumer, which tended to force a reduction in the price of American-made automobiles to meet foreign competition and enable American auto manufacturers to retain or increase their share of the market.

During the oil shortage, the oligopolistic oil suppliers of the Middle East acted as a monopoly and maximized their profits to such a level that buyers of oil were forced to look for substitute forms of energy. There was an increase in research efforts and exploration activities for new sites of oil reserves. Energy users also looked at coal, solar, and nuclear sources.

This sudden increase in activity in quest of new oil sites caused the Middle East oil suppliers to lower their prices to a level that would"equalize" the expenditures made for research and development activities.

Some exploration projects were halted, but others continued so that we have now developed new sources of crude oil at lower prices. This sudden glut of oil caused some disintegration of the Middle East unity when several of these nations lowered their price to regain and retain their share in the crude market.

The normal imperfect competition exists when there are a great number of sellers of similar products, but each with its own distinguishing feature. These distinguishing features are used by suppliers as persuasive arguments in their attempts to influence buyer's decision.

FAIR AND REASONABLE PRICES

One method of determining what is a fair and reasonable price by securing quotations from several potential suppliers. In all governmental agencies, as required by law, purchase contracts are the result of public bidding.

There are exceptions to formal bidding - when there is an emergency, when time is too short to obtain formal quotes, when a patent is involved, or other conditions prescribed under the charter under which the agency or department operates.

In industry, formal competition bidding is used in very limited situations or for special projects. Industrial buyers use the b ding system to build their lists of potential suppliers, especially suppliers of new goods, to seek a replacement for their present supplier, or to seek a quote to use in negotiations.

No two suppliers have identical costs of operation or the same eagerness for that purchase order, resulting in a wide range price quotes.

The buyer should use quotations as a tool in the determination of what is a fair and reasonable price, keeping in Mind our quality and service of that product.

The supplier must quote a price high enough to recover fixed and variable costs plus a profit, sometimes fair and reasonable, sometimes maximized, in order to grow in his business venture. The supplier's profit portion of the price contains what believes his superior manufacturing capabilities are worth for his product.

FACTORS INFLUENCING PRICE

It should be recognized that the quoted price reflects more than just costs plus profit. The price is influenced by many factors. Particularly pertinent is competition among the suppliers of that commodity and the buyers of that commodity.

The supplier who faces a limited number of competitors will react differently in his pricing than the supplier who faces many active competitors. Also, the supplier's price is influenced by the number of prospective buyers.

Psychological factors also influence price. One is the prediction of future supply-demand relationships. If there is confidence in the guture of the relationship, there is a tendency towrds higher pricing. In an atmosphere of pessimism, there may be a decline in the pricing. This attitude about the future is a sort of"sixth sense" that buyers develop through experience. An alert buyer can verify his personal attitude by talking with other buyers individually or collectively at meetings.

Another psychological factor is knowing how far you can

press a bargaining advantage. Don't press too hard. You may eliminate a good source by attempting to force prices so low that the supplier may refuse to do any business with you. This will force you to look elsewhere to other suppliers whose prices may be higher than you present good supplier's.

A third psychological factor is the practice of haggling over every price quoted. Price haggling has reappeared, especially in the retail market, due to effects of discount outlets on regular retail dealers.

This type of bargaining diverts attention from the quality of the product and services offered. Look at the food supermarts, especially in the produce part, where a low price will often result in poor quality or lesser size, giving rise to a suspicion about future"bargains" that works against the good will between seller and buyer.

Another psychological factor is non business considerations - gifts, entertainment, bribes, etc,. The buyer should be wary of these overtures, for the seller, in the long run, will always recoup these considerations in future prices.

SUPPLY AND DEMAND RELATIONSHIPS

Let us explore the concept of the supply and demand law and how prices are set under competitive conditions. These will show the relationship between the price and the quantity sold at a specific time. The higher the price requested, the smaller the amount desired, and vice versa.

When a buyer is concerned about some basic material that is used on a continuous bais in the production process, that buyer will be on the lookout for any market signs that will influence buying decisions. The awareness is not only for the price at the moment but also for the future availability of the basic and essential material, which could affect the trend in pricing.

Price-quantity or demand-supply relations are at the heart of economic analysis. The principle of supply and demand will tell us the pressures of each on the formation of prices.

The price for item-X paid by buyers can signal suppliers

that Item-X is a profitable item to make and sell. When there is a price change, it can be an indication that the buyers have changed their preference. When the price goes up, the suppliers produce more; however, the buyers purchase less. When there is a price reduction, the supplier does not want to produce more, for his profit margin declines despite the buyer's desire to purchase. Each price change reflects the influence of supply and demand on the economic market.

THE DEMAND SCHEDULE

This is the demand of quantities of an item that buyers will purchase at certain prices at specific times. That is, the demand schedule indicates the price-quantity demand by buyers at a specific time.

Table represents the number of units the buyers will demand at five different prices.

Three principal reasons exist for an increase in demand:

Table. The Demand Table

Price per Unit ($)	Quantity Demanded	Value of Sale
$5.00	600	$3000.00
4.00	1200	4800.00
3.00	2400	7200.00
2.00	3000	6000.00
1.00	4500	4500.00

- At lower prices, the buyer will be able to purchase a larger quantity for the same amount of dollars, increasing the inventory level. The buyer must keep in mind the additional carrying costs.
- The lower price may be assumed to be temporary, and the buyer purchases more in anticipation of soon-to-be higher prices. The buyer must justify the additional carrying costs.
- At the lower price, some buyers may find it advantageous to substitute this item for another whose price s quite high, has not changed for some time, and is suitable for use in the production process.

Figure represents the variation in quantity that buyers will demand at the different prices.

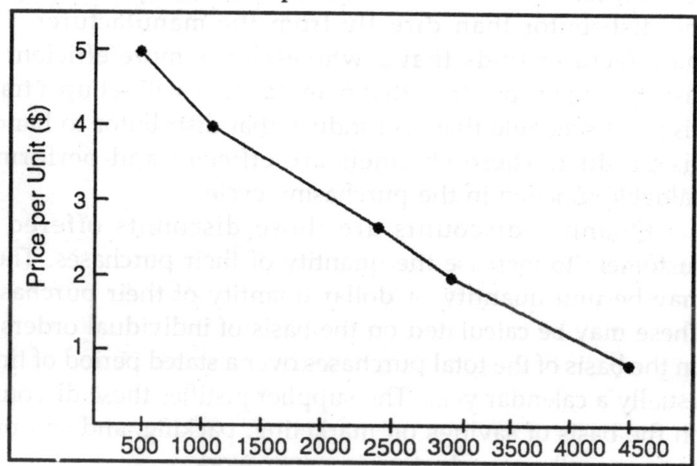

Fig. Demand Curve for Item X

COMPETITION PRICING

When there is a demand for a product or service at a definite price, it is competition that helps determine the price. Don't forget to take not of the various discounts offered by potential suppliers in their quotes. Discounts are offered as an inducement to purchasing agents to increase their purchase quantities or to meet competition. There are trade discounts and quantity discounts in addition to the usual cash discount.

Before you send that request for quotations, look in the various catalogs to not the packaging quantities of various suppliers. For example, you may wish to purchase eight dozen of Item Z, and that is the quantity you request for quotation. Many suppliers will quote on that amount only. Had you looked the item up to note the packaging, you would have discovered the various packaging and discount scales offered by the different suppliers. Some may offer a price break at quantities of 100 units or more. Others may have other packing variations.

Trade discounts are discounts from a supplier's catalog granted for the purpose of protecting certain channels of distribution. This is accomplished by making it more economical for certain classes of customers to purchase from the distributor than directly from the manufacturer. If a manufacturer finds that a wholesaler is more efficient in distributing his product, that manufacturer will set up a trade discount schedule that will induce that distributor to handle his product. These channels are efficient and perform a valuable function in the purchasing cycle.

Quantity discounts are those discounts offered to customers to increase the quantity of their purchases. These may be unit quantity or dollar quantity of their purchases. These may be calculated on the basis of individual orders or on the basis of the total purchases over a stated period of time, usually a calendar year. The supplier justifies these discounts on the basis of savings on marketing, packing, and shipping costs as well as a reduction in paper work.

For example, in non-cumulative purchase orders, that is, single orders, the discount offered can be on the number of units ordered. This can be a 5 per cent discount for one gross of an item, 10 per cent on five gross, and even 15 per cent on 12 gross. Dollar amount discounts for single orders are usually given by firms with a large variety of items, each with small dollar value. The offer can be a 5 per cent discount on orders amounting to $500, 10 per cent on $2000, and 15 per cent on orders totaling $10,000. In a cumulative agreement, the buyer's company pays for the individual purchase orders during the agreed period, usually one year, and the supplier offeres a rebate on the total sum of the purchases. For example, there can be a 5 per cent rebate on purchases totaling $2,500 to $4,999.99, 7.5 per cent to $7,499.99, and 15 per cent on over $7,500. Rebate amounts can be negotiated by both buyer and seller.

Some firms offer a series of discounts on various dollar amounts of purchase orders. These can be calculated several ways. For example, on orders amounting to $5,000 the supplier allows discounts of 40, 10, and 5 per cent from list price. This means that on orders of $5,000 the buyer receives a 40 per cent discount from list, that intermediate sum is subject to a 10 per cent discount and that sum is further discounted by 5 per cent.

The calculations are:

- $5,000.00 less 40% = 5,000 - (5,000 x 0.40) = $3,000
- $3,000.00 less 10% = 3000 - (3,000 x 0.10) = $2,700
- $2,700.00 less 5% = 2,700 - (2,700 x 0.05) = $2,565

A simpler method is to multiply the decimal complements to form a single rate discount and this multiplied by $5,000 to arrive at the net cost.

Series of multiple discounts are never added to arrive at a single discount rate. In the example, we find the actual discount to be 48.7 per cent not 55 per cent (40 + 10 + 5).

PRICE DISCRIMINATION

Price discrimination, or price differentiation, exists when sales of identical goods or services are transacted at different prices from the same provider. In general, the practice of charging different customers different prices is called price discrimination.

In a theoretical market with perfect information, perfect substitutes, and no transaction costs or prohibition on secondary exchange to prevent arbitrage, price discrimination can only be a feature of monopolistic and oligopolistic markets, where market power can be exercised. Otherwise, the moment the seller tries to sell the same good at different prices, the buyer at the lower price can arbitrage by selling to the consumer buying at the higher price but with a tiny discount. However, product heterogeneity, market frictions or high fixed costs can allow for some degree of differential pricing to different consumers, even in fully competitive retail or industrial markets. Price discrimination also occurs when the same price is charged to customers which have different supply costs.

The effects of price discrimination on social efficiency are unclear; typically such behaviour leads to lower prices for some consumers and higher prices for others. Output can be expanded when price discrimination is very efficient, but output can also decline when discrimination is more effective at extracting surplus from high-valued users than expanding sales to low valued users. Even if output remains constant, price discrimination can reduce efficiency by misallocating output among consumers.

Price discrimination requires market segmentation and some means to discourage discount customers from becoming resellers and, by extension, competitors. This usually entails using one or more means of preventing any resale, keeping the different price groups separate, making price comparisons difficult, or restricting pricing information. The boundary set up by the marketer to keep segments separate are referred to as a rate fence.

Price discrimination is thus very common in services, where resale is not possible; an example is student discounts at museums. Price discrimination in intellectual property is also enforced by law and by technology. In the market for DVDs, DVD players are designed - by law - with chips to prevent use of an inexpensive copy of the DVD from being used in a higher price market. The Digital Millenium Copyright Act has provisions to outlaw circumventing of such devices to protect the enhanced monopoly profits that copyright holders can obtain from price discrimination against higher price market segments.

Price discrimination can also be seen where the requirement that goods be identical is relaxed. For example, so-called"premium products" have a price differential that is not explained by the cost of production. Some economists have argued that this is a form of price discrimination exercised by providing a means for consumers to reveal their willingness to pay.

TYPES OF PRICE DISCRIMINATION

First Degree Price Discrimination

In first degree price discrimination, price varies by customer's willingness or ability to pay. This arises from the fact that the value of goods is subjective. A customer with low price elasticity is less deterred by a higher price than a customer with high price elasticity of demand. As long as the price elasticity for a customer is less than one, it is very advantageous to increase the price: the seller gets more money for fewer goods. With an increase of the price elasticity tends to rise above one. One can show that in the optimum the price, as it varies by customer, is inversely proportional to one minus the reciprocal of the price elasticity of that customer at that price.

This assumes that the consumer passively reacts to the price set by the seller, and that the seller knows the demand curve of the customer. In practice however there is a bargaining situation, which is more complex: the customer may try to influence the price, such as by pretending to like the product less than he or she really does or by threatening not to buy it.

An alternative way to understand First Degree Price Discrimination is as follows: This type of price discrimination is primarily theoretical because it requires the seller of a good or service to know the absolute maximum price that every consumer is willing to pay. It is true that consumers have different price elasticities, but the seller is not concerned with such. The seller is concerned with the maximum willingness to pay of each customer.

By knowing the reservation price, the seller is able to absorb the entire market surplus, thus taking all of the consumer's surplus from the consumer and transforming it into revenues. From a social welfare perspective though, first degree price discrimination is not necessarily undesirable. That is, the market is still entirely efficient and there is no deadweight loss to society.

In a market with first degree price discrimination, the seller(s) simply captures all surplus. Efficiency is unchanged but the wealth is transferred. This type of market does not exist much in reality, hence it is primarily theoretical. Examples of where this might be observed are in markets where consumers bid for tenders, though still, in this case, the practice of collusive tendering undermines efficiency.

Second Degree Price Discrimination

In second degree price discrimination, price varies

according to quantity sold. Larger quantities are available at a lower unit price. This is particularly widespread in sales to industrial customers, where bulk buyers enjoy higher discounts.

Additionally to second degree price discrimination, sellers are not able to differentiate between different types of consumers. Thus, the suppliers will provide incentives for the consumers to differentiate themselves according to preference. Quantity"discounts", or non-linear pricing, is a means by which suppliers use consumer preference to distinguish classes of consumers. This allows the supplier to set different prices to the different groups and capture a larger portion of the total market surplus.

In reality, different pricing may apply to differences in product quality as well as quantity. For example, airlines often offer multiple classes of seats on flights, such as first class and economy class. This is a way to differentiate consumers based on preference, and therefore allows the airline to capture more producer's surplus.

Third Degree Price Discrimination

In third degree price discrimination, price varies by attributes such as location or by customer segment, or in the most extreme case, by the individual customer's identity; where the attribute in question is used as a proxy for ability/ willingness to pay.

Additionally to third degree price discrimination, the supplier(s) of a market where this type of discrimination is exhibited are capable of differentiating between consumer classes.

Examples of this differentiation are student or senior discounts. For example, a student or a senior consumer will have a different willingness to pay than an average consumer, where the reservation price is presumably lower because of budget constraints.

Thus, the supplier sets a lower price for that consumer because the student or senior has a more elastic price elasticity of demand. The supplier is once again capable of capturing more market surplus than would be possible without price discrimination.

Note that it is not always advantageous to the company to price discriminate even if it is possible, especially for second and third degree discrimination. In some circumstances, the demands of different classes of consumers will encourage suppliers to simply ignore one/some class(es) and target entirely to the other(s). Whether it is profitable to price discriminate is determined by the specifics of a particular market.

Price Skimming

In price skimming, price varies over time. Typically a company starts selling a new product at a relatively high price then gradually reduces the price as the low price elasticity segment gets satiated. Price skimming is closely related to the concept of yield management.

Combination

These types are not mutually exclusive. Thus a company may vary pricing by location, but then offer bulk discounts as well.

Airlines use several different types of price discrimination, including:

- Bulk discounts to wholesalers, consolidators, and tour operators
- Incentive discounts for higher sales volumes to travel agents and corporate buyers
- Seasonal discounts, incentive discounts, and even general prices that vary by location. The price of a flight from say, Singapore to Beijing can vary widely if one buys the ticket in Singapore compared to Beijing. In online ticket sales this is achieved by using the customer's credit card billing address to determine his location.
- Discounted tickets requiring advance purchase and/ or Saturday stays. Both restrictions have the effect of excluding business travellers, who typically travel

during the workweek and arrange trips on shorter notice.

- First degree price discrimination based on customer. It is not accidental that hotel or car rental firms may quote higher prices to their loyalty program's top tier members than to the general public.

MODERN TAXONOMY

The first/second/third degree taxonomy of price discrimination is due to Pigou suggests an alternative taxonomy:

- *Complete discrimination*: Where each user purchases up to the point where the user's marginal benefit equals the marginal cost of the item;
- *Direct segmentation*: Where the seller can condition price on some attribute that directly segments the buyers;
- *Indirect segmentation*: Where the seller relies on some proxy to structure a choice that indirectly segments the buyers.

The hierarchy-complete/direct/indirect-is in decreasing order of:

- Profitability and
- Information requirement.

Complete price discrimination is most profitable, and requires the seller to have the most information about buyers. Indirect segmentation is least profitable, and requires the seller to have the least information about buyers.

EXPLANATION

The purpose of price discrimination is generally to capture the market's consumer surplus. This surplus arises because, in a market with a single clearing price, some customers would have been prepared to pay more than the single market price. Price discrimination transfers some of this surplus from the consumer to the producer/marketer.

Strictly, a consumer surplus need not exist, for example where some below-cost selling is beneficial due to fixed costs or economies of scale.

An example is a high-speed internet connection shared by two consumers in a single building; if one is willing to pay less than half the cost, and the other willing to make up the rest but not to pay the entire cost, then price discrimination is necessary for the purchase to take place.

It can be proved mathematically that a firm facing a downward sloping demand curve that is convex to the origin will always obtain higher revenues under price discrimination than under a single price strategy. This can also be shown diagrammatically.

In the top diagram, a single price (P) is available to all customers. The amount of revenue is represented by area P, A,Q, O. The consumer surplus is the area above line segment P, A but below the demand curve (D).

With price discrimination, the demand curve is divided into two segments. A higher price is charged to the low elasticity segment, and a lower price is charged to the high elasticity segment.

The total revenue from the first segment is equal to the area P1,B, Q1,O. The total revenue from the second segment is equal to the area E, C,Q2,Q1. The sum of these areas will always be greater than the area without discrimination assuming the demand curve resembles a rectangular hyperbola with unitary elasticity.

The more prices that are introduced, the greater the sum of the revenue areas, and the more of the consumer surplus is captured by the producer.

Note the requires both first and second degree price discrimination: the right segment corresponds partly to different people than the left segment, partly to the same people, willing to buy more if the product is cheaper.

It is very useful for the price discriminator to determine the optimum prices in each market segment. This is done in the next diagram where each segment is considered as a separate market with its own demand curve.

As usual, the profit maximizing output (Qt) is determined by the intersection of the marginal cost curve (MC) with the marginal revenue curve for the total market (MRt).

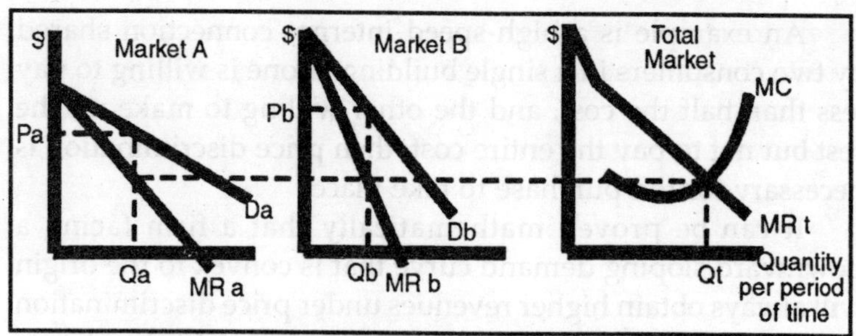

Fig. Multiple Market Price Determination

The firm decides what amount of the total output to sell in each market by looking at the intersection of marginal cost with marginal revenue. This output is then divided between the two markets, at the equilibrium marginal revenue level. Therefore, the optimum outputs are Qa and Qb. From the demand curve in each market we can determine the profit maximizing prices of Pa and Pb.

It is also important to note that the marginal revenue in both markets at the optimal output levels must be equal, otherwise the firm could profit from transferring output over to whichever market is offering higher marginal revenue.

Given that Market 1 has a price elasticity of demand of E1 and Market of E2, the optimal pricing ration in Market 1 versus Market 2 is P1/P2 = [1 – 1/E2]/[1 – 1/E1].

EXAMPLES OF PRICE DISCRIMINATION

Retail Price Discrimination

In certain circumstances, it is a violation of the Robinson-Patman Act, for manufacturers of goods to sell their products to similarly situated retailers at different prices based solely on the volume of products purchased.

Travel Industry

Airlines and other travel cozmpanies use differentiated pricing regularly, as they sell travel products and services simultaneously to different market segments. This is often done by assigning capacity to various booking classes, which sell for different prices and which may be linked to fare restrictions. The restrictions or"fences" help ensure that market segments buy in the booking class range that has been established for them. For example, schedule-sensitive business passengers who are willing to pay $300 for a seat from city A to city B cannot purchase a $150 ticket because the $150 booking class contains a requirement for a Saturday night stay, or a 15-day advance purchase, or another fare rule that discourages, minimizes, or effectively prevents a sale to business passengers.

Notice however that in this example"the seat" is not really always the same product. That is, the business person who purchases the $300 ticket may be willing to do so in return for a seat on a high-demand morning flight, for full refundability if the ticket is not used, and for the ability to upgrade to first class if space is available for a nominal fee. On the same flight are price-sensitive passengers who are not willing to pay $300, but who are willing to fly on a lower-demand flight or via a connection city, and who are willing to forgo refundability.

On the other hand, an airline may also apply differential pricing to"the same seat" over time, e.g. by discounting the price for an early or late booking. This could present an arbitrage opportunity in the absence of any restriction on reselling. However, passenger name changes are typically prevented or financially penalized by contract.

Since airlines often fly multi-leg flights, and since no-show rates vary by segment, competition for the seat has to take in the spatial dynamics of the product. Someone trying to fly A-B is competing with people trying to fly A-C through city B on the same aircraft. This is one reason airlines use yield management technology to determine how many seats to allot for A-B passengers, B-C passengers, and A-B-C passengers, at their varying fares and with varying demands and no-show rates.

With the rise of the Internet and the growth of low fare airlines, airfare pricing transparency has become far more pronounced. Passengers discovered it is quite easy to compare fares across different flights or different airlines. This helped put pressure on airlines to lower fares. Meanwhile, in the recession following the September 11, 2001, attacks on the U.S., business travellers and corporate buyers made it clear to airlines that they were not going to be buying air travel at rates high enough to subsidize lower fares for non-business travellers. This prediction has come true, as vast numbers of business travellers are buying airfares only in economy class for business travel.

There are sometimes group discounts on rail tickets and passes. This may be in view of the alternative of going by car together.

Premium Pricing

For certain products, premium products are priced at a level that is well beyond their marginal cost of production. For example, a coffee chain may price regular coffee at $1, but"premium" coffee at $2.50.

Economists such as Tim Harford in the Undercover Economist have argued that this is a form of price discrimination: by providing a choice between a regular and premium product, consumers are being asked to reveal their degree of price sensitivity for comparable products. Similar techniques are used in pricing business class airline tickets and premium alcoholic drinks, for example.

This effect can lead to perverse incentives for the producer. If, for example, potential business class customers will pay a large price differential only if economy class seats are uncomfortable while economy class customers are more sensitive to price than comfort, airlines may have substantial incentives to purposely make economy seating uncomfortable. In the example of coffee, a restaurant may gain more economic profit by making poor quality regular coffee-more profit is gained from up-selling to premium customers than is lost from customers who refuse to purchase inexpensive but poor quality coffee. In such cases, the net social utility should also account for the"lost" utility to consumers of the regular product, although determining the magnitude of this foregone utility may not be feasible.

Segmentation by Age Group and Student Status

Many movie theaters, amusement parks, tourist attractions, and other places have different admission prices per market segment: typical groupings are Youth, Student, Adult, and Senior. Each of these groups typically have a much different demand curve. Children, people living on student wages, and people living on retirement generally have much less disposable income.

Discounts for Members of Certain Occupations

Many businesses, especially in the Southern United States, offer reduced prices to active military members. In addition to increased sales to the target group, businesses benefit from the resulting positive publicity, leading to increased sales to the general public. Less publicized are discounts to other service workers such as police; off-duty police customers in high-crime areas are said to constitute free security.

Employee Discounts

Discounts that businesses give to their own employees are also a form of price discrimination.

Retail Incentives

A variety of incentive techniques may be used to increase market share or revenues at the retail level. These include discount coupons, rebates, bulk and quantity pricing, seasonal discounts, and frequent buyer discounts.

Incentives for Industrial Buyers

Many methods exist to incentivize wholesale or industrial buyers. These may be quite targeted, as they are designed to generate specific activity, such as buying more frequently, buying more regularly, buying in bigger quantities, buying new products with established ones, and so on. Thus, there are bulk discounts, special pricing for long-term commitments, non-peak discounts, discounts on high-demand goods to incentivize buying lower-demand goods, rebates, and many others. This can help the relations between the firms involved.

TWO NECESSARY CONDITIONS FOR PRICE DISCRIMINATION

There are two conditions that must be met if a price discrimination plan is to work. First the firm must be able to identify market segments by their price elasticity of demand and second the firms must be able to enforce the plan. For example, airlines routinely engage in price discrimination by charging high prices for customers with relatively inelastic demand - business travellers - and discount prices for tourist who have relatively elastic demand, The airlines enforce the plan by making the tickets non-transferable thus preventing a tourist from buying a ticket at a discounted price and selling it to a business traveller.

Airlines must also prevent business travellers from directly buying discount tickets. Airlines accomplish this by imposing advance ticketing requirements or minimum stay requirements conditions that it would be difficult for average business traveller to meet.

SELLING COST

The cost used to make a sale. Basically to compare the ROI of an operation or transaction(s). This cost can be sales employee wages, building lease, postage, sales calls, etc.

PRODUCT DIFFERENTIATION

SIGNIFICANCE

Offered under different brands by competing firms, products fulfilling the same need typically do not have identical features. The differentiation of goods along key features and minor details is an important strategy for firms to defend their price from levelling down to the bottom part of the price spectrum. Within firms, product differentiation is the way multi-product firms build their own supplied products' range. At market level, differentiation is the way through which the quality of goods is improved over time thanks to innovation. Launching new goods with entirely new performances is a radical change, often leading to changes in market shares and industry structures.

In an evolutionary sense, differentiation is a strategy to adapt to a moving environment and its social groups.

VERTICAL DIFFERENTIATION

Vertical differentiation occurs in a market where the several goods that are present can be ordered according to their objective quality from the highest to the lowest. It's possible to say in this case that one good is"better" than another.

Vertical differentiation can be obtained:

- Along one decisive feature;
- Along a few features, each of which has a wide possible range of values;
- Across a large number of features, each of which has only a presence/absence"flag".

In the second and third cases, it is possible to find out a product that is better than another one according to one criteria but worse than it in respect to another feature.

Vertical differentiation is a property of the supplied goods but, as it is maybe needless to say, the perceived difference in quality by different consumer will play a crucial role in the purchase decisions. In particular, potential consumers can have a biased perception of the features of the good.

When evaluating a real market, a good starting point is a top-down grid of interpretation, we shall present first in 3 segments.

Class	Price	Crucial Feature
Low	Low	The price is low, the product simply works
Middle	Middle	Use of the good is comfortable. Most people use it. Mass market brand.
High	High	Quality, exclusivity, durability (= low life-long price),

To this basic classification, one should add two intermediate classes:

Class	Price	Crucial feature
Middle-low	Low	The cheapest nation-wide brand
Middle-high	Middle	The cheapest product of high quality

Two extreme classes should finally be added:

Class	Price	Crucial feature
Extremely low	Low	It usually does not work, it does not last, and it has important defects
Extremely High	High	Exclusivity, non practical, status symbol

In this way, you can vertically position different brands and product versions, also using clues from advertising campaigns.

If you compare widely different goods fulfilling the same need, you may distinguish at the extreme of your spectrum necessity goods and at the other luxury goods. In other cases, what makes this difference is, instead, the nature of the need fulfilled. As a general rule, better products have a higher price, both because of higher production costs and bigger expected advantages for clients, partly reflected in higher margins.

Thus, the quality-price relationship is typically upwards sloped. This means that consumers without their own opinion nor the capability of directly judging quality may rely on the price to infer quality. They will prefer to pay a higher price because they expect quality to be better.

This important flaw in knowledge and information processing capability - an instance of bounded rationality - can be purposefully exploited by the seller, with the result that not all highly priced products are of good quality.

Through this mechanism, the demand curve - that in the neoclassical model - is always downward sloped, can instead turn out to be in the opposite direction.

HORIZONTAL DIFFERENTIATION

When products are different according to features that

can't be ordered, a horizontal differentiation emerges in the market. A typical example is the ice-cream offered in different tastes. Chocolate is not"better" than lemon.

Horizontal differentiation can be linked to differentiation in colours, in styles, in tastes. This does not prevent specific consumers to have a stable preference for one or the other version, since you should always distinguish what belongs to the supply structure and what is due to consumers' subjectivity. It is quite common that, in horizontal differentiation, the supplier of many versions decide a unique price for all of them. Chocolate ice-creams cost as much as lemon ones. When consumers don't have strong stable preferences, a rule of behaviour can be to change often the chosen good, looking for variety itself. An example is when you go to a fast food and ask for what you haven't eaten the previous time.

Fashion waves often emerge in horizontally-differentiated markets with imitation behaviours among consumers and specific styles going"in" and"out".

DETERMINANTS

How a product rates according to different measures of quality or taste depends on its physical and immaterial characteristics. The raw material from which it has been built, the share of high/low quality ingredients/components, its engineered design, its production process are typical determinants of product specificity. Contrary to the neoclassical approach of technique choice along isoquants, every change in proportion in productive inputs entering in the final product results in product differentiation.

More broadly, product differentiation can be:

- The indirect effect of different endowments in raw materials, know-how, style preference of different firms ignoring each others;
- The conscious choice, out of firm strategies, to position each product against competitors;
- The costly, uncertain, and difficult outcome of innovation efforts.

In perspective 2, how to achieve product differentiation? The steps are the following:

- To map all competitors' products and compare them couplewise or in groups;
- To identify explicit and implicit axes of differentiation, qualitative or quantitative;
- To identify the accumulation points where most competitors are focused;
- To highlight"empty spaces" where combination of features are abstent;
- To brainstorm around which consumer segment could be interested in such combination of features;
- To preliminarily estimate the size of the segment;
- To explore if the firm has the capability of offering such product and at which cost;
- To transform the segment into a viable niche by offering a price, an advertising strategy and a distribution channel such that the supply of the product is profitable over a reasonable time

IMPACT ON OTHER VARIABLES

Differentiated versions of a good can have widely different costs of production. Upstream, they may be produced using different raw materials and semi-manufactured parts, thus referring to diverse suppliers and their relative market power. Import of exotic substances can be the effect of the attempt to introduce new goods on the market.

Downstream, the supply of different and better goods allows for deeper fulfilment of consumption needs, for production processes at higher productivity as well as for the opening of export opportunities to other countries.

For the firms introducing the new version of the product, the expected results are mainly improvements of profits, sales, and market shares.

For the consumer, product differentiation can increase the satisfaction from its consumption. At the same time, he will be confronted with a wider spectrum of prices. Test whether how much quality is expensive by playing this business game.

When faced with the burgeoning choice spectrum at supermarket premises among product varieties of the same category, the consumer can react with several rules of selection; retailers take them into account to assure profits and profitability, as you can experiment with this spreadsheet.

At the same time, product differentiation can lead to the exploration of the product space by unloyal customers, who use the repurchase occasions to try new versions.

LONG-TERM TRENDS

The ever growing product differentiation process due to new emergent firms/countries and the innovation efforts of incumbents has encountered in the last decades some form of brake due to the pressure of globalized, standardized homogeneous goods with a dominant design.

BEHAVIOUR DURING THE INDUSTRY LIFE-CYCLE

High product differentiation with radically different proposals is typical of the early stage of an infant industry, until a dominant design will replace technically imperfect or simply unlucky models.

Afterwards, when the industry reaches the maturity stage with few main competitors, differentiation re-emerge as an attempt to soften price competition and to reach new niches of consumers.

VARIOUS PRICING METHODS

As we said earlier, there is no"one right way" to calculate your pricing. Once you've considered the various factors involved and determined your objectives for your pricing strategy, now you need some way to crunch the actual numbers. Here are four ways to calculate prices:

COST-PLUS PRICING

Set the price at your production cost, including both cost of goods and fixed costs at your current volume, plus a certain profit margin. For example, your widgets cost $20 in raw materials and production costs, and at current sales volume, your fixed costs come to $30 per unit. Your total cost is $50 per unit. You decide that you want to operate at a 20% markup, so you add $10 to the cost and come up with a price of $60 per unit. So long as you have your costs calculated correctly and have accurately predicted your sales volume, you will always be operating at a profit.

TARGET RETURN PRICING

Set your price to achieve a target return-on-investment. For example, let's use the same situation, and assume that you have $10,000 invested in the company. Your expected sales volume is 1,000 units in the first year. You want to recoup all your investment in the first year, so you need to make $10,000 profit on 1,000 units, or $10 profit per unit, giving you again a price of $60 per unit.

VALUE-BASED PRICING

Price your product based on the value it creates for the customer. This is usually the most profitable form of pricing, if you can achieve it. The most extreme variation on this is"pay for performance" pricing for services, in which you charge on a variable scale according to the results you achieve. Let's say that your widget above saves the typical customer $1,000 a year in energy costs. In that case, $60 seems like a bargain - maybe even too cheap. If your product reliably produced that kind of cost savings, you could easily charge $200, $300 or more for it, and customers would gladly pay it, since they would get their money back in a matter of months. However, there is one more major factor that must be considered.

PSYCHOLOGICAL PRICING

Ultimately, you must take into consideration the consumer's perception of your price, figuring things like:

POSITIONING

If you want to be the"low-cost leader", you must be priced lower than your competition. If you want to signal high quality, you should probably be priced higher than most of your competition.

POPULAR PRICE POINTS

There are certain"price points" at which people become much more willing to buy a certain type of product. For example,"under $100" is a popular price point."Enough under $20 to be under $20 with sales tax" is another popular price point, because it's"one bill" that people commonly carry. Meals under $5 are still a popular price point, as are entree or snack items under $1. Dropping your price to a popular price point might mean a lower margin, but more than enough increase in sales to offset it.

FAIR PRICING

- Sometimes it simply doesn't matter what the value of the product is, even if you don't have any direct competition. There is simply a limit to what consumers perceive as"fair". If it's obvious that your product only cost $20 to manufacture, even if it delivered $10,000 in value, you'd have a hard time charging two or three thousand dollars for it -- people would just feel like they were being gouged. A little market testing will help you determine the maximum price consumers will perceive as fair.

Now, how do you combine all of these calculations to come up with a price? Here are some basic guidelines:

- Your price must be enough higher than costs to cover reasonable variations in sales volume. If your sales forecast is inaccurate, how far off can you be and still be profitable? Ideally,. you want to be able to be off by a factor of two or more and still be profitable.
- You have to make a living. Have you figured salary for yourself in your costs? If not, your profit has to be enough for you to live on and still have money to reinvest in the company.
- Your price should almost never be lower than your costs or higher than what most consumers

consider"fair". This may seem obvious, but many entrepreneurs seem to miss this simple concept, either by miscalculating costs or by inadequate market research to determine fair pricing. Simply put, if people won't readily pay enough more than your cost to make you a fair profit, you need to reconsider your business model entirely. How can you cut your costs substantially? Or change your product positioning to justify higher pricing?

Pricing is a tricky business. You're certainly entitled to make a fair profit on your product, and even a substantial one if you create value for your customers. But remember, something is ultimately worth only what someone is willing to pay for it.

TRANSFER PRICING

Transfer pricing refers to the pricing of contributions transferred within an organization. For example, goods from the production division may be sold to the marketing division, or goods from a parent company may be sold to a foreign subsidiary. Since the prices are set within an organization, the typical market mechanisms that establish prices for such transactions between third parties may not apply. The choice of the transfer price will affect the allocation of the total profit among the parts of the company. This is a major concern for fiscal authorities who worry that multi-national entities may set transfer prices on cross-border transactions to reduce taxable profits in their jurisdiction. This has led to the rise of transfer pricing regulations and enforcement, making transfer pricing a major tax compliance issue for multi-national companies.

ECONOMIC THEORY

The discussion in this part explains an economic theory behind optimal transfer pricing with optimal defined as transfer pricing that maximizes overall firm profits in a non-realistic world with no taxes, no capital risk, no development risk, no externalities or any other frictions which exist in the real world. In practice a great many factors influence the transfer prices that are used by multinational corporations, including performance measurement, capabilities of accounting systems, import quotas, customs duties, VAT, taxes on profits, and simple lack of attention to the pricing.

From marginal price determination theory, the optimum level of output is that where marginal cost equals marginal revenue. That is to say, a firm should expand its output as long as the marginal revenue from additional sales is greater than their marginal costs. In the diagram that follows, this intersection is represented by point A, which will yield a price of P*, given the demand at point B.

When a firm is selling some of its product to itself, and only to itself then the picture gets more complicated, but the outcome remains the same. The demand curve remains the same. The optimum price and quantity remain the same. But marginal cost of production can be separated from the firm's total marginal costs. Likewise, the marginal revenue associated with the production division can be separated from the marginal revenue for the total firm. This is referred to as the Net Marginal Revenue in production and is calculated as the marginal revenue from the firm minus the marginal costs of distribution.

It can be shown algebraically that the intersection of the firm's marginal cost curve and marginal revenue curve must occur at the same quantity as the intersection of the production division's marginal cost curve with the net marginal revenue from production. If the production division is able to sell the transfer good in a competitive market, then again both must operate where their marginal costs equal their marginal revenue, for profit maximization. Because the external market is competitive, the firm is a price taker and must accept the transfer price determined by market forces. If the market price is relatively high, then the firm will experience an internal surplus equal to the amount Qt1 minus Qf1. The actual marginal cost curve is defined by points A,C,D.

If the firm is able to sell its transfer goods in an imperfect market, then it need not be a price taker. There are two markets each with its own price. The aggregate market is constructed from the first two. That is, point C is a horizontal summation of points A and B. The total optimum quantity (Q) is the sum of Qf plus Qt.

PRACTICAL APPLICATION

Role of Legislation, Regulations and Administrative Guidelines

Although there is sound economic theory behind the selection of a transfer pricing method, the fact remains that it can be advantageous to arbitrarily select prices such that, in terms of bookkeeping, most of the profit is made in a country with low taxes, e.g. tax havens, thus shifting the profits to reduce overall taxes paid by a multinational group. However, most countries enforce tax laws based on the arm's length principle as defined in the OECD Transfer Pricing Guidelines for Multinational Enterprises and Tax Administrations, limiting how transfer prices can be set and ensuring that that country gets to tax its"fair" share. In the United States, the pricing of transactions between related parties that are reported for tax purposes is governed by Section 482 of the Internal Revenue Code and the regulations thereunder. In Canada, it is governed by section 247 of the Income Tax Act.

It should be noted that tax authorities, such as the IRS in the United States and the Canada Revenue Agency in Canada, often differ in interpretation of transfer pricing policy with their corresponding national customs agency, such as the Bureau of Customs and Border Protection in the United States. In many cases the objectives of these agencies in assessing a multinational's transfer pricing policies are opposed to each other.

From the corporation's position, running afoul of such regulations can prove to be a costly mistake, as illustrated by GlaxoSmithKline's announcement on September 11, 2006 that they had settled a long-running transfer pricing dispute with the US tax authorities, agreeing to pay $3.1 billion in taxes related to an assessed income adjustment due to improper transfer pricing. However, proper use of the regulations also provides a method of protecting against double taxation, provided that the transactions are carried out between divisions in countries bound by bilateral tax treaties. In the GlaxoSmithKline case, however, the company has indicated that they will not pursue competent authority negotiations for the relief of U.S.-U.K. double taxation.

Application of the Arm's Length Principle

Although there are discrepancies in the specifics of each country's laws concerning the application of the arm's length principle, most countries have based their transfer pricing laws and regulations on the OECD Guidelines. Further, most double-tax treaties contain provisions that force both taxing authorities to resolve transfer pricing disputes on the basis of the arm's length principle.

Thus, multi-national companies should be able to devise global transfer pricing policies that can be effectively used to determine appropriate ranges representing the arm's length prices for transactions carried out across a global enterprise without necessarily running afoul of local laws and regulations.

However, different countries may accept different methods of calculating the transfer prices so care must be taken in such circumstances. In addition, some countries may have immature transfer pricing regimes or apply the arm's length principle in different ways-Brazil, for example, does not apply the arm's length principle despite the existence of transfer pricing legislation.

The following definitions are thus based on the OECD Guidelines.

Traditional Transaction Methods

The OECD Guidelines refer to the following methods as'traditional transaction method':

- Comparable Uncontrolled Price method (CUP);
- Resale Price Method (RPM); and
- Cost Plus Method (CP method or C+);

These are different from the transactional profit methods:

- Profit split method; and
- Transactional Net Margin Method (TNMM).

The OECD Guidelines prefer the use of the traditional transaction methods, whereby the other methods should be used as methods of last resort. However, the Guidelines stress there is no best-method rule: a taxpayer is only required to show that the method used delivers a reasonable result and is not required to disprove the use of each other method than the method used. Regarding the'reasonable outcome', the Guidelines note that transfer pricing is not an exact science.

Comparable Uncontrolled Price Method

Comparable Uncontrolled Price method compares the price at which a controlled transaction is conducted to the price at which a comparable uncontrolled transaction is conducted. Comparability between a controlled and uncontrolled transaction exists when there are no differences between these transactions or, if there are differences, when such differences do not have a material effect or for which reasonable adjustments can be made. Hence, an at arm's length transfer price can be determined through a comparison with the sales price between two unrelated corporations executing a transaction However, the fact that virtually any minor difference in the circumstances of trade may have a significant effect on the price makes it exceedingly difficult to find a transaction--much less transactions--that are sufficiently comparable.In short CUP determines price through Comparing sales Price charged to Related Party with the sales price been charged to two Unrelated parties

Should they exist, such comparable transactions fall into two categories: external comparables and internal comparables. The former is a comparable uncontrolled transaction in the purest sense of the term--if Company A, in France, sells widgets to its subsidiary A(sub) in Turkey, then an external comparable transaction would be the sale of widgets from an unrelated French Company B to an unrelated Turkish Company C on comparable terms as the trade between Company A and its subsidiary A(sub). An internal comparable transaction, then, would be either the trade of widgets between Company A and an unrelated Company C, or the trade of widgets between an unrelated Company B and Company A's subsidiary, with the term"internal" referring to the fact that one of the parties involved in the tested transaction is also involved in the comparable uncontrolled transaction

Cost Plus Method

The Cost Plus method, generally used for the trade of finished goods, is determined by adding an appropriate markup to the costs incurred by the selling party in manufacturing/purchasing the goods or services provided, with the appropriate markup being based on the profits of other companies comparable to the tested party. For example, the arm's length price for a transaction involving the sale of finished clothing to a related distributor would be determined by adding an appropriate markup to the cost of materials, labour, manufacturing, and so on. Cost-based method calculates transfer price on the cost of the goods or services available as per the cost accounting records of the company. The method is generally accepted by the tax customs authorities, since it provides some indication that the transfer price approximates the real cost of item. Cost-based approaches are, however, not as transparent as they appear. A company can easily manipulate its cost accounts to alter the magnitude of the transfer price. Companies that adopt the cost-based transfer pricing method have to choose between alternative approaches which are listed:

- Actual cost approach
- Standard cost approach
- Variable cost approach
- Marginal cost approach

Apart from this, companies also have to decide on the treatment of fixed cost and research and development cost. These issues can prove problematic for the company that adopts a cost-based transfer pricing method. Cost-based method usually creates difficulties for the selling profit centre.

As their incentives to be cost effective may fall, if they know that they can recover increased cost simply by raising the transfer price without an incentive. To produce efficiently, the transfer price may erode the competitiveness of the final product in the market place.

Resale Price Method

The Resale Price, while similar to the CP method, is found by working backwards from transactions taking place at the next stage in the supply chain, and is determined by subtracting an appropriate gross markup from the sale price to an unrelated third party, with the appropriate gross margin being determined by examining the conditions under which the goods or services are sold and comparing said transaction to other, third-party transactions. In our clothing example, then, the arm's length price would be determined by subtracting an appropriate gross margin from the price at which the distributor sold the products received from the manufacturer to third-party retailers--department stores, boutiques, etc.

In this example, both the CP and RP methods are being used to examine the same transaction--the one between the manufacturer and the distributor--meaning that the selection of one for use is ultimately dependent on the availability of data and comparable transactions. This flexibility is not available in other transactions, particularly those involving intangible goods.

Transactional Profit Methods

The OECD Guidelines consider the following transactional profit methods: the Profit Split method and the Transactional Net Margin Method. In principle, application of any other method which would deliver a reasonable at arm's length transfer price should not be disallowed.

Profit Split Method

The PS method is applied when the businesses involved in the examined transaction are too integrated to allow for separate evaluation, and so the ultimate profit derived from the endeavor is split-based on the level of contribution--itself often determined by some measurable factor such as employee compensation, payment of administration expenses, etc.--of each of the participants in the project.

To present a highly simplified example, if Company A above sent three researchers to Company A(sub) to aid in the development of widgets tailored for the Turkish market while Company A(sub) allocated seven identically-compensated researchers to aid in the development, we would expect that Company A(sub) would pay Company A 30% of the royalty fee portion of the ultimate profits for the technical knowledge provided by Company A's researchers.

The residual profit split method initially focuses on the company in a controlled transaction which performs the most routine functions, for example toll-manufacturing or distributing services. Routine functions are functions which are low value-added compared to the overall profitability. Such company is generally referred to as'least-complex entity'. The residual profit split method seeks to set the appropriate arm's length remuneration for such least-complex entity, whereby the remaining profit is allocated to the other company of the controlled transaction.

An example: Company A sells widgets through its subsidiary, a limited-risk distributor, in the Turkish market. Assume that an overall profit of 100 is made on the sale. The limited-risk distributor should receive an at arm's length return of 5. Then, the residual profit of 95 would be allocated to Company A, being the complex entity or entrepreneur. In case of an overall loss, the Turkish subsidiary should, in principle, continue to receive the arm's length return of 5.

Transactional Net Margin Method

TNMM, meanwhile, is a method that focuses on the arm's length operating profit earned by one of the entities in the transaction. It stipulates that relative operating profit may be a more robust measure of an arm's length result when close comparables, as required for the traditional methods, are not available. For example, two distributors may sell different products that require different sales efforts per unit sold. This may lead to very different gross margins. However, the operating margins would not be expected to be materially different since the margins reflects a competitive return only.

The margin is measured pre-interest since the level of interest expense is a function of how a company decides to finance its operations and unrelated to the transfer pricing.

Although not one of the traditional three methods, the TNMM and its counterpart under the U.S. transfer pricing regulations, the Comparable Profits Method or CPM is one of the most-widely used transfer pricing methods.

Advance Pricing Agreement

An Advance Pricing Agreement/Arrangement or APA, is an agreement between the taxpayer and the competent taxation authorities that a future transaction will be conducted at the agreed-upon price, which is recognized as the arm's length price for the period designated. Although retroactive APAs can be used to reduce tax exposure in past years, APAs are primarily used to avoid the risk of future income assessment adjustments which, as in the case of GlaxoSmithKline, could lead to hefty payments in the future.

There are two types of APAs: unilateral and bilateral/ multilateral APAs. A unilateral APA is, as its name suggests, an agreement between a corporation and the authority of the country where it is subject to taxation. Although simpler to implement than a bilateral/multilateral APA, a unilateral APA will not be recognized by a foreign tax authority, meaning that a U.S. company securing a unilateral APA for trade with its British subsidiary would still run the risk of being assessed should the foreign tax authorities not agree with the method of calculating the arm's length price, resulting in double taxation.

Bilateral/multilateral APAs, however, do provide such coverage, although their implementation requires a more lengthy application process, including consultation between and the agreement of all competent authorities involved.

Mutual Agreement Procedures

A mutual agreement procedure is an instrument used for relieving international tax grievances, including double taxation. Although the specifics vary based on the laws of each country, they are only carried out between authorities of countries or principalities with existing tax treaties--for example, it is impossible to relieve double taxation by holding mutual agreement procedures between the authorities of People's Republic of China and Taiwan.

Although most conventions require that each party to put forth all reasonable effort to resolve such disputes, they are generally not required to come to any sort of agreement. This means that although mutual agreement procedures can be an effective tool for the relief of taxation grievances, they are not fail-safes.

Some countries are beginning to insert into their tax treaties provisions for the mandatory arbitration of mutual agreement procedures that do not reach resolution after a period of time. Such arbitration provisions, for example Article 25 of the OECD model tax treaty as at 2008, are intended to ensure that double taxation disputes under tax treaties reach a final and relatively independent resolution within a fixed period of time.

BREAK-EVEN ANALYSIS

Break-even analysis is a technique widely used by production management and management accountants. It is based on categorising production costs between those which are"variable" and those that are"fixed".

Total variable and fixed costs are compared with sales revenue in order to determine the level of sales volume, sales value or production at which the business makes neither a profit nor a loss.

THE BREAK-EVEN CHART

In its simplest form, the break-even chart is a graphical representation of costs at various levels of activity shown on the same chart as the variation of income with the same variation in activity. The point at which neither profit nor loss is made is known as the"break-even point" and is represented on the chart by the intersection of the two lines:

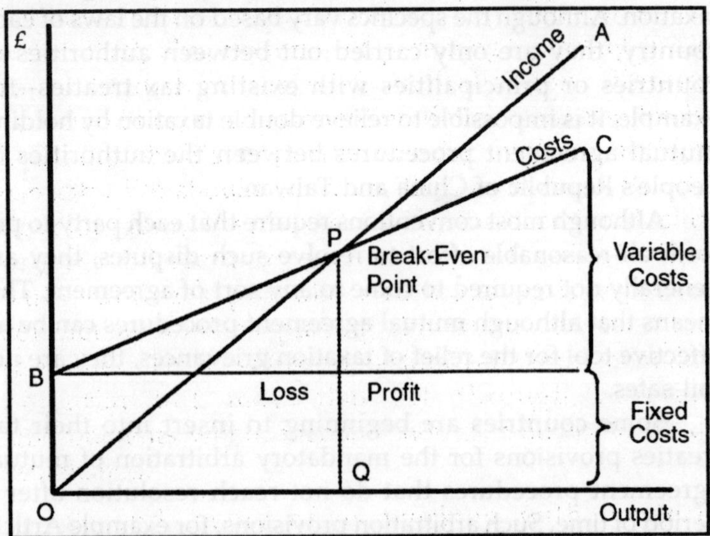

In the diagram, the line OA represents the variation of income at varying levels of production activity. OB represents the total fixed costs in the business. As output increases, variable costs are incurred, meaning that total costs also increase. At low levels of output, Costs are greater than Income. At the point of intersection, P, costs are exactly equal to income, and hence neither profit nor loss is made.

FIXED COSTS

Fixed costs are those business costs that are not directly related to the level of production or output. In other words, even if the business has a zero output or high output, the level of fixed costs will remain broadly the same. In the long term fixed costs can alter - perhaps as a result of investment in production capacity or through the growth in overheads required to support a larger, more complex business.

Examples of fixed costs:

- Rent and rates
- Depreciation

- Research and development
- Marketing costs
- Administration costs

VARIABLE COSTS

Variable costs are those costs which vary directly with the level of output. They represent payment output-related inputs such as raw materials, direct labour, fuel and revenue-related costs such as commission. A distinction is often made between"Direct" variable costs and"Indirect" variable costs.

Direct variable costs are those which can be directly attributable to the production of a particular product or service and allocated to a particular cost centre. Raw materials and the wages those working on the production line are good examples. Indirect variable costs cannot be directly attributable to production but they do vary with output. These include depreciation, maintenance and certain labour costs.

SEMI-VARIABLE COSTS

Whilst the distinction between fixed and variable costs is a convenient way of categorising business costs, in reality there are some costs which are fixed in nature but which increase when output reaches certain levels. These are largely related to the overall"scale" and/or complexity of the business. For example, when a business has relatively low levels of output or sales, it may not require costs associated with functions such as human resource management or a fully-resourced finance department. However, as the scale of the business grows then more resources are required. If production rises suddenly then some short-term increase in warehousing and/or transport may be required. In these circumstances, we say that part of the cost is variable and part fixed.

PROFIT PLANNING

Profit planning is simply the development of your operating plan for the coming period. Your plan is summarized in the form of an income statement that serves as your sales and profit objective and your budget for cost.

HOW IS IT USED?

The profit plan is used in the following ways:

- Evaluating operations. Each time you prepare an income statement, actual sales and costs are compared with those you projected in your original profit plan. This permits detection of areas of unsatisfactory performance so that corrective action can be taken.
- Determining the need for additional resources such as facilities or personnel. For example, the profit plan may show that a sharp increase in expected sales will overload the company's billing personnel. A decision can then be made to add additional invoicing personnel, to retain an EDP service, or to pursue some other alternative.
- Planning purchasing requirements. The volume of expected sales may be more than the business' usual suppliers can handle or expected sales may be sufficient to permit taking advantage of quantity discounts. In either case, advance knowledge of purchasing requirements will permit taking advantage of cost savings and ensure that purchased goods are readily available when needed.
- Anticipating any additional financing needs. With planning, the search for needed funds can begin as early as possible. In this way, financial crises are avoided and financing can be arranged on more favourable terms.

ADVANTAGES OF PROFIT PLANNING

Profit planning offers many advantages to your business. The modest investment in time required to develop and implement the plan will pay liberal dividends later.

Among the benefits that your business can enjoy from profit planning are the following:

- Performance evaluation. The profit plan provides a continuing standard against which sales performance and cost control can quickly be evaluated.

- Awareness of responsibilities. With the profit plan, personnel are readily aware of their responsibilities for meeting sales objectives, controlling costs, and the like.
- Cost consciousness. Since cost excesses can quickly be identified and planned, expenditures can be compared with budgets even before they are incurred, cost consciousness is increased, reducing unnecessary costs and overspending.
- Disciplined approach to problem-solving. The profit plan permits early detection of potential problems so that their nature and extent are known. With this information, alternate corrective actions can be more easily and accurately evaluated.
- Thinking about the future. Too often, small businesses neglect to plan ahead: thinking about where they are today, where they will be next year, or the year after. As a result, opportunities are overlooked and crises occur that could have been avoided. Development of the profit plan requires thinking about the future so that many problems can be avoided before they arise.
- Financial planning. The profit plan serves as a basis for financial planning. With the information developed from the profit plan, you can anticipate the need for increased investment in receivables, inventory, or facilities as well as any need for additional capital.
- Confidence of lenders and investors. A realistic profit plan, supported by a description of specific steps proposed to achieve sales and profit objectives, will inspire the confidence of potential lenders and investors. This confidence will not only influence their judgment of you as a business manager, but also the prospects of your business' success and its worthiness for a loan or an investment.

LIMITATIONS OF PROFIT PLANNING

Profit plans are based upon estimates. Inevitably, many

conditions you expected when the plan was prepared will change. Crystal balls are often cloudy. The further down the road one attempts to forecast, the cloudier they become. In a year, any number of factors can change, many of them beyond the control of the company. Customers' economic fortunes may decline, suppliers' prices may increase, or suppliers' inability to deliver may disrupt your plan.

The profit plan requires the support of all responsible parties. Sales quotas must be agreed upon with those responsible for meeting them. Expense budgets must be agreed upon with the people who must live with them. Without mutual agreement on objectives and budgets, they will quickly be ignored and serve no useful purpose.

Finally, profit plans must be changed from time to time to meet changing conditions. There is no point in trying to operate a business according to a plan that is no longer realistic because conditions have changed.

ADVANTAGES VS. DISADVANTAGES

Despite the limitations of profit planning, the advantages far outweigh the disadvantages. A realistic plan, established yearly and re-evaluated as changing conditions require will provide performance guidelines that will help you control every aspect of your business with a minimum of analysis and digging for financial facts.

5

National Income Analysis

TECHNIQUES OF SOCIAL ACCOUNTING

Social accounting is the process of communicating the social and environmental effects of organizations' economic actions to particular interest groups within society and to society at large. Social accounting is commonly used in the context of business, or corporate social responsibility, although any organisation, including NGOs, charities, and government agencies may engage in social accounting.

Social accounting emphasises the notion of corporate accountability. D. Crowther defines social accounting in this sense as"an approach to reporting a firm's activities which stresses the need for the identification of socially relevant behaviour, the determination of those to whom the company is accountable for its social performance and the development of appropriate measures and reporting techniques."

Social accounting is often used as an umbrella term to describe a broad field of research and practice. The use of more narrow terms to express a specific interest is thus not uncommon. Environmental accounting may e.g. specifically refer to the research or practice of accounting for an organisation's impact on the natural environment. Sustainability accounting is often used to express the measuring and the quantitative analysis of social and economic sustainability.

PURPOSE

Social accounting challenges conventional accounting, in

particular financial accounting, for giving a narrow image of the interaction between society and organizations, and thus artificially constraining the subject of accounting.

Social accounting, a largely normative concept, seeks to broaden the scope of accounting in the sense that it should:

- Concern itself with more than only economic events;
- Not be exclusively expressed in financial terms;
- Be accountable to a broader group of stakeholders;
- Broaden its purpose beyond reporting financial success.

It points to the fact that companies influence their external environment through their actions and should therefore account for these effects as part of their standard accounting practices. Social accounting is in this sense closely related to the economic concept of externality.

Social accounting offers an alternative account of significant economic entities. It has the"potential to expose the tension between pursuing economic profit and the pursuit of social and environmental objectives".

The purpose of social accounting can be approached from two different angles, namely for management control purposes or accountability purposes.

Accountability

Social accounting for accountability purposes is designed to support and facilitate the pursuit of society's objectives. These objectives can be manifold but can typically be described in terms of social and environmental desirability and sustainability. In order to make informed choices on these objectives, the flow of information in society in general, and in accounting in particular, needs to cater for democratic decision-making. In democratic systems, Gray argues, there must then be flows of information in which those controlling the resources provide accounts to society of their use of those resources: a system of corporate accountability.

Society is seen to profit from implementing a social and environmental approach to accounting in a number of ways, e.g:

- Honouring stakeholders' rights of information;

- Balancing corporate power with corporate responsibility;
- Increasing transparency of corporate activity;
- Identifying social and environmental costs of economic success.

Management Control

Social accounting for the purpose of management control is designed to support and facilitate the achievement of an organization's own objectives.

Because social accounting is concerned with substantial self-reporting on a systemic level, individual reports are often referred to as social audits.

Organizations are seen to benefit from implementing social accounting practices in a number of ways, e.g:

- Increased information for decision-making;
- More accurate product or service costing;
- Enhanced image management and Public Relations;
- Identification of social responsibilities;
- Identification of market development opportunities;
- Maintaining legitimacy.

BITC the"process of reporting on responsible businesses performance to stakeholders" helps integrate such practices into business practices, as well as identifying future risks and opportunities.

The management control view thus focuses on the individual organization. Critics of this approach point out that the benign nature of companies is assumed. Here, responsibility, and accountability, is largely left in the hands of the organization concerned.

SCOPE

Formal Accountability

In social accounting the focus tends to be on larger organisations such as multinational corporations and their visible, external accounts rather than informally produced accounts or accounts for internal use. The need for formality in making MNCs accountability is given by the spatial, financial and cultural distance of these organisations to those who are affecting and affected by it.

Social accounting also questions the reduction of all meaningful information to financial form. Financial data is seen as only one element of the accounting language.

Self-reporting and Third Party Audits

In most countries, existing legislation only regulates a fraction of accounting for socially relevant corporate activity. In consequence, most available social, environmental and sustainability reports are produced voluntarily by organisations and in that sense often resemble financial statements. While companies' efforts in this regard are usually commended, there seems to be a tension between voluntary reporting and accountability, for companies are likely to produce reports favouring their interests.

The re-arrangement of social and environmental data companies already produce as part of their normal reporting practice into an independent social audit is called a silent or shadow account.

An alternative phenomenon is the creation of external social audits by groups or individuals independent of the accountable organisation and typically without its encouragement. External social audits thus also attempt to blur the boundaries between organisations and society and to establish social accounting as a fluid two-way communication process. Companies are sought to be held accountable regardless of their approval. It is in this sense that external audits part with attempts to establish social accounting as an intrinsic feature of organisational behaviour. The reports of Social Audit Ltd in the 1970s on e.g. Tube Investments, Avon Rubber and Coalite and Chemical, laid the foundations for much of the later work on social audits.

Reporting Areas

Unlike in financial accounting, the matter of interest is by definition less clear-cut in social accounting; this is due to an aspired all-encompassing approach to corporate activity. It is generally agreed that social accounting will cover an organisations relationship with the natural environment, its employees, and ethical issues concentrating upon consumers and products, as well as local and international communities. Other issues include corporate action on questions of ethnicity and gender.

Audience

Social accounting supersedes the traditional audit audience, which is mainly composed of a company's shareholders and the financial community, by providing information to all of the organisation's stakeholders. A stakeholder of an organisation is anyone who can influence or is influenced by the organisation.

This often includes, but is not limited to, suppliers of inputs, employees and trade unions, consumers, members of local communities, society at large and governments. Different stakeholders have different rights of information. These rights can be stipulated by law, but also by non-legal codes, corporate values, mission statements and moral rights. The rights of information are thus determined by"society, the organisation and its stakeholders".

ENVIRONMENTAL ACCOUNTING

Environmental accounting, is a subset of social accounting, focuses on the cost structure and environmental performance of a company. It principally describes the preparation, presentation, and communication of information related to an organisation's interaction with the natural environment. Although environmental accounting is most commonly undertaken as voluntary self-reporting by companies, third-party reports by government agencies, NGOs and other bodies posit to pressure for environmental accountability.

Accounting for impacts on the environment may occur within a company's financial statements, relating to liabilities, commitments and contingencies for the remediation of contaminated lands or other financial concerns arising from pollution. Such reporting essentially expresses financial issues arising from environmental legislation. More typically, environmental accounting describes the reporting of quantitative and detailed environmental data within the non-financial parts of the annual report or in separate environmental reports. Such reports may account for pollution emissions, resources used, or wildlife habitat damaged or re-established.

In their reports, large companies commonly place primary emphasis on eco-efficiency, referring to the reduction of resource and energy use and waste production per unit of product or service.

A complete picture which accounts for all inputs, outputs and wastes of the organisation, must not necessarily emerge. Whilst companies can often demonstrate great success in eco-efficiency, their ecological footprint, that is an estimate of total environmental impact, may move independently following changes in output.

Legislation for compulsory environmental reporting exists in some form e.g. in Denmark, Netherlands, Australia and Korea. The United Nations has been highly involved in the adoption of environmental accounting practices, most notably in the United Nations Division for Sustainable Development publication Environmental Management Accounting Procedures and Principles.

APPLICATIONS

Social accounting is a widespread practice in a number of large organisations in the United Kingdom. Royal Dutch Shell, BP, British Telecom, The Co-operative Bank, The Body Shop, and United Utilities all publish independently audited social and sustainability accounts. In many instances the reports are produced in compliance with the sustainability reporting guidelines set by the Global Reporting Initiative.

Traidcraft plc, the fair trade organisation, claims to be the first public limited company to publish audited social accounts in the UK, starting in 1993.

Format

Companies and other organisations may publish annual corporate responsibility reports, in print or online. The reporting format can also include summary or overview documents for certain stakeholders, a corporate responsibility or sustainability part on its corporate website, or integrate social accounting into its annual report and accounts.

Companies may seek to adopt a social accounting format that is audience specific and appropriate. For example, H&M, asks stakeholders how they would like to receive reports on its website; Vodafone publishes separate reports for 11 of its operating companies as well as publishing an internal report in 2005; Weyerhaeuser produced a tabloid-size, four-page mini-report in addition to its full sustainability report.

THEORIES OF INCOME

A body of economic analysis concerned with the relative levels of output, employment, and prices in an economy. By defining the interrelation of these macroeconomic factors, governments try to create policies that contribute to economic stability.

Modern interest in income and employment theory was triggered by the severity of the Great Depression of the 1930s in the United States and Europe. In its failure to explain the persistent high levels of unemployment and the low levels of business productivity, the prevailing school of classical economics lacked solutions for the problems of that era.

John Maynard Keynes offered new thinking on income and employment theory with the publication of General Theory of Employment, Interest and Money. Building on his theory, Keynesians have stressed the relationship between income, output, and expenditure. Since transactions are two-sided-in that one person's income is another person's expenditure-the relationship could be expressed in the form of a simple equation: Y = O = D, where Y is the national income, O is the value of the national output, and D is national expenditure. What this equation means is that effective demand is equal to income as well as to output. Since consumers can either spend or save their income, Y = C + S, where C is consumption and S is savings.

Similarly, on the output side, production is either sold to final customers or invested in inventory or new capital equipment,. So O = C + I, where C represents sales to final customers and I investment. Thus, C + S = C + I and, therefore, S = I. However, while savings and investment may thus be equated from an accounting standpoint, in fact, actual planned savings and planned investment may differ in real life. Keynesians, that economic instability stems from this discrepancy between savings and investment.

Suppose, for example, that in a given period savings rise above their previous levels. The effect will be a reduction in present demand with a prospect of increased future demand. If, by coincidence, additional capital formation rises by the same amount, productive resources will continue to operate at capacity; there will be no change in the level of activity, and the economy will remain in equilibrium. However, if capital formation does not rise, then the demand for labour will fall and, assuming that wages do not fall, some workers will become unemployed and lose some of their current income.

The fall in incomes further reduces consumer demand while also reducing the rate of savings. Provided manufacturers do not alter their investment plans, equilibrium will be established at a lower level of income. In reality, then, it is not savings that are unstable but the level of investment: a fall in investment and an increase in savings will both produce a dampening effect on the economy. Conversely, a rise in investment or an increase in consumer spending will tend to stimulate the economy.

This example illustrates how changes in savings or investment will affect changes in national income, but it does not show the extent of those changes. The actual degree of change is determined by what Keynes called the"consumption function". Keynes's primary aim in developing his theory was to show that, under certain conditions the economy could become stuck in a disequilibrium, with productive resources in surplus but income and output unable to rise sufficiently to reach an equilibrium. Put simply, Keynes argued that, when business was unwilling or unable to increase investment because of low demand, additional government spending could spur new spending and eventually pull the economy out of disequilibrium. Keynesians believe that fiscal policy-such as an increase in government expenditure or a reduction in taxation-is the most effective way to offset the lack of private demand.

A competing theory of income and employment, the monetarist approach, places the quantity of money in the controlling role. The analysis of the effects of increasing or decreasing the money supply is approximately parallel to that of the consumption-and-savings relation. The rules of thumb derived from the two theories may, in fact, be combined: an excess demand for goods or an excess supply of money will be associated with rising income; similarly, an excess supply of goods or an excess demand for money will be associated with falling income. Monetarists, such as Milton Friedman, have advocated monetary policy as the proper countercyclical tool of government.

Both the Keynesian and the monetarist theories have two notable shortcomings. First, both are demand-side theories and are therefore incapable of contributing towrds the long-term considerations of economic growth. Second, both assume that people can be fooled over and over again; in reality, as they learn to anticipate government policies based on the monetarist or Keynesian models, people act in ways to offset these policies and thus negate the government actions.

KEYNESIAN ECONOMICS

Keynesian economics is a macroeconomic theory based on the ideas of 20th century British economist John Maynard Keynes. Keynesian economics argues that private sector decisions sometimes lead to inefficient macroeconomic outcomes and therefore, advocates active policy responses by the public sector, including monetary policy actions by the central bank and fiscal policy actions by the government to stabilize output over the business cycle. The theories forming the basis of Keynesian economics were first presented in The General Theory of Employment, Interest and Money, published in 1936; the interpretations of Keynes are contentious, and several schools of thought claim his legacy.

Keynesian economics advocates a mixed economy-predominantly private sector, but with a large role of government and public sector-and served as the economic model during the latter part of the Great Depression, World War II, and the post-war economic expansion, though it lost some influence following the stagflation of the 1970s. The advent of the global financial crisis in 2007 has caused a resurgence in Keynesian thought. The former British Prime Minister Gordon Brown and other world leaders have used Keynesian economics to justify government stimulus programmes for their economies.

Keynesian theory, some microeconomic-level actions - if taken collectively by a large proportion of individuals and firms - can lead to inefficient aggregate macroeconomic outcomes, where the economy operates below its potential output and growth rate. Such a situation had previously been referred to by classical economists as a general glut. There was disagreement among classical economists on whether a general glut was possible.

Keynes contended that a general glut would occur when aggregate demand for goods were insufficient, leading to an economic downturn with unnecessarily high unemployment and losses of potential output. In such a situation, government policies could be used to increase aggregate demand, thus increasing economic activity and reducing unemployment and deflation.

Keynes argued that the solution to the Great Depression was to stimulate the economy through some combination of two approaches: a reduction in interest rates and government investment in infrastructure. Investment by government injects income, which results in more spending in the general economy, which in turn stimulates more production and investment involving still more income and spending and so forth. The initial stimulation starts a cascade of events, whose total increase in economic activity is a multiple of the original investment.

A central cease of Keynesian economics is that, in some situations, no strong automatic mechanism moves output and employment towards full employment levels. This cease conflicts with economic approaches that assume a strong general tendency towards equilibrium. In the'neoclassical synthesis', which combines Keynesian macro concepts with a micro foundation, the conditions of general equilibrium allow for price adjustment to eventually achieve this goal. More broadly, Keynes saw his theory as a general theory, in which utilization of resources could be high or low, whereas previous economics focused on the particular case of full utilization.

The new classical macroeconomics movement, which began in the late 1960s and early 1970s, criticized Keynesian theories, while New Keynesian economics have sought to base Keynes's idea on more rigorous theoretical foundations.

Some interpretations of Keynes have emphasized his stress on the international coordination of Keynesian policies, the need for international economic institutions, and the ways in which economic forces could lead to war or could promote peace.

PRECURSORS

Keynes's work was part of a long-running debate within economics over the existence and nature of general gluts. While a number of the policies Keynes advocated and the theoretical ideas he proposed were advanced by various authors in the 19th and early 20th century, Keynes's unique contribution was to provide a general theory of these, which proved acceptable to the political and economic establishments.

Schools

An intellectual precursor of Keynesian economics was underconsumption theory in classical economics, dating from such 19th century economists as Thomas Malthus, the Birmingham School of Thomas Attwood, and the American economists William Trufant Foster and Waddill Catchings, who were influential in the 1920s and 1930s. Underconsumptionists were, like Keynes after them, concerned with failure of aggregate demand to attain potential output, calling this"underconsumption", rather than"overproduction", and advocating economic interventionism.

Numerous concepts were developed earlier and independently of Keynes by the Stockholm school during the 1930s; these accomplishments were described in a 1937, General Theory, sharing the Swedish discoveries.

Concepts

The multiplier dates to work in the 1890s by the Australian economist Alfred De Lissa, the Danish economist Julius Wulff, and the German American economist Nicholas Johannsen, the latter being cited in a footnote of Keynes. Nicholas Johannsen also proposed a theory of effective demand in the 1890s.

The paradox of thrift was stated in 1892 by John M. Robertson in his The Fallacy of Savings, in earlier forms by mercantilist economists since the 16th century, and similar sentiments date to antiquity:

Today these ideas, regardless of provenance, are referred to in academia under the rubric of"Keynesian economics", due to Keynes's role in consolidating, elaborating, and popularizing them.

KEYNES AND THE CLASSICS

Keynes sought to distinguish his theories from and oppose them to"classical economics," by which he meant the economic theories of David Ricardo and his followers, including John Stuart Mill, Alfred Marshall, Francis Ysidro Edgeworth, and Arthur Cecil Pigou. A central tenet of the classical view, known as Say's law, states that"supply creates its own demand". Say's Law can be interpreted in two ways. First, the claim that the total value of output is equal to the sum of income earned in production is a result of a national income accounting identity, and is therefore indisputable. A second and stronger claim, however, that the"costs of output are always covered in the aggregate by the sale-proceeds resulting from demand" depends on how consumption and saving are linked to production and investment. In particular, Keynes argued that the second, strong form of Say's Law only holds if increases in individual savings exactly match an increase in aggregate investment.

Keynes sought to develop a theory that would explain determinants of saving, consumption, investment and production. In that theory, the interaction of aggregate demand and aggregate supply determines the level of output and employment in the economy.

Because of what he considered the failure of the"Classical Theory" in the 1930s, Keynes firmly objects to its main theory-adjustments in prices would automatically make demand tend to the full employment level.

Neo-classical theory supports that the two main costs that shift demand and supply are labour and money. Through the distribution of the monetary policy, demand and supply can be adjusted. If there were more labour than demand for it, wages would fall until hiring began again. If there was too much saving, and not enough consumption, then interest rates would fall until people either cut their savings rate or started borrowing.

Wages and Spending

During the Great Depression, the classical theory defined economic collapse as simply a lost incentive to produce, and the mass unemployment as a result of high and rigid real wages.

To Keynes, the determination of wages is more complicated. First, he argued that it is not real but nominal wages that are set in negotiations between employers and workers, as opposed to a barter relationship. Second, nominal wage cuts would be difficult to put into effect because of laws and wage contracts. Even classical economists admitted that these exist; unlike Keynes, they advocated abolishing minimum wages, unions, and long-term contracts, increasing labour-market flexibility. However, to Keynes, people will resist nominal wage reductions, even without unions, until they see other wages falling and a general fall of prices. He also argued that to boost employment, real wages had to go down: nominal wages would have to fall more than prices. However, doing so would reduce consumer demand, so that the aggregate demand for goods would drop. This would in turn reduce business sales revenues and expected profits. Investment in new plants and equipment would then become more risky, less likely. Instead of raising business expectations, wage cuts could make matters much worse.

Further, if wages and prices were falling, people would start to expect them to fall. This could make the economy spiral downward as those who had money would simply wait as falling prices made it more valuable-rather than spending. As Irving Fisher argued in 1933, in his Debt-Deflation Theory of Great Depressions, deflation can make a depression deeper as falling prices and wages made pre-existing nominal debts more valuable in real terms.

Excessive Saving

To Keynes, excessive saving, i.e. saving beyond planned investment, was a serious problem, encouraging recession or even depression. Excessive saving results if investment falls, perhaps due to falling consumer demand, over-investment in earlier years, or pessimistic business expectations, and if saving does not immediately fall in step, the economy would decline.

The classical economists argued that interest rates would fall due to the excess supply of"loanable funds". The first diagram, adapted from the only graph in The General Theory, shows this process. Assume that fixed investment in capital goods falls from"old I" to"new I". Second, the resulting excess of saving causes interest-rate cuts, abolishing the excess supply: so again we have saving equal to investment. The interest-rate fall prevents that of production and employment.

Keynes had a complex argument against this laissez-faire response. The graph summarizes his argument, assuming again that fixed investment falls. First, saving does not fall much as interest rates fall, since the income and substitution effects of falling rates go in conflicting directions. Second, since planned fixed investment in plant and equipment is mostly based on long-term expectations of future profitability, that spending does not rise much as interest rates fall. So S and I are drawn as steep in the graph. Given the inelasticity of both demand and supply, a large interest-rate fall is needed to close the saving/investment gap. As drawn, this requires a negative interest rate at equilibrium. However, this negative interest rate is not necessary to Keynes's argument.

Third, Keynes argued that saving and investment are not the main determinants of interest rates, especially in the short run. Instead, the supply of and the demand for the stock of money determine interest rates in the short run. Neither changes quickly in response to excessive saving to allow fast interest-rate adjustment.

Finally, because of fear of capital losses on assets besides money, Keynes suggested that there may be a"liquidity trap" setting a floor under which interest rates cannot fall. While in this trap, interest rates are so low that any increase in money supply will cause bond-holders to sell their bonds to attain money. The equilibrium suggested by the new I line and the old S line cannot be reached, so that excess saving persists. Some see this latter kind of liquidity trap as prevailing in Japan in the 1990s. Most economists agree that nominal interest rates cannot fall zero, however, some economists reject the existence of a liquidity trap.

Even if the liquidity trap does not exist, there is a fourth element to Keynes's critique. Saving involves not spending all of one's income. It thus means insufficient demand for business output, unless it is balanced by other sources of demand, such as fixed investment. Thus, excessive saving corresponds to an unwanted accumulation of inventories, or what classical economists called a general glut. This pile-up of unsold goods and materials encourages businesses to decrease both production and employment. This in turn lowers people's incomes. For Keynes, the fall in income did most of the job by ending excessive saving and allowing the loanable funds market to attain equilibrium. Instead of interest-rate adjustment solving the problem, a recession does so.

Whereas the classical economists assumed that the level of output and income was constant and given at any one time, Keynes saw this as the key variable that adjusted to equate saving and investment.

Finally, a recession undermines the business incentive to engage in fixed investment. With falling incomes and demand for products, the desired demand for factories and equipment will fall. This accelerator effect would shift the I line to the left again. This recreates the problem of excessive saving and encourages the recession to continue.

In sum, to Keynes there is interaction between excess supplies in different markets, as unemployment in labour markets encourages excessive saving-and vice-versa. Rather than prices adjusting to attain equilibrium, the main story is one of quantity adjustment allowing recessions and possible attainment of underemployment equilibrium.

Active Fiscal Policy

As noted, the classicals wanted to balance the government budget. To Keynes, this would exacerbate the underlying problem: following either policy would raise saving and thus lower the demand for both products and labour. For example, Keynesians, Herbert Hoover's June 1932 tax increase as making the Depression worse.

Keynes? ideas influenced Franklin D. Roosevelt's view that insufficient buying-power caused the Depression. During his presidency, Roosevelt adopted some aspects of Keynesian economics, especially after 1937, when, in the depths of the Depression, the United States suffered from recession yet again following fiscal contraction. But to many the true success of Keynesian policy can be seen at the onset of World War II, which provided a kick to the world economy, removed uncertainty, and forced the rebuilding of destroyed capital. Keynesian ideas became almost official in social-democratic Europe after the war and in the U.S. in the 1960s.

Keynes? theory suggested that active government policy could be effective in managing the economy. Rather than seeing unbalanced government budgets as wrong, Keynes advocated what has been called countercyclical fiscal policies, that is policies which acted against the tide of the business cycle: deficit spending when a nation's economy suffers from recession or when recovery is long-delayed and unemployment is persistently high-and the suppression of inflation in boom times by either increasing taxes or cutting back on government outlays. He argued that governments should solve problems in the short run rather than waiting for market forces to do it in the long run, because"in the long run, we are all dead."

This contrasted with the classical and neoclassical economic analysis of fiscal policy. Fiscal stimulus could actuate production. But to these schools, there was no reason to believe that this stimulation would outrun the side-effects that"crowd out" private investment: first, it would increase the demand for labour and raise wages, hurting profitability; Second, a government deficit increases the stock of government bonds, reducing their market price and encouraging high interest rates, making it more expensive for business to finance fixed investment. Thus, efforts to stimulate the economy would be self-defeating.

The Keynesian response is that such fiscal policy is only appropriate when unemployment is persistently high, the non-accelerating inflation rate of unemployment. In that case, crowding out is minimal. Further, private investment can be"crowded in": fiscal stimulus raises the market for business output, raising cash flow and profitability, spurring business optimism. To Keynes, this accelerator effect meant that government and business could be complements rather than substitutes in this situation. Second, as the stimulus occurs, gross domestic product rises, raising the amount of saving, helping to finance the increase in fixed investment. Finally, government outlays need not always be wasteful: government investment in public goods that will not be provided by profit-seekers will encourage the private sector's growth. That is, government spending on such things as basic research, public health, education, and infrastructure could help the long-term growth of potential output.

A Keynesian economist might point out that classical and neoclassical theory does not explain why firms acting as"special interests" to influence government policy are assumed to produce a negative outcome, while those same firms acting with the same motivations outside of the government are supposed to produce positive outcomes. Libertarians counter that because both parties consent, free trade increases net happiness, but government imposes its will by force, decreasing happiness. Therefore firms that manipulate the government do net harm, while firms that respond to the free market do net good.

In Keynes' theory, there must be significant slack in the labour market before fiscal expansion is justified. Both conservative and some neoliberal economists question this assumption, unless labour unions or the government"meddle" in the free market, creating persistent supply-side or classical unemployment. Their solution is to increase labour-market flexibility, e.g., by cutting wages, busting unions, and deregulating business.

Deficit spending is not Keynesianism. Keynesianism recommends counter-cyclical policies to smooth out fluctuations in the business cycle.

An example of a counter-cyclical policy is raising taxes to cool the economy and to prevent inflation when there is abundant demand-side growth, and engaging in deficit spending on labour-intensive infrastructure projects to stimulate employment and stabilize wages during economic downturns.

Classical economics, on the other hand, argues that one should cut taxes when there are budget surpluses, and cut spending-or, less likely, increase taxes-during economic downturns.

Keynesian economists believe that adding to profits and incomes during boom cycles through tax cuts, and removing income and profits from the economy through cuts in spending and/or increased taxes during downturns, tends to exacerbate the negative effects of the business cycle. This effect is especially pronounced when the government controls a large fraction of the economy, and is therefore one reason fiscal conservatives advocate a much smaller government.

"Multiplier Effect" and Interest Rates

Two aspects of Keynes' model had implications for policy:

First, there is the"Keynesian multiplier", first developed by Richard F. Kahn in 1931. Exogenous increases in spending, such as an increase in government outlays, increases total spending by a multiple of that increase.

A government could stimulate a great deal of new production with a modest outlay if:

- The people who receive this money then spend most on consumption goods and save the rest.
- This extra spending allows businesses to hire more people and pay them, which in turn allows a further increase consumer spending.

This process continues. At each step, the increase in spending is smaller than in the previous step, so that the multiplier process tapers off and allows the attainment of an equilibrium.

This story is modified and moderated if we move beyond a"closed economy" and bring in the role of taxation: the rise in imports and tax payments at each step reduces the amount of induced consumer spending and the size of the multiplier effect.

Second, Keynes re-analysed the effect of the interest rate on investment. In the classical model, the supply of funds determined the amount of fixed business investment. That is, since all savings was placed in banks, and all business investors in need of borrowed funds went to banks, the amount of savings determined the amount that was available to invest. To Keynes, the amount of investment was determined independently by long-term profit expectations and, to a lesser extent, the interest rate.

The latter opens the possibility of regulating the economy through money supply changes, via monetary policy. Under conditions such as the Great Depression, Keynes argued that this approach would be relatively ineffective compared to fiscal policy. But during more"normal" times, monetary expansion can stimulate the economy.

POSTWAR KEYNESIANISM

In the post-WWII years, Keynes's policy ideas were widely accepted. Governments prepared high quality economic statistics on an ongoing basis and tried to base their policies on the Keynesian theory that had become the norm. In the early era of new liberalism and social democracy, most western capitalist countries enjoyed low, stable unemployment and modest inflation, an era called the Golden Age of Capitalism.

In terms of policy, the twin tools of post-war Keynesian economics were fiscal policy and monetary policy. While these are credited to Keynes, others, such as economic historian David Colander, argue that they are rather due to the interpretation of Keynes by Abba Lerner in his theory of Functional Finance, and should instead be called"Lernerian" rather than"Keynesian".

Through the 1950s, moderate degrees of government demand leading industrial development, and use of fiscal and monetary counter-cyclical policies continued, and reached a peak in the"go go" 1960s, where it seemed to many Keynesians that prosperity was now permanent. In 1971, Republican US President Richard Nixon even proclaimed"we are all Keynesians now".

However, with the oil shock of 1973, and the economic problems of the 1970s, modern liberal economics began to fall out of favour. During this time, many economies experienced high and rising unemployment, coupled with high and rising inflation, contradicting the Phillips curve's prediction.

This stagflation meant that the simultaneous application of expansionary and contractionary policies appeared to be necessary, a clear impossibility. This dilemma led to the end of the Keynesian near-consensus of the 1960s, and the rise throughout the 1970s of ideas based upon more classical analysis, including monetarism, supply-side economics and new classical economics.

At the same time Keynesians began during the period to

reorganize their thinking; one strategy, utilized also as a critique of the notably high unemployment and potentially disappointing GNP growth rates associated with the latter two theories by the mid-1980s, was to emphasize low unemployment and maximal economic growth at the cost of somewhat higher inflation.

Currently, multiple schools of economic thought exist that trace their legacy to Keynes, notably Neo-Keynesian economics, New Keynesian economics, and Post-Keynesian economics. Keynes' biographer Robert Skidelsky writes that the post-Keynesian school has remained closest to the spirit of Keynes' work in following his monetary theory and rejecting the neutrality of money.

In the postwar era Keynesian analysis was combined with neoclassical economics to produce what is generally termed the"neoclassical synthesis", yielding Neo-Keynesian economics, which dominated mainstream macroeconomic thought.

Though it was widely held that there was no strong automatic tendency to full employment, many believed that if government policy were used to ensure it, the economy would behave as neoclassical theory predicted. This post-war domination by Neo-Keynesian economics was broken during the stagflation of the 1970s. There was a lack of consensus among macroeconomists in the 1980s. However, the advent of New Keynesian economics in the 1990s, modified and provided microeconomic foundations for the neo-Keynesian theories. These modified models now dominate mainstream economics.

Post-Keynesian economists on the other hand, reject the neoclassical synthesis, and more generally, neoclassical economics applied to the macroeconomy. Post-Keynesian economics is a heterodox school which holds that both Neo-Keynesian economics and New Keynesian economics are incorrect, and a misinterpretation of Keynes's ideas. The Post-Keynesian school encompasses a variety of perspectives, but has been far less influential than the other more mainstream Keynesian schools.

Main Theories

The two key theories of mainstream Keynesian economics are the IS-LM model of John Hicks, and the Phillips curve; both of these are rejected by Post-Keynesians.

It was with John Hicks that Keynesian economics produced a clear model which policy-makers could use to attempt to understand and control economic activity. This model, the IS-LM model is nearly as influential as Keynes' original analysis in determining actual policy and economics education. It relates aggregate demand and employment to three exogenous quantities, i.e., the amount of money in circulation, the government budget, and the state of business expectations. This model was very popular with economists after World War II because it could be understood in terms of general equilibrium theory.

The second main part of a Keynesian policy-maker's theoretical apparatus was the Phillips curve. This curve, which was more of an empirical observation than a theory, indicated that increased employment, and decreased unemployment, implied increased inflation. Keynes had only predicted that falling unemployment would cause a higher price, not a higher inflation rate. Thus, the economist could use the IS-LM model to predict, for example, that an increase in the money supply would raise output and employment-and then use the Phillips curve to predict an increase in inflation.

CRITICISM

Mone Arist Criticism

One school began in the late 1940s with Milton Friedman. Instead of rejecting macro-measurements and macro-models of the economy, the monetarist school embraced the techniques of treating the entire economy as having a supply and demand equilibrium. However, because of Irving Fisher's equation of exchange, they regarded inflation as solely being due to the variations in the money supply, rather than as being a consequence of aggregate demand. They argued that the"crowding out" effects would hobble or deprive fiscal policy of its positive effect. Instead, the focus should be on monetary policy, which was considered ineffective by early Keynesians.

Monetarism had an ideological as well as a practical appeal: monetary policy does not, at least on the surface, imply as much government intervention in the economy as other measures. The monetarist critique pushed Keynesians towrds a more balanced view of monetary policy, and inspired a wave of revisions to Keynesian theory.

New Classical Macroeconomics Criticism

Another influential school of thought was based on the Lucas critique of Keynesian economics. This called for greater consistency with microeconomic theory and rationality, and particularly emphasized the idea of rational expectations. Lucas and others argued that Keynesian economics required remarkably foolish and short-sighted behaviour from people, which totally contradicted the economic understanding of their behaviour at a micro level. New classical economics introduced a set of macroeconomic theories which were based on optimising microeconomic behaviour. These models have been developed into the Real Business Cycle Theory, which argues that business cycle fluctuations can to a large extent be accounted for by real shocks.

Austrian School Criticism

Austrian economist Friedrich Hayek criticized Keynesian economic policies for what he called their fundamentally collectivist approach, arguing that such theories encourage centralized planning, which leads to malinvestment of capital, which is the cause of business cycles. Hayek also argued that Keynes' study of the aggregate relations in an economy is fallacious, as recessions are caused by micro-economic factors. Hayek claimed that what starts as temporary governmental fixes usually become permanent and expanding government programmes, which stifle the private sector and civil society.

Other Austrian school economists have also attacked Keynesian economics. Henry Hazlitt criticized, paragraph by paragraph, Keynes' General Theory. Murray Rothbard accuses

Keynesianism of having"its roots deep in medieval and mercantilist thought."

Methodological Disagreement and Different Results that Emerge

Beginning in the late 1950s neoclassical macroeconomists began to disagree with the methodology employed by Keynes and his successors. Keynesians emphasized the dependence of consumption on disposable income and, also, of investment on current profits and current cash flow. In addition Keynesians posited a Phillips curve that tied nominal wage inflation to unemployment rate. To buttress these theories Keynesians typically traced the logical foundations of their model and buttressed their assumptions with statistical evidence. Neoclassical theorists demanded that macroeconomics be grounded on the same foundations as microeconomic theory, profit-maximizing firms and utility maximizing consumers.

The result of this shift in methodology produced several important divergences from Keynesian Macroeconomics:

- Independence of Consumption and current Income
- Irrelevance of Current Profits to Investment
- Long run independence of inflation and unemployment
- The inability of monetary policy to stabilize output
- Irrelevance of Taxes and Budget Deficits to Consumption

KEYNESIAN RESPONSES TO THE CRITICS

The heart of the'new Keynesian' view rests on microeconomic models that indicate that nominal wages and prices are"sticky," i.e., do not change easily or quickly with changes in supply and demand, so that quantity adjustment prevails. Economist Paul Krugman,"while I regard the evidence for such stickiness as overwhelming, the assumption of at least temporarily rigid nominal prices is one of those things that works beautifully in practice but very badly in theory." This integration is further spurred by the work of other economists which questions rational decision-making in a perfect information environment as a necessity for micro-economic theory. Imperfect decision making such as that investigated by Joseph Stiglitz underlines the importance of management of risk in the economy.

Over time, many macroeconomists have returned to the IS-LM model and the Phillips curve as a first approximation of how an economy works. New versions of the Phillips curve, such as the"Triangle Model", allow for stagflation, since the curve can shift due to supply shocks or changes in built-in inflation. In the 1990s, the original ideas of"full employment" had been modified by the NAIRU doctrine, sometimes called the"natural rate of unemployment." NAIRU advocates suggest restraint in combating unemployment, in case accelerating inflation should result. However, it is unclear exactly what the value of the NAIRU should be-or whether it even exists.

6

Multiplier

THEORY OF MULTIPLIER

In economics, a multiplier is a factor of proportionality that measures how much an endogenous variable changes in response to a change in some exogenous variable. For example, suppose a one-unit change in some variable x causes another variable y to change by M units. Then the multiplier is M.

COMMON USES

Two multipliers are commonly discussed in introductory macroeconomics.

Money Multiplier

In monetary macroeconomics and banking, the money multiplier measures how much the money supply increases in response to a change in the monetary base.

The multiplier may vary across countries, and will also vary depending on what measures of money are considered. For example, consider M2 as a measure of the U.S. money supply, and M0 as a measure of the U.S. monetary base. If a $1 increase in M0 by the Federal Reserve causes M2 to increase by $10, then the money multiplier is 10.

Fiscal Multipliers

Multipliers can be calculated to analyse the effects of fiscal policy, or other exogenous changes in income and spending, on aggregate output. For example, if an increase in German government spending by €100, with no change in taxes, causes

German GDP to increase by €150, then the spending multiplier is 1.5. Other types of fiscal multipliers can also be calculated, like multipliers that describe the effects of changing taxes.

Keynesian Multiplier

Keynesian economists often calculate multipliers that measure the effect on aggregate demand only. Opponents of Keynesianism have sometimes argued that Keynesian multiplier calculations are misleading; for example, the theory of rational expectations, it is impossible to calculate the effect of deficit-financed government spending on demand without specifying how people expect the deficit to be paid off in the future. American Economist Paul Samuelson credits Alvin Hansen for the inspiration behind his seminal 1939 contribution. The original Samuelson multiplier-accelerator model relies on a multiplier mechanism which is based on a simple Keynesian consumption function with a Robertsonian lag:

$$C_t = c_0 + cY_t - 1$$

so present consumption is a function of past income. Investment, in turn, is assumed to be composed of three parts:

$$I_t = I_0 + I(r) + b(C_t - C_t - 1)$$

The first part is autonomous investment, the second is investment induced by interest rates and the final part is investment induced by changes in consumption demand. It is assumed that $0 < b$. As we are concentrating on the income-expenditure side, let us assume $I(r) = 0$ (or alternatively, constant interest), so that:

$$I_t = I_0 + b(C_t - C_t - 1)$$

Now, assuming away government and foreign sector, aggregate demand at time t is:

$$Ytd = C_t + I_t = c_0 + I_0 + cY_t - 1 + b(C_t - C_t - 1)$$

assuming goods market equilibrium (so Yt = Ytd), then in equilibrium:

$$Yt = c_0 + I_0 + cY_t - 1 + b(C_t - C_t - 1)$$

But we know the values of C_t and $C_t - 1$ are merely $C_t = c_0 + cY_{t-1}$ and $C_{t-1} = c_0 + cY_{t-2}$ respectively, then substituting these in:

$$Yt = c_0 + I_0 + cY_{t-1} + b(c_0 + cY_{t-1} - c_0 - cY_{t-2})$$

or, rearranging and rewriting as a second order linear difference equation:

$$Y_t - (1 + b)cY_{t-1} + bcY_{t-2} = (c_0 + I_0)$$

The solution to this system then becomes elementary. The equilibrium level of Y (call it Yp, the particular solution) is easily solved by letting $Yt = Y_{t-1} = Y_{t-2} = Y_p$, or:

$$(1 - c - bc + bc)Y_p = (c_0 + I_0)$$

so:

$$Y_p = (c_0 + I_0)/(1 - c)$$

The complementary function, Y_c is also easy to determine. Namely, we know that it will have the form $Y_c = A_1r_1t + A_2r_2t$ where A_1 and A_2 are arbitrary constants to be defined and where r_1 and r_2 are the two eigenvalues (characteristic roots) of the following characteristic equation:

$$r^2 - (1 + b)cr + bc = 0$$

Thus, the entire solution is written as $Y = Y_c + Y_p$

GENERAL METHOD

The general method for calculating long-run multipliers is called comparative statics. That is, comparative statics calculates how much one or more endogenous variables change in the long run, given a permanent change in one or more exogenous variables. The comparative statics method is an application of the Implicit Function Theorem.

Dynamic multipliers can also be calculated. That is, one can ask how a change in some exogenous variable in year t affects endogenous variables in year t, in year t+1, in year t+2, and so forth. A graph showing the impact on some endogenous variable, over time is called an impulse-response function. The general method for calculating impulse response functions is sometimes called comparative dynamics.

BALANCED-BUDGET MULTIPLIER

The balanced-budget multiplier measures the change in aggregate production triggered by an autonomous change in government taxes. This multiplier is useful in the analysis of fiscal policy changes that involves both government purchases and taxes. The logic behind this multiplier comes from the government's budget, which includes both spending and taxes. In general, a balanced budget has an equality between spending and taxes.

As such, the balanced-budget multiplier analyses what happens when there is an equality between changes in government purchases and taxes, that is, actions that keep the budget"balanced."

In other words, the balanced-budget multiplier indicates the overall impact on aggregate production of a change in government purchases that is matched by an equivalent change in taxes. The balanced-budget multiplier, as such, is actually the sum of the expenditures multiplier and the tax multiplier.

The balanced-budget multiplier is equal to one. The"positive" impact on aggregate production caused by a change in government purchases is largely, but not completely, offset by the"negative" impact of the change in taxes. The only part of the impact of the change in government purchases NOT offset by the change in taxes is the purchase of aggregate production made by the initial injection. Hence, the change in aggregate production is equal to the initial change in government purchases.

A SIMPLE FORMULATION

The balanced-budget multiplier, like the expenditures multiplier and tax multiplier can come in several different varieties based on assumptions concerning the structure of the economy and what components are induced by aggregate production.

However, the value of the balanced-budget multiplier is the same whether consumption is the only induced expenditure or all components are assumed to be induced. The reason is that all of the"induced" changes in aggregate production caused by changes in government purchases are cancelled out by opposite changes in taxes. So it matters not what components are induced.

As such, here is the balanced-budget multiplier based on

the combination of the simple expenditures multiplier and the simple tax multiplier.

$$m[bb] = \frac{1}{MPS} + \frac{-MPC}{MPS} = \frac{1 - MPC}{MPS} = \frac{MPS}{MPS} = 1$$

Where MPC is the marginal propensity to consume and MPS is the marginal propensity to save.

WHY ONE?

The most obvious and most important point is that the balanced-budget multiplier has a value of 1. This value indicates that the change in aggregate production is caused by the initial injection of government purchases. The subsequent changes in aggregate production that might be result as government purchases trigger cumulatively reinforcing induced changes in factor payments, income, and consumption are cancelled out by an opposite impact from the change in taxes. Suppose, for example, that government purchases are increased by $1 trillion using fiscal policy designed to correct a business-cycle contraction. By itself, this $1 trillion government purchases increase would be expected to trigger a $4 trillion increase in aggregate production.

However, further suppose that this $1 trillion increase in government purchases is matched by, and paid for with, an equal $1 trillion increase in taxes. By itself, this $1 trillion increase in taxes is expected to trigger a $3 trillion decrease in aggregate production. The net impact on aggregate production of both changes is only $1 trillion, not $4 trillion. If a $4 trillion increase in aggregate production is needed to achieve full employment, then this strategy falls $3 trillion short.

Why does this happen?

- First, the increase in aggregate production triggered by the increase in government purchases is offset by a decrease in aggregate production triggered by the increase in taxes.
- Second, the increase in aggregate production stimulated by government purchases is only partially offset by the decrease aggregate production stimulated by taxes.

The offset is only partial and there is a net impact on production due to the way taxes and government purchases affect aggregate expenditures. All $1 trillion of the government purchases act to increase aggregate expenditures. However, only $750 billion of the taxes work their way through consumption to decrease aggregate expenditures.

As such, there remains a net increase in aggregate expenditures of $250 billion. Evaluating this net increase of $250 billion using the simple expenditures multiplier of 4 identifies an increase in aggregate production of $1 trillion.

Is it just a coincidence that this net increase in aggregate production is exactly equal to the original change in government purchases?

Not at all: Only the initial $1 trillion government purchase triggers an increase in aggregate production. Each subsequent round of increased consumption that would be otherwise induced by the multiplier process is offset by decreased consumption resulting by higher taxes. The only expenditure that does not go through the household sector and is not cancelled by taxes is the original government purchase.

OTHER MULTIPLIERS

The tax multiplier is one of several Keynesian multipliers. Two other related multipliers are expenditures multiplier and tax multiplier.

- *Expenditures Multiplier*: The expenditures multiplier measures changes in aggregate production caused by changes in an autonomous expenditure. Like the tax multiplier this comes in several varieties, simple and complex, depending on which expenditures and other components are induced by aggregate production and income. It differs from the tax multiplier in that aggregate expenditures change by full amount of the autonomous change.
- *Tax Multiplier*: The tax multiplier measures changes in aggregate production caused by changes in taxes. Like the expenditures multiplier this comes in several varieties, simple and complex, depending on which

expenditures and other components are induced by aggregate production and income. It differs from the expenditures multiplier in that aggregate expenditures change by less than the change in taxes.

Two other multipliers arise from the financial, or money, side of the economy. They are the deposit expansion multiplier and the money multiplier. The deposit expansion multiplier measures the change in bank deposits caused by a change in bank reserves. The money multiplier measures the change in money caused by a change in bank reserves. Both are useful in the analysis of monetary policy.

FISCAL MULTIPLIER

In economics, the multiplier effect or spending multiplier is the idea that an initial amount of spending leads to increased consumption spending and so results in an increase in national income greater than the initial amount of spending. In other words, an initial change in aggregate demand causes a change in aggregate output for the economy that is a multiple of the initial change.

However, multiplier values less than one have been empirically measured, suggesting that certain types of government spending crowd out private investments and spending that would have otherwise happened.

The existence of a multiplier effect was initially proposed by Ralph George Hawtrey in 1931. It is particularly associated with Keynesian economics Some other schools of economic thought reject or downplay the importance of multiplier effects, particularly in terms of the long run. The multiplier effect has been used as an argument for the efficacy of government spending or taxation relief to stimulate aggregate demand.

For example: a company spends $1 million to build a factory. The money does not disappear, but rather becomes wages to builders, revenue to suppliers etc. The builders will have higher disposable income as a result, consumption rises as well, and hence aggregate demand will also rise. Suppose further that recipients of the new spending by the builder in turn spend their new income, this will raise consumption and demand further, and so on.

The increase in the gross domestic product is the sum of the increases in net income of everyone affected. If the builder receives $1 million and pays out $800,000 to sub contractors, he has a net income of $200,000 and a corresponding increase in disposable income.

This process proceeds down the line through subcontractors and their employees, each experiencing an increase in disposable income to the degree the new work they perform does not displace other work they are already performing. Each participant who experiences an increase in disposable income then spends some portion of it on final goods, according to his or her marginal propensity to consume, which causes the cycle to repeat an arbitrary number of times, limited only by the spare capacity available.

Another example: when tourists visit somewhere they need to buy the plane ticket, catch a taxi from the airport to the hotel, book in at the hotel, eat at the restaurant and go to the movies or tourist destination. The taxi driver needs petrol for his cab, the hotel needs to hire the staff, the restaurant needs attendants and chefs, and the movies and tourist destinations need staff and cleaners.

APPLICATIONS

The multiplier effect is a tool used by governments to attempt to stimulate aggregate demand. This can be done in a period of recession or economic uncertainty. The money invested by a government creates more jobs, which in turn will mean more spending and so on.

The idea is that the net increase in disposable income by all parties throughout the economy will be greater than the original investment. When that is the case, the government can increase the gross domestic product by an amount that is greater than an increase in the amount it spends relative to the amount it collects in taxes.

The difference is the fiscal stimulus. The net fiscal stimulus may be increased by raising spending above the level of tax revenues, reducing taxes below the level of government spending, or any combination of the two that results in the government taxing less than it spends.

The resulting deficit spending must be financed from government reserves or net borrowing from private or foreign investors. If the money is borrowed, it must eventually be paid back with interest, such that the long term effect on the economy depends on the trade off between the immediate increase to the GDP and the long term cost of servicing the resulting government debt.

It must be noted that the extent of the multiplier effect is dependent upon the marginal propensity to consume and marginal propensity to import. Also that the multiplier can work in reverse as well, so an initial fall in spending can trigger further falls in aggregate output.

The concept of the economic multiplier on a macroeconomic scale can be extended to any economic region. For example, building a new factory may lead to new employment for locals, which may have knock-on economic effects for the city or region.

VARIOUS TYPES OF FISCAL MULTIPLIERS

The following values are theoretical values based on simplified models, and the empirical values corresponding to the reality have been found to be lower.

Note: In the following examples the multiplier is the right-hand-side equation without the first component.

- y is original output
- b_C is marginal propensity of consumption
- b_T is original income tax rate
- b_M is marginal propensity to import
- Δ_y is change in income
- Δa_T is change in lump-sum tax rate
- Δb_T is change in income tax rate
- ΔG is change in government spending
- ΔT is change in aggregate taxes
- ΔI is change in investment
- ΔX is change in exports

Standard Income Tax Equation

$$\Delta y = \Delta b_T * \frac{-b_C * y}{1 - b_C(1 - b_T) + b_M}$$

Note: only ΔbT is here because if this is a change in income tax rate then ΔaT is implied to be 0.

Standard Government Spending Equation

$$\Delta y = \Delta G * \frac{1}{1 - b_C(1 - b_T) + b_M}$$

Standard Investment Equation

$$\Delta y = \Delta I * \frac{1}{1 - b_C(1 - b_T) + b_M}$$

Standard Exports Equation

$$\Delta y = \Delta X * \frac{1}{1 - b_C(1 - b_T) + b_M}$$

Balanced-Budget Government Spending Equation

$$\Delta y = \Delta G * 1$$
$$\Delta y = \Delta T * 1$$

MONEY MULTIPLIER

In monetary economics, a money multiplier is one of various closely related ratios of commercial bank money to central bank money under a fractional-reserve banking system. Most often, it measures the maximum amount of commercial bank money that can be created by a given unit of central bank money. That is, in a fractional-reserve banking system, the total amount of loans that commercial banks are allowed to extend is a multiple of reserves; this multiple is the reciprocal of the reserve ratio, and it is an economic multiplier.

If banks lend out close to the maximum allowed by their reserves, then the inequality becomes an approximate equality, and commercial bank money is central bank money times the multiplier. If banks instead lend less than the maximum, accumulating excess reserves, then commercial bank money will be less than central bank money times the multiplier.

In the United States since 1959, banks lent out close to the maximum allowed for the 49-year period from 1959 until August 2008, maintaining a low level of excess reserves, then accumulated significant excess reserves over the period September 2008 through the present. Thus, in the first period, commercial bank money was almost exactly central bank money times the multiplier, but this relationship broke down from September 2008.

In equations, writing M for commercial bank money, R for reserves and RR for the reserve ratio, the reserve ratio requirement is that $R/M \geq RR$; the fraction of reserves must be at least the reserve ratio. Taking the reciprocal, $M/R \leq 1/RR$, which yields $M \leq R \times (1/RR)$ meaning that commercial bank money is at most reserves times, the latter being the multiplier.

As a formula and legal quantity, the money multiplier is not controversial - it is simply the maximum that commercial banks are allowed to lend out. The mechanism of money creation in a fractional-reserve banking system, and the implication for monetary policy differ between different schools of economics, however.

The money multiplier is defined in various ways. Most simply, it can be defined either as the statistic of"commercial bank money"/"central bank money", based on the actual observed quantities of various empirical measures of money supply, such as M2 over M0 or it can be the theoretical" maximum commercial bank money/central bank money" ratio, defined as the reciprocal of the reserve ratio, 1/RR. The multiplier in the first sense fluctuates continuously based on changes in commercial bank money and central bank money while the multiplier in the second sense depends only on the reserve ratio, and thus does not change unless the law changes.

For purposes of monetary policy, what is of most interest is the predicted impact of changes in central bank money on commercial bank money, and in various models of monetary creation, the associated multiple is called the money multiplier. For example, if one assumes that people hold a constant fraction of deposits as cash, one may add a"currency drain" variable and obtain a multiplier of (1 + CD)/(RR + CD).

These concepts are not generally distinguished by different names; if one wishes to distinguish them, one may gloss them by names such as empirical multiplier, legal multiplier, or model multiplier, but these are not standard usages.

Similarly, one may distinguish the observed reserve-deposit ratio from the legal reserve ratio, and the observed currency-deposit ratio from an assumed model one. Note that in this case the reserve-deposit ratio and currency-deposit ratio are outputs of observations, and fluctuate over time. If one then uses these observed ratios as model parametres for the predictions of effects of monetary policy and assumes that they remain constant, computing a constant multiplier, the resulting predictions are valid only if these ratios do not in fact change. Sometimes this holds, and sometimes it does not; for example, increases in central bank money may result in increases in commercial bank money - and will, if these ratios stay constant - or may result in increases in excess reserves but little or no change in commercial bank money, in which case the reserve-deposit ratio will grow and the multiplier will fall.

MECHANISM

There are two suggested mechanisms for how money creation occurs in a fractional-reserve banking system: either reserves are first injected by the central bank, and then lent on by the commercial banks, or loans are first extended by commercial banks, and then backed by reserves borrowed from the central bank. The"reserves first" model is that taught in mainstream economics textbooks, while the"loans first" model is supported by econometric data and advanced by endogenous money theories.

Reserves First

In the"reserves first" model of money creation, a given

reserve is lent out by a bank, then deposited at a bank, which is then relent, the process repeating and the ultimate result being a geometric series.

Formula

The money multiplier, m, is the inverse of the reserve requirement, RR:

$$m = \frac{1}{RR}$$

This formula stems from the fact that the sum of the"amount loaned out" column can be expressed mathematically as a geometric series with a common ratio of $1 - RR$.

To correct for currency drain and for banks' desire to hold reserves in excess of the required amount, the formula

$$m = \frac{(1 + \text{Curency Drain Ratio})}{(\text{Currency Drain Ratio} + \text{Desired Re serve Ratio})}$$

can be used, where Currency Drain Ratio is the percentage of money that people want to hold as cash and the Desired Reserve Ratio is the sum of the Required Reserve Ratio and the Excess Reserve Ratio.

The formula is derived from the following procedure. Define the legal reserve ratio, $\alpha \in (0,1)$, the excess reserves ratio, $\beta \in (0,1)$, , the currency drain ratio with respect to deposits, $\gamma \in (0,1)$, ; suppose the demand for funds is unlimited; then the theoretical superior limit for deposits is defined by the following series:

$$\text{Deposite} = \sum_{n=0}^{\infty} [(1 - \alpha - \beta - \gamma)]^n = \frac{1}{\alpha + \beta + \gamma}$$

Analogously, the theoretical superior limit for the money held by public is defined by the following series:

$$\text{Publicly Held Currency} = \gamma \cdot \text{Deposits} = \frac{\gamma}{\alpha + \beta + \gamma}$$

and the theoretical superior limit for the totale loans lent in the market is defined by the following series:

$$\text{Loans} = (1-\alpha-\beta)\cdot \text{Deposits} = \frac{1-\alpha-\beta}{\alpha+\beta+\gamma}$$

By summing up the two quantities, the theoretical money multiplier is defined as,

$$m = \frac{\text{Money Stock}}{\text{Monetary Base}} = \frac{\text{Deposits} + \text{Publicly Held Currency}}{\text{Monetary Base}} = \frac{1+\gamma}{\alpha+\beta+\gamma}$$

where $\alpha+\beta$ = DesiredReserveRatio and γ = Currency Drain Ratio.

The process described by the geometric series can be represented in the following table, where,

- Loans at stage k are a function of the deposits at the precedent stage:

$$L_k = (1-\alpha-\beta)\cdot D_{k-1}$$

- Publicly held money at stage K is a function of the deposits at the precedent stage:

$$PHM_k = \gamma \cdot D_{k-1}$$

- Deposits at stage K are the difference between additional loans and publicly held money relative to the same stage:

$$D_k = L_k - PHM_k$$

Process of money multiplication:

n	Deposits	Loans	Publicly Held Money
n=0	$D_0 = 1$	-	-
n=1	$D_1 = (1-\alpha-\beta-\gamma)$	$L_1 = (1-\alpha-\beta)$	$PHM_1 = \gamma$
n=2	$D_2 = (1-\alpha-\beta-\gamma^2)$	$L_2 = (1-\alpha-\beta)\ (1-\alpha-\beta-\gamma)$	$PHM_2 = \gamma\ (1-\alpha-\beta-\gamma)$
n=3	$D_3 = (1-\alpha-\beta-\gamma^3)$	$L_3 = (1-\alpha-\beta)\ (1-\alpha-\beta-\gamma)^2$	$PHM_3 = \gamma\ (1-\alpha-\beta-\gamma)$
...	...	...	...
n=k	$D_k = (1-\alpha-\beta-\gamma)^k$	$L_k = (1-\alpha-\beta)\ (1-\alpha-\beta-\gamma)^{k-1}$	$PHM_k = \gamma\ (1-\alpha-\beta-\gamma)$
...	...	...	...
$n \to \infty$	$D\infty = 0$	$L\infty = 0$	$PHM\infty = 0$
	Total Deposits:	*Total Loans*:	*Total Publicly Held Money*:
	$D = \frac{1}{\alpha+\beta+\gamma}$	$L = \frac{1-\alpha-\beta}{\alpha+\beta+\gamma}$	$PHM = \frac{\gamma}{\alpha+\beta+\gamma}$

Table

This re-lending process can be depicted as follows, assuming a 20% reserve ratio and a $100 initial deposit:

Individual Bank	Amount Deposited	Lent Out	Reserves
A	100.00	80.00	20.00
B	80.00	64.00	16.00
C	64.00	51.20	12.80
D	51.20	40.96	10.24
E	40.96	32.77	8.19
F	32.77	26.21	6.55
G	26.21	20.97	5.24
H	20.97	16.78	4.19
I	16.78	13.42	3.36
J	13.42	10.74	2.68
K	10.74		
			Total Reserves:
			89.26
	Total Amount of Deposits:	Total Amount Lent Out:	Total Reserves + Last Amount Deposited:
	457.05	357.05	100.00

Example

For example, with the reserve ratio of 20 per cent, this reserve ratio, RR, can also be expressed as a fraction:

$$RR = \frac{1}{5}$$

So then the money multiplier, m, will be calculated as:

$$m = 1/\frac{1}{5} = 5$$

This number is multiplied by the initial deposit to show the maximum amount of money it can be expanded to.

Another way to look at the monetary multiplier is derived from the concept of money supply and money base. It is the number of dollars of money supply that can be created for every dollar of monetary base. Money supply, denoted by M, is the stock of money held by public. It is measured by the amount of currency and deposits. Money Base, denoted by B, is the summation of currency and reserves. Currency and Reserves are monetary policy that can be affected by the Federal Reserve. For example, the Federal Reserve can increase currency by printing more money and they can similarly increase reserve by requiring a higher percentage of deposits to be stored in the Federal Reserve.

Mathematically:

- M=C+D
- B=C+R
- M=Money Supply
- C=Currency
- D=Deposits
- B=Money Base
- R=Reserve

So that money supply over money base: M/B = (C+D)/(C+R)

Multiply the right side by [(D/CR)/(D/CR)]. Since this equals to 1, it is mathematically justified to multiply it to only the right side.

Then multiple the right side of the equation by the Money Base,

So we get:

$$M=B * [(D/R)(1+D/C)/(D/R + D/C)]$$

$$[(D/R)(1+D/C)/(D/R + D/C)]$$

is the multiplier. Therefore, if money base is held constant, the ratio of D/R and D/C affects the money supply. When the ratio of deposits to reserves reduces, the multiplier reduces. Similarly, if the ratio of deposits to currency falls, the multiplier falls as well.

The multiplier effect is relevant to considering monetary and fiscal policies, as well how the banking system works. For example, the deposit, the monetary amount a customer deposits at a bank, is used by the bank to loan out to others, thereby generating the money supply. Most banks are FDIC insured so that customers are assured that their savings, up to a certain amount, is insured by the federal government. Banks are required to reserve a certain ratio of the customer's deposits in reserve, either in the form of vault cash or of a deposit maintained by a Federal Reserve Bank.. Therefore, if the Federal Reserve Bank requires a higher percentage of reserve, then it lowers the bank's financial ability to loan.

Loans First

In the alternative model of money creation, loans are first extended by commercial banks -$1,000 of loans, which then require that the bank borrow $100 of reserves either from depositors or from the central bank. This view is advanced in endogenous money theories, such as the Post-Keynesian school of monetary circuit theory, as advanced by such economists as Basil Moore and Steve Keen.

The view that loans lead reserves finds econometric support in neoclassical economics in who found that increases in broad money supply preceded increases in reserves, rather than reserves first being injected, and then gradually increasing broad money supply, as in the mainstream relending model.

IMPLICATIONS FOR MONETARY POLICY

The multiplier plays a key role in monetary policy, and the distinction between the multiplier being the maximum amount of commercial bank money created by a given unit of central bank money and approximately equal to the amount created has important implications in monetary policy.

If banks maintain low levels of excess reserves, as they did in the US from 1959 to August 2008, then central banks can finely control broad money supply by controlling central bank money creation, as the multiplier gives a direct and fixed connection between these.

Restated, increases in central bank money may not result in commercial bank money because the money is not required to be lent out - it may instead result in a growth of unlent reserves. This situation is referred to as"pushing on a string": withdrawal of central bank money compels commercial banks to curtain lending but input of central bank money does not compel commercial banks to lend.

This described growth in excess reserves has indeed occurred in the Financial crisis of 2007-2010, US bank excess reserves growing over 500-fold, from under $2 billion in August 2008 to over $1,000 billion in November 2009.

7

Theories of Inflation

INFLATION

In economics, inflation is a rise in the general level of prices of goods and services in an economy over a period of time. When the price level rises, each unit of currency buys fewer goods and services; consequently, annual inflation is also an erosion in the purchasing power of money - a loss of real value in the internal medium of exchange and unit of account in the economy. A chief measure of price inflation is the inflation rate, the annualized percentage change in a general price index over time.

Inflation's effects on an economy are manifold and can be simultaneously positive and negative. Negative effects of inflation include a decrease in the real value of money and other monetary items over time; uncertainty about future inflation may discourage investment and saving, or may lead to reductions in investment of productive capital and increase savings in non-producing assets. e.g. selling stocks and buying gold. This can reduce overall economic productivity rates, as the capital required to retool companies becomes more elusive or expensive. High inflation may lead to shortages of goods if consumers begin hoarding out of concern that prices will increase in the future. Positive effects include a mitigation of economic recessions, and debt relief by reducing the real level of debt.

High rates of inflation and hyperinflation can be caused by an excessive growth of the money supply. Views on which factors determine low to moderate rates of inflation are more varied. Low or moderate inflation may be attributed to fluctuations in real demand for goods and services, or changes in available supplies such as during scarcities, as well as to growth in the money supply. However, the consensus view is that a long sustained period of inflation is caused by money supply growing faster than the rate of economic growth.

Today, most mainstream economists favour a low steady rate of inflation. Low inflation may reduce the severity of economic recessions by enabling the labour market to adjust more quickly in a downturn, and reduce the risk that a liquidity trap prevents monetary policy from stabilizing the economy.

The task of keeping the rate of inflation low and stable is usually given to monetary authorities. Generally, these monetary authorities are the central banks that control the size of the money supply through the setting of interest rates, through open market operations, and through the setting of banking reserve requirements.

The term"inflation" originally referred to increases in the amount of money in circulation. Today, the term monetary inflation is generally used to distinguish such an occurrence from a general rise in prices, sometimes called price inflation. The occurrence of an increase of the quantity of money and the overall money supply has occurred in many different societies throughout history, changing with different forms of money used.

For instance, when gold was used as currency, the government could collect gold coins, melt them down, mix them with other metals such as silver, copper or lead, and reissue them at the same nominal value. By diluting the gold with other metals, the government could issue more coins without also needing to increase the amount of gold used to make them. When the cost of each coin is lowered in this way, the government profits from an increase in seigniorage. This practice would increase the money supply but at the same time the relative value of each coin would be lowered. As the relative value of the coins becomes less, consumers would need to give more coins in exchange for the same goods and services as before. These goods and services would experience a price increase as the value of each coin is reduced.

From second half of the 15th century to the first half of the 17th, Western Europe experienced a major inflationary cycle referred to as"price revolution", with prices on average rising perhaps sixfold over 150 years. It was thought that this was caused by the increase in wealth of Habsburg Spain, with a large influx of gold and silver from the New World. The spent silver, suddenly spread throughout a previously cash starved Europe, caused widespread inflation. Demographic factors also contributed to upward pressure on prices, with European population growth after depopulation caused by the Black Death pandemic.

By the nineteenth century, economists categorized three separate factors that cause a rise or fall in the price of goods: a change in the value or resource costs of the good, a change in the price of money which then was usually a fluctuation in the commodity price of the metallic content in the currency, and currency depreciation resulting from an increased supply of currency relative to the quantity of redeemable metal backing the currency. Following the proliferation of private bank note currency printed during the American Civil War, the term"inflation" started to appear as a direct reference to the currency depreciation that occurred as the quantity of redeemable bank notes outstripped the quantity of metal available for their redemption. The term inflation then referred to the devaluation of the currency, and not to a rise in the price of goods.

This relationship between the over-supply of bank notes and a resulting depreciation in their value was noted by earlier classical economists such as David Hume and David Ricardo, who would go on to examine and debate to what effect a currency devaluation has on the price of goods.

The term"inflation" usually refers to a measured rise in a broad price index that represents the overall level of prices in goods and services in the economy. The Consumer Price Index, the Personal Consumption Expenditures Price Index and the GDP deflator are some examples of broad price indices. The term inflation may also be used to describe the rising level of prices in a narrow set of assets, goods or services within the economy, such as commodities, financial assets, and services. The Reuters-CRB Index, the Producer Price Index, and Employment Cost Index are examples of narrow price indices used to measure price inflation in particular sectors of the economy.

Asset price inflation is a rise in the price of assets, as opposed to goods and services. Core inflation is a measure of price fluctuations in a sub-set of the broad price index which excludes food and energy prices. The Federal Reserve Board uses the core inflation rate to measure overall inflation, eliminating food and energy prices to mitigate against short term price fluctuations that could distort estimates of future long term inflation trends in the general economy.

Other related economic concepts include: deflation - a fall in the general price level; disinflation - a decrease in the rate of inflation; hyperinflation - an out-of-control inflationary spiral; stagflation - a combination of inflation, slow economic growth and high unemployment; and reflation - an attempt to raise the general level of prices to counteract deflationary pressures.

MEASURES

Inflation is usually estimated by calculating the inflation rate of a price index, usually the Consumer Price Index. The Consumer Price Index measures prices of a selection of goods and services purchased by a"typical consumer". The inflation rate is the percentage rate of change of a price index over time.

For instance, in January 2007, the U.S. Consumer Price Index was 202.416, and in January 2008 it was 211.080. The formula for calculating the annual percentage rate inflation in the CPI over the course of 2007 is,

$$\left(\frac{211.080 - 202,416}{202.416}\right) \times 100 = 4.28\%$$

The resulting inflation rate for the CPI in this one year period is 4.28%, meaning the general level of prices for typical U.S. consumers rose by approximately four per cent in 2007.

Other widely used price indices for calculating price inflation include the following:

- Producer price indices which measures average changes in prices received by domestic producers for their output. This differs from the CPI in that price subsidization, profits, and taxes may cause the amount received by the producer to differ from what the consumer paid. There is also typically a delay between an increase in the PPI and any eventual increase in the CPI. Producer price index measures the pressure being put on producers by the costs of their raw materials. This could be"passed on" to consumers, or it could be absorbed by profits, or offset by increasing productivity. In India and the United States, an earlier version of the PPI was called the Wholesale Price Index.
- Commodity price indices, which measure the price of a selection of commodities. In the present commodity price indices are weighted by the relative importance of the components to the"all in" cost of an employee.
- Core price indices: because food and oil prices can change quickly due to changes in supply and demand conditions in the food and oil markets, it can be difficult to detect the long run trend in price levels when those prices are included. Therefore most statistical agencies also report a measure of'core inflation', which removes the most volatile components from a broad price index like the CPI. Because core inflation is less affected by short run supply and demand conditions in specific markets, central banks rely on it to better measure the inflationary impact of current monetary policy.

Other common measures of inflation are:

- GDP deflator is a measure of the price of all the goods and services included in Gross Domestic Product. The US Commerce Department publishes a deflator series for US GDP, defined as its nominal

GDP measure divided by its real GDP measure.

- Regional inflation The Bureau of Labour Statistics breaks down CPI-U calculations down to different regions of the US.
- Historical inflation Before collecting consistent econometric data became standard for governments, and for the purpose of comparing absolute, rather than relative standards of living, various economists have calculated imputed inflation figures. Most inflation data before the early 20th century is imputed based on the known costs of goods, rather than compiled at the time. It is also used to adjust for the differences in real standard of living for the presence of technology.
- Asset price inflation is an undue increase in the prices of real or financial assets, such as stock and real estate. While there is no widely accepted index of this type, some central bankers have suggested that it would be better to aim at stabilizing a wider general price level inflation measure that includes some asset prices, instead of stabilizing CPI or core inflation only. The reason is that by raising interest rates when stock prices or real estate prices rise, and lowering them when these asset prices fall, central banks might be more successful in avoiding bubbles and crashes in asset prices.

Issues in Measuring

Measuring inflation in an economy requires objective means of differentiating changes in nominal prices on a common set of goods and services, and distinguishing them from those price shifts resulting from changes in value such as volume, quality, or performance. For example, if the price of a 10 oz. can of corn changes from \$0.90 to \$1.00 over the course of a year, with no change in quality, then this price difference represents inflation. This single price change would not, however, represent general inflation in an overall economy. To measure overall inflation, the price change of a large"basket" of representative goods and services is measured. This is the purpose of a price index, which is the combined price of a"basket" of many goods and services. The combined price is the sum of the weighted average prices of items in the"basket". A weighted price is calculated by multiplying the unit price of an item to the number of those items the average consumer purchases. Weighted pricing is a necessary means to measuring the impact of individual unit price changes on the economy's overall inflation. The Consumer Price Index, for example, uses data collected by surveying households to determine what proportion of the typical consumer's overall spending is spent on specific goods and services, and weights the average prices of those items accordingly. Those weighted average prices are combined to calculate the overall price. To better relate price changes over time, indexes typically choose a"base year" price and assign it a value of 100. Index prices in subsequent years are then expressed in relation to the base year price.

Inflation measures are often modified over time, either for the relative weight of goods in the basket, or in the way in which goods and services from the present are compared with goods and services from the past. Over time adjustments are made to the type of goods and services selected in order to reflect changes in the sorts of goods and services purchased by'typical consumers'. New products may be introduced, older products disappear, the quality of existing products may change, and consumer preferences can shift. Both the sorts of goods and services which are included in the"basket" and the weighted price used in inflation measures will be changed over time in order to keep pace with the changing marketplace.

Inflation numbers are often seasonally adjusted in order to differentiate expected cyclical cost shifts. For example, home heating costs are expected to rise in colder months, and seasonal adjustments are often used when measuring for inflation to compensate for cyclical spikes in energy or fuel demand. Inflation numbers may be averaged or otherwise subjected to statistical techniques in order to remove statistical noise and volatility of individual prices.

When looking at inflation economic institutions may focus only on certain kinds of prices, or special indices, such as the core inflation index which is used by central banks to formulate monetary policy.

Most inflation indices are calculated from weighted averages of selected price changes. This necessarily introduces distortion, and can lead to legitimate disputes about what the true inflation rate is. This problem can be overcome by including all available price changes in the calculation, and then choosing the median value.

EFFECTS

General

An increase in the general level of prices implies a decrease in the purchasing power of the currency. That is, when the general level of prices rises, each monetary unit buys fewer goods and services. The effect of inflation is not distributed evenly in the economy, and as a consequence there are hidden costs to some and benefits to others from this decrease in the purchasing power of money. For example, with inflation, lenders or depositors who are paid a fixed rate of interest on loans or deposits will lose purchasing power from their interest earnings, while their borrowers benefit. Individuals or institutions with cash assets will experience a decline in the purchasing power of their holdings. Increases in payments to workers and pensioners often lag behind inflation, especially for those with fixed payments.

Increases in the price level erodes the real value of money and other items with an underlying monetary nature. However, inflation has no effect on the real value of non-monetary items,.

Negative

High or unpredictable inflation rates are regarded as harmful to an overall economy. They add inefficiencies in the market, and make it difficult for companies to budget or plan long-term. Inflation can act as a drag on productivity as companies are forced to shift resources away from products and services in order to focus on profit and losses from currency inflation.

Uncertainty about the future purchasing power of money discourages investment and saving. And inflation can impose hidden tax increases, as inflated earnings push taxpayers into higher income tax rates unless the tax brackets are indexed to inflation.

With high inflation, purchasing power is redistributed from those on fixed nominal incomes, such as some pensioners whose pensions are not indexed to the price level, towards those with variable incomes whose earnings may better keep pace with the inflation.

This redistribution of purchasing power will also occur between international trading partners. Where fixed exchange rates are imposed, higher inflation in one economy than another will cause the first economy's exports to become more expensive and affect the balance of trade. There can also be negative impacts to trade from an increased instability in currency exchange prices caused by unpredictable inflation.

Cost-push Inflation

High inflation can prompt employees to demand rapid wage increases, to keep up with consumer prices. Rising wages in turn can help fuel inflation. In the case of collective bargaining, wage growth will be set as a function of inflationary expectations, which will be higher when inflation is high. This can cause a wage spiral. In a sense, inflation begets further inflationary expectations, which beget further inflation.

Hoarding

People buy consumer durables as stores of wealth in the absence of viable alternatives as a means of getting rid of excess cash before it is devalued, creating shortages of the hoarded objects.

Hyperinflation

If inflation gets totally out of control in the upward

direction), it can grossly interfere with the normal workings of the economy, hurting its ability to supply goods. Hyperinflation can lead to the abandonment of the use of the country's currency, leading to the inefficiencies of barter.

Allocative Efficiency

A change in the supply or demand for a good will normally cause its relative price to change, signalling to buyers and sellers that they should re-allocate resources in response to the new market conditions. But when prices are constantly changing due to inflation, price changes due to genuine relative price signals are difficult to distinguish from price changes due to general inflation, so agents are slow to respond to them. The result is a loss of allocative efficiency.

Shoe Leather Cost

High inflation increases the opportunity cost of holding cash balances and can induce people to hold a greater portion of their assets in interest paying accounts. However, since cash is still needed in order to carry out transactions this means that more"trips to the bank" are necessary in order to make withdrawals, proverbially wearing out the"shoe leather" with each trip.

Menu Costs

With high inflation, firms must change their prices often in order to keep up with economy-wide changes. But often changing prices is itself a costly activity whether explicitly, as with the need to print new menus, or implicitly.

Business Cycles

The Austrian Business Cycle Theory, inflation sets off the business cycle. Austrian economists hold this to be the most damaging effect of inflation. Austrian theory, artificially low interest rates and the associated increase in the money supply lead to reckless, speculative borrowing, resulting in clusters of malinvestments, which eventually have to be liquidated as they become unsustainable.

Positive

Labour-market Adjustments

Keynesians believe that nominal wages are slow to adjust downwards. This can lead to prolonged disequilibrium and high unemployment in the labour market. Since inflation would lower the real wage if nominal wages are kept constant, Keynesians argue that some inflation is good for the economy, as it would allow labour markets to reach equilibrium faster.

Debt Relief

Debtors who have debts with a fixed nominal rate of interest will see a reduction in the"real" interest rate as the inflation rate rises. The"real" interest on a loan is the nominal rate minus the inflation rate. (R=n-i) For example if you take a loan where the stated interest rate is 6% and the inflation rate is at 3%, the real interest rate that you are paying for the loan is 3%. It would also hold true that if you had a loan at a fixed interest rate of 6% and the inflation rate jumped to 20% you would have a real interest rate of -14%. Banks and other lenders adjust for this inflation risk either by including an inflation premium in the costs of lending the money by creating a higher initial stated interest rate or by setting the interest at a variable rate.

Room to Maneuver

The primary tools for controlling the money supply are the ability to set the discount rate, the rate at which banks can borrow from the central bank, and open market operations which are the central bank's interventions into the bonds market with the aim of affecting the nominal interest rate. If an economy finds itself in a recession with already low, or even zero, nominal interest rates, then the bank cannot cut these rates further in order to stimulate the economy - this situation is known as a liquidity trap. A moderate level of inflation tends to ensure that nominal interest rates stay sufficiently above zero so that if the need arises the bank can cut the nominal interest rate.

Tobin Effect

The Nobel prize winning economist James Tobin at one point had argued that a moderate level of inflation can increase investment in an economy leading to faster growth or at least higher steady state level of income. This is due to the fact that inflation lowers the return on monetary assets relative to real assets, such as physical capital. To avoid inflation, investors would switch from holding their assets as money to investing in real capital projects.

CAUSES

Historically, a great deal of economic literature was concerned with the question of what causes inflation and what effect it has. There were different schools of thought as to the causes of inflation. Most can be divided into two broad areas: quality theories of inflation and quantity theories of inflation. The quality theory of inflation rests on the expectation of a seller accepting currency to be able to exchange that currency at a later time for goods that are desirable as a buyer. The quantity theory of inflation rests on the quantity equation of money, that relates the money supply, its velocity, and the nominal value of exchanges. Adam Smith and David Hume proposed a quantity theory of inflation for money, and a quality theory of inflation for production.

Currently, the quantity theory of money is widely accepted as an accurate model of inflation in the long run. Consequently, there is now broad agreement among economists that in the long run, the inflation rate is essentially dependent on the growth rate of money supply. However, in the short and medium term inflation may be affected by supply and demand pressures in the economy, and influenced by the relative elasticity of wages, prices and interest rates. The question of whether the short-term effects last long enough to be important is the central topic of debate between monetarist and Keynesian economists. In monetarism prices and wages adjust quickly enough to make other factors merely marginal behaviour on a general trend-line. In the Keynesian view, prices and wages adjust at different rates, and these differences have enough effects on real output to be"long term" in the view of people in an economy.

KEYNESIAN VIEW

Keynesian economic theory proposes that changes in money supply do not directly affect prices, and that visible inflation is the result of pressures in the economy expressing themselves in prices. The supply of money is a major, but not the only, cause of inflation.

There are three major types of inflation, as part of what Robert J. Gordon calls the"triangle model":

- Demand-pull inflation is caused by increases in aggregate demand due to increased private and government spending, etc. Demand inflation is constructive to a faster rate of economic growth since the excess demand and favourable market conditions will stimulate investment and expansion.
- Cost-push inflation, also called"supply shock inflation," is caused by a drop in aggregate supply. This may be due to natural disasters, or increased prices of inputs. For example, a sudden decrease in the supply of oil, leading to increased oil prices, can cause cost-push inflation. Producers for whom oil is a part of their costs could then pass this on to consumers in the form of increased prices.
- Built-in inflation is induced by adaptive expectations, and is often linked to the"price/wage spiral". It involves workers trying to keep their wages up with prices and firms passing these higher labour costs on to their customers as higher prices, leading to a'vicious circle'. Built-in inflation reflects events in the past, and so might be seen as hangover inflation.

Demand-pull theory states that the rate of inflation accelerates whenever aggregate demand is increased beyond the ability of the economy to produce. Hence, any factor that increases aggregate demand can cause inflation. However, in the long run, aggregate demand can be held above productive capacity only by increasing the quantity of money in circulation faster than the real growth rate of the economy. Another cause can be a rapid decline in the demand for money, as happened in Europe during the Black Death, or in the Japanese occupied territories just before the defeat of Japan in 1945.

The effect of money on inflation is most obvious when governments finance spending in a crisis, such as a civil war, by printing money excessively. This sometimes leads to hyperinflation, a condition where prices can double in a month or less. Money supply is also thought to play a major role in determining moderate levels of inflation, although there are differences of opinion on how important it is. For example, Monetarist economists believe that the link is very strong; Keynesian economists, by contrast, typically emphasize the role of aggregate demand in the economy rather than the money supply in determining inflation. That is, for Keynesians, the money supply is only one determinant of aggregate demand.

Some Keynesian economists also disagree with the notion that central banks fully control the money supply, arguing that central banks have little control, since the money supply adapts to the demand for bank credit issued by commercial banks. This is known as the theory of endogenous money, and has been advocated strongly by post-Keynesians as far back as the 1960s. It has today become a central focus of Taylor rule advocates. This position is not universally accepted - banks create money by making loans, but the aggregate volume of these loans diminishes as real interest rates increase. Thus, central banks can influence the money supply by making money cheaper or more expensive, thus increasing or decreasing its production.

A fundamental concept in inflation analysis is the relationship between inflation and unemployment, called the Phillips curve. This model suggests that there is a trade-off between price stability and employment. Therefore, some level of inflation could be considered desirable in order to minimize unemployment. The Phillips curve model described the U.S. experience well in the 1960s but failed to describe the combination of rising inflation and economic stagnation experienced in the 1970s.

Thus, modern macroeconomics describes inflation using a Phillips curve that shifts because of such matters as supply shocks and inflation becoming built into the normal workings of the economy. The former refers to such events as the oil shocks of the 1970s, while the latter refers to the price/wage spiral and inflationary expectations implying that the economy"normally" suffers from inflation. Thus, the Phillips curve represents only the demand-pull component of the triangle model.

Another concept of note is the potential output, a level of GDP, where the economy is at its optimal level of production given institutional and natural constraints. If GDP exceeds its potential, the theory says that inflation will accelerate as suppliers increase their prices and built-in inflation worsens. If GDP falls below its potential level, inflation will decelerate as suppliers attempt to fill excess capacity, cutting prices and undermining built-in inflation.

However, one problem with this theory for policy-making purposes is that the exact level of potential output is generally unknown and tends to change over time. Inflation also seems to act in an asymmetric way, rising more quickly than it falls. Worse, it can change because of policy: for example, high unemployment under British Prime Minister Margaret Thatcher might have led to a rise in the NAIRU because many of the unemployed found themselves as structurally unemployed, unable to find jobs that fit their skills. A rise in structural unemployment implies that a smaller percentage of the labour force can find jobs at the NAIRU, where the economy avoids crossing the threshold into the realm of accelerating inflation.

MONETARIST VIEW

Monetarists believe the most significant factor influencing inflation or deflation is the management of money supply through the easing or tightening of credit. They consider fiscal policy, or government spending and taxation, as ineffective in controlling inflation. The famous monetarist economist Milton Friedman,"Inflation is always and everywhere a monetary phenomenon."

Monetarists assert that the empirical study of monetary history shows that inflation has always been a monetary phenomenon. The quantity theory of money, simply stated, says that any change the amount of money in a system will change the price level. This theory begins with the equation of exchange:

$$M.V = P.Q$$

where:

M is the quantity of money.

V is the velocity of money in final expenditures;

P is the general price level;

Q is an index of the real value of final expenditures;

In this formula, the general price level is affected by the level of economic activity (Q), the quantity of money (M) and the velocity of money (V). The formula is an identity because the velocity of money (V) is defined to be the ratio of final expenditure (P.Q) to the quantity of money (M).

Monetarists assume that the velocity of money is constant, and the real value of output is determined in the long run by the productive capacity of the economy. Under these assumptions, the primary driver of the change in the general price level is changes in the quantity of money. With constant velocity, the money supply determines the value of nominal output in the short run. In practice, velocity is not constant, and can only be measured indirectly and so the formula does not necessarily imply a stable relationship between money supply and nominal output. However, in the long run, changes in money supply and level of economic activity usually dwarf changes in velocity. If velocity is relatively constant, the long run rate of increase in prices is equal to the difference between the long run growth rate of money supply and the long run growth rate of real output.

UNEMPLOYMENT

A connection between inflation and unemployment has

been drawn since the emergence of large scale unemployment in the 19th century, and connections continue to be drawn this today. In Marxian economics, the unemployed serve as a reserve army of labour, which restrain wage inflation. In the 20th century, similar concepts in Keynesian economics include the NAIRU and the Phillips curve.

RATIONAL EXPECTATIONS THEORY

Rational expectations theory holds that economic actors look rationally into the future when trying to maximize their well-being, and do not respond solely to immediate opportunity costs and pressures. In this view, while generally grounded in monetarism, future expectations and strategies are important for inflation as well.

A core assertion of rational expectations theory is that actors will seek to"head off" central-bank decisions by acting in ways that fulfill predictions of higher inflation. This means that central banks must establish their credibility in fighting inflation, or have economic actors make bets that the economy will expand, believing that the central bank will expand the money supply rather than allow a recession.

AUSTRIAN THEORY

The Austrian School asserts that inflation is an increase in the money supply, rising prices are merely consequences and this semantic difference is important in defining inflation. Austrian economists believe there is no material difference between the concepts of monetary inflation and general price inflation. Austrian economists measure monetary inflation by calculating the growth of new units of money that are available for immediate use in exchange, that have been created over time. This interpretation of inflation implies that inflation is always a distinct action taken by the central government or its central bank, which permits or allows an increase in the money supply. In addition to state-induced monetary expansion, the Austrian School also maintains that the effects of increasing the money supply are magnified by credit expansion, as a result of the fractional-reserve banking system employed in most economic and financial systems in the world.

Austrians argue that the state uses inflation as one of the three means by which it can fund its activities, the other two being taxation and borrowing. Various forms of military spending is often cited as a reason for resorting to inflation and borrowing, as this can be a short term way of acquiring marketable resources and is often favoured by desperate, indebted governments.

In other cases, Austrians argue that the government actually creates economic recessions and depressions, by creating artificial booms that distort the structure of production. The central bank may try to avoid or defer the widespread bankruptcies and insolvencies which cause economic recessions or depressions by artificially trying to"stimulate" the economy through"encouraging" money supply growth and further borrowing via artificially low interest rates. Many Austrian economists support the abolition of the central banks and the fractional-reserve banking system, and advocate returning to a 100 per cent gold standard, or less frequently, free banking. They argue this would constrain unsustainable and volatile fractional-reserve banking practices, ensuring that money supply growth would never spiral out of control.

REAL BILLS DOCTRINE

Within the context of a fixed specie basis for money, one important controversy was between the quantity theory of money and the real bills doctrine. Within this context, quantity theory applies to the level of fractional reserve accounting allowed against specie, generally gold, held by a bank. Currency and banking schools of economics argue the RBD, that banks should also be able to issue currency against bills of trading, which is"real bills" that they buy from merchants. This theory was important in the 19th century in debates between"Banking" and"Currency" schools of monetary soundness, and in the formation of the Federal Reserve. In the wake of the collapse of the international gold standard post

1913, and the move towards deficit financing of government, RBD has remained a minor topic, primarily of interest in limited contexts, such as currency boards.

It is generally held in ill repute today, with Frederic Mishkin, a governor of the Federal Reserve going so far as to say it had been"completely discredited." Even so, it has theoretical support from a few economists, particularly those that see restrictions on a particular class of credit as incompatible with libertarian principles of laissez-faire, even though almost all libertarian economists are opposed to the RBD.

The debate between currency, or quantity theory, and banking schools in Britain during the 19th century prefigures current questions about the credibility of money in the present. In the 19th century the banking school had greater influence in policy in the United States and Great Britain, while the currency school had more influence"on the continent", that is in non-British countries, particularly in the Latin Monetary Union and the earlier Scandinavia monetary union.

ANTI-CLASSICAL OR BACKING THEORY

Another issue associated with classical political economy is the anti-classical hypothesis of money, or"backing theory". The backing theory argues that the value of money is determined by the assets and liabilities of the issuing agency. Unlike the Quantity Theory of classical political economy, the backing theory argues that issuing authorities can issue money without causing inflation so long as the money issuer has sufficient assets to cover redemptions. There are very few backing theorists, making quantity theory the dominant theory explaining inflation.

CONTROLLING

A variety of methods have been used in attempts to control inflation.

MONETARY POLICY

Today the primary tool for controlling inflation is

monetary policy. Most central banks are tasked with keeping the federal funds lending rate at a low level, normally to a target rate around 2% to 3% per annum, and within a targeted low inflation range, somewhere from about 2% to 6% per annum. A low positive inflation is usually targeted, as deflationary conditions are seen as dangerous for the health of the economy.

There are a number of methods that have been suggested to control inflation. Central banks such as the U.S. Federal Reserve can affect inflation to a significant extent through setting interest rates and through other operations. High interest rates and slow growth of the money supply are the traditional ways through which central banks fight or prevent inflation, though they have different approaches. For instance, some follow a symmetrical inflation target while others only control inflation when it rises above a target, whether express or implied.

Monetarists emphasize keeping the growth rate of money steady, and using monetary policy to control inflation. Keynesians emphasize reducing aggregate demand during economic expansions and increasing demand during recessions to keep inflation stable. Control of aggregate demand can be achieved using both monetary policy and fiscal policy.

FIXED EXCHANGE RATES

Under a fixed exchange rate currency regime, a country's currency is tied in value to another single currency or to a basket of other currencies. A fixed exchange rate is usually used to stabilize the value of a currency, vis-a-vis the currency it is pegged to. It can also be used as a means to control inflation. However, as the value of the reference currency rises and falls, so does the currency pegged to it. This essentially means that the inflation rate in the fixed exchange rate country is determined by the inflation rate of the country the currency is pegged to. In addition, a fixed exchange rate prevents a government from using domestic monetary policy in order to achieve macroeconomic stability.

Under the Bretton Woods agreement, most countries around the world had currencies that were fixed to the US dollar.

This limited inflation in those countries, but also exposed them to the danger of speculative attacks. After the Bretton Woods agreement broke down in the early 1970s, countries gradually turned to floating exchange rates. However, in the later part of the 20th century, some countries reverted to a fixed exchange rate as part of an attempt to control inflation. This policy of using a fixed exchange rate to control inflation was used in many countries in South America in the later part of the 20th century.

GOLD STANDARD

The gold standard is a monetary system in which a region's common media of exchange are paper notes that are normally freely convertible into pre-set, fixed quantities of gold.

The standard specifies how the gold backing would be implemented, including the amount of specie per currency unit. The currency itself has no innate value, but is accepted by traders because it can be redeemed for the equivalent specie. A U.S. silver certificate, for example, could be redeemed for an actual piece of silver.

The gold standard was partially abandoned via the international adoption of the Bretton Woods System. Under this system all other major currencies were tied at fixed rates to the dollar, which itself was tied to gold at the rate of $35 per ounce. The Bretton Woods system broke down in 1971, causing most countries to switch to fiat money - money backed only by the laws of the country. Austrian economists strongly favour a return to a 100 per cent gold standard.

Under a gold standard, the long term rate of inflation would be determined by the growth rate of the supply of gold relative to total output. Critics argue that this will cause arbitrary fluctuations in the inflation rate, and that monetary policy would essentially be determined by gold mining, which some believe contributed to the Great Depression.

WAGE AND PRICE CONTROLS

Another method attempted in the past have been wage and price controls. Wage and price controls have been successful in wartime environments in combination with rationing. However, their use in other contexts is far more mixed. Notable failures of their use include the 1972 imposition of wage and price controls by Richard Nixon. More successful examples include the Prices and Incomes Accord in Australia and the Wassenaar Agreement in the Netherlands.

In general wage and price controls are regarded as a temporary and exceptional measure, only effective when coupled with policies designed to reduce the underlying causes of inflation during the wage and price control regime, for example, winning the war being fought. They often have perverse effects, due to the distorted signals they send to the market.

Artificially low prices often cause rationing and shortages and discourage future investment, resulting in yet further shortages. The usual economic analysis is that any product or service that is under-priced is overconsumed. For example, if the official price of bread is too low, there will be too little bread at official prices, and too little investment in bread making by the market to satisfy future needs, thereby exacerbating the problem in the long term.

Temporary controls may complement a recession as a way to fight inflation: the controls make the recession more efficient as a way to fight inflation, while the recession prevents the kinds of distortions that controls cause when demand is high. However, in general the advice of economists is not to impose price controls but to liberalize prices by assuming that the economy will adjust and abandon unprofitable economic activity.

The lower activity will place fewer demands on whatever commodities were driving inflation, whether labour or resources, and inflation will fall with total economic output. This often produces a severe recession, as productive capacity is reallocated and is thus often very unpopular with the people whose livelihoods are destroyed.

COST-OF-LIVING ALLOWANCE

The real purchasing-power of fixed payments is eroded by inflation unless they are inflation-adjusted to keep their real values constant. In many countries, employment contracts, pension benefits, and government entitlements are tied to a cost-of-living index, typically to the consumer price index. A cost-of-living allowance adjusts salaries based on changes in a cost-of-living index. Salaries are typically adjusted annually. They may also be tied to a cost-of-living index that varies by geographic location if the employee moves.

Annual escalation clauses in employment contracts can specify retroactive or future percentage increases in worker pay which are not tied to any index. These negotiated increases in pay are colloquially referred to as cost-of-living adjustments or cost-of-living increases because of their similarity to increases tied to externally determined indexes.

Many economists and compensation analysts consider the idea of predetermined future"cost of living increases" to be misleading for two reasons:

- For most recent periods in the industrialized world, average wages have increased faster than most calculated cost-of-living indexes, reflecting the influence of rising productivity and worker bargaining power rather than simply living costs, and
- Most cost-of-living indexes are not forward-looking, but instead compare current or historical data.

8

Productivity and Supply

PRODUCTION AND SUPPLY

In investigating the foundations of supply and demand, we will look at demand and supply as separate headings. It doesn't matter much, logically, which we take first. Historically, the first stages of the economists' Reasonable Dialog were focused more on supply. In investigating the foundations of supply, we are investigating the economics of production and that was the central topic for the classical economists.

Adam Smith, we recall, had been very optimistic about the future economic development of the industrializing countries. With increased division of labour leading to higher wages and growing demand, he felt, production could continue to grow. However, Thomas Malthus criticized Smith's optimism.

Malthus spoke for the pessimistic view and, of course, Malthus is best known for his claim that increasing population would lead to poverty. In supporting this idea, Malthus began to study the limits on production. It was this study that has made his work important particularly for Neoclassical economics.

Limits on production stem from limited resources with a given technology. With a given technology, limited quantities of inputs will yield only limited quantities of outputs. The relationship between the quantities of inputs and the maximum quantities of outputs produced is called the "production function."

The "production function." is a relationship between quantities of input and quantities of output that tells us, for each quantity of input, the greatest output that can be produced with those inputs. Malthus didn't work out the details, but he clearly had this idea in mind as he originated the key concept of Diminishing Returns.

DIMINISHING RETURNS

As we recall, Malthus is best known for his pessimistic idea that population growth would force incomes down to the subsistence level. What we are interested in here is not his conclusion, but the reasoning that took him there.

Malthus argued that l and is a fixed input, but the growth of population makes labour a variable input. Malthus proposed a general law of economics, the Law of Diminishing Returns: when a fixed input is combined in production with a variable input, using a given technology, increases in the quantity of the variable input will eventually depress the productivity of the variable input. (Malthus argued that decreasing productivity of labour would depress incomes). Was Malthus right? The answer is, of course, yes and no.

There is plenty of evidence, both observational and statistical, that the Law of Diminishing Returns is valid. For example, agricultural economists have carried out experimental tests of the theory. They have selected plots of l and of identical size and fertility and used different quantities of fertilizer on the different plots of l and. In this example, l and was the fixed input and fertilizer the variable input. They found that, as the quantity of fertilizer increased, the productivity of fertilizer declines. This is only one of many bits of evidence that the Law of Diminishing Returns is true in general.

On the other h and, in the two hundred years since Malthus wrote, on the whole, population has increased but labour productivity and incomes have not declined. On the whole, they have risen. What seems to have happened is that technology has improved. Malthus recognized that if technology improved (in agriculture, at least), that might postpone what he saw as the inevitable poverty as a consequence of rising population. Some economists and other people, believe that the Malthusian prediction will eventually come true.

Perhaps: what is clear is that in two hundred years it has not. But that doesn't mean the Law of Diminishing Returns is wrong! A "law" such as this can be true in general but cannot be applied when its assumptions (such as an unchanging technology) aren't true.

The "Law" isn't wrong—just inapplicable to that case.There are many valid and useful applications of the Law of Diminishing Returns in economics. In this chapter we will look at two.

- We will use Diminishing Returns and related concepts to get a better idea of the meaning of the phrase "efficient allocation of resources" and some guidelines for efficiency in that sense.
- We will explore how a business firm should direct its production in order to get maximum profits and that will give us a basis for a better underst anding of the economics of supply.

First, though, we will need to look at production and diminishing returns in general in a little more detail.

PRODUCTION FUNCTION

Production is the transformation of inputs into outputs. Inputs are the factors of production—l and, labour and capital—plus raw materials and business services. The transformation of inputs into outputs is determined by the technology in use. Limited quantities of inputs will yield only limited quantities of outputs.

The relationship between the quantities of inputs and the maximum quantities of outputs produced is called the "production function."But how do these outputs change when the input quantities vary? Let's take a look at an example of a production function.In general, we would allow for varying amounts of l and, labour and capital. However, in this example, labour will be the only input, for the sake of simplicity.

A PRODUCTION FUNCTION EXAMPLE

The production function thus contains the limitations that technology places on the firm. The mathematical forms of the production function and the utility function are identical. In one case, inputs of goods and services combine to produce utility; in the other, inputs of resources combine to produce goods or services.

As one moves to the right, one reaches higher levels of production. If one can visualize this as a three-dimensional graph, one can see that the production surface rises increasingly high above the surface of the page; the isoquants indicate a hill.

Marginal Productivity

Productivity, by definition, is a ratio of output to labour input. In most statistical discussions of productivity, we refer to the average productivity of labour:

$$AP = \frac{\text{Output}}{\text{Labor Input}}$$

Average labour productivity is an important concept, especially in macroeconomics. In microeconomics, however, we will focus more on the marginal productivity. We can think of the marginal productivity of labour as the additional output as a result of adding one unit of labour, with all other inputs held steady and ceteris paribus.

In algebraic terms, an equally correct definition is:

$$MP = \frac{\Delta\text{Output}}{\Delta\text{Labor}}$$

Let's have a numerical example to illustrate the application of the theory. Suppose that:

- When 300 labour-days per week are employed the firm produces 2505 units of output per week.
- When 400 labour-days per week are employed the firm produces 3120 units of output per week.
- It follows that the change in labour input, ýÿLabour, is 100.
- It also follows that the change in output, ýÿOutput, is 615.

- Applying the formula above, we approximate the marginal productivity of labour by the quotient 615/ 100 = 6.15.
- We can interpret this result as follows: over the range of 300 to 400 man-days of labour per week, each additional worker adds approximately 6.15 units to output.

Of course, if we had more information, we could get a closer approximation. For example, if we had the outputs for 310, 320,... 390 man-days of labour, we could see how MP varies within the range 300-400. But we can be sure that the values will be in the neighbourhood of 6.15.

Now let's think a little further about the Law of Diminishing Returns.

THE LAW OF DIMINISHING MARGINAL PRODUCTIVITY

In his discussions of the Law of Diminishing Returns, Malthus did not distinguish between average and marginal productivity. However, in modern economics, we think of diminishing returns primarily in terms of marginal, not average, productivity.

Law of Diminishing Returns (Modern Statement): When the technology of production and some of the inputs are held constant and the quantity of a variable input increases continually, the marginal productivity of the variable input will eventually decline.

The inputs that are held steady are called the "fixed inputs." In these pages we are treating l and and capital as fixed inputs. The inputs that are allowed to vary are called the "variable inputs." In these pages we are treating labour as the variable input. Another way to express the law of diminishing returns, is that, as the variable input increases, the output also increases, but at a decreasing rate. The marginal productivity of labour is the rate of increase in output as the labour input increases. To say that output increases at a decreasing rate when the variable input increases is another way to say that the marginal productivity declines.

Marginal Productivity

Let's extend the numerical example in the page before last and see how marginal productivity varies over a wide range of labour inputs. Here is a hypothetical example of production with the inputs of l and and labour held steady and varying quantities of labour and the output and average and marginal productivities.

Table

Labour	Output Productivity	Average Productivity	Marginal
0	0	0	0
100	945	9.45	9.45
200	1780	8.90	8.35
300	2505	8.35	7.25
400	3120	7.80	6.15
500	3625	7.25	5.05
600	4020	6.70	3.95
700	4305	6.15	2.85
800	4480	5.60	1.75
900	4545	5.05	0.65
1000	4500	4.50	-0.45

OUTPUT DIAGRAM

Here is a picture of the relationship between the variable input and the output in the numerical example in the previous table. Notice how the slope gets flatter: as the variable input increases, output increases at a decreasing rate. This is a visualization of the Law of Diminishing Marginal Productivity.

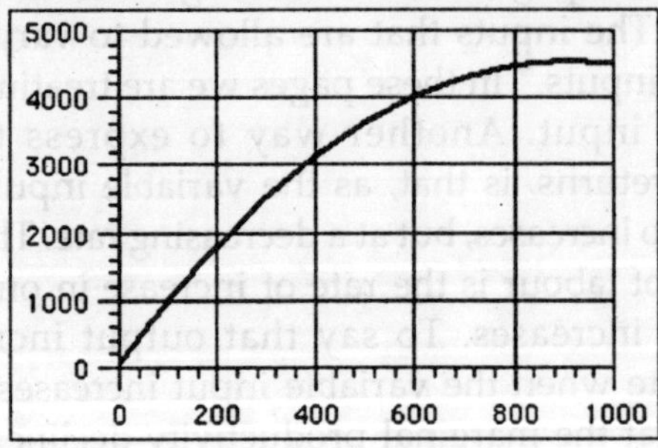

Fig: Production with Diminishing Returns

Average and Marginal Productivity Diagram

We have put some stress on the difference between average and marginal productivity. Both are important, but for a model of short-run profit-maximizing supply, marginal productivity is the more important. and the two are quite different. Here are the average and marginal productivities for the same numerical example in the page before last. Notice how both average and marginal productivity decrease as the labour input increases. But the marginal productivity declines faster than the average productivity, pulling the average productivity down after it. The downward slope of the marginal productivity line expresses the Law of Diminishing Returns and the downward slope of the average productivity is also a result of the law.

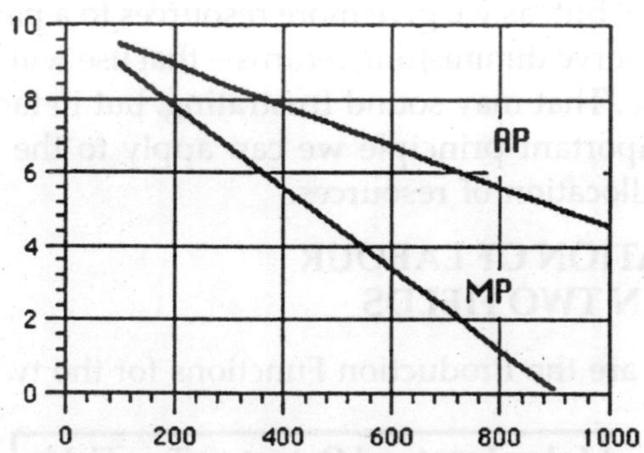

Fig: Average and Marginal Productivity

The relationship between average and marginal productivity in the diagram is important in itself and we will see similar relationships in future chapters. So let's look at it a little more closely. Average and marginal productivity will not always have the same slope. In general,

- Whenever average productivity is greater than marginal productivity, average productivity will slope downward.
- Whenever average productivity is less than marginal productivity, average productivity will slope upward.

The diagram does not show any values where average

productivity is less, but a more complicated example might and then we would see the second part of the relationship visualized. To underst and the relationship, think of it this way: as we add labour input, one unit after another, we add a bit more to output at each step. When the addition is greater than the average, it pulls the average up towrds it. When the addition is less than the average, it pulls the average down towrds it.

EFFICIENT ALLOCATION OF RESOURCES

Diminishing returns plays an important part in the efficient allocation of resources. For efficiency, of course, we want to give more resources to the use in which they are more productive. But, as we give more resources to a particular use, we will observe diminishing returns—that use will become less productive. That may sound frustrating, but in fact it leads to a very important principle we can apply to the problem of efficient allocation of resources.

ALLOCATION OF LABOUR BETWEEN TWO FIELDS

Here are the Production Functions for the two Fields.

Labor Input and Output on Two Fields			
North Field		South Field	
labor	output	labor	output
0	0	0	0
100	9500	100	12107
200	18000	200	23429
300	25500	300	33964
400	32000	400	43714
500	37500	500	52679
600	42000	600	60857
700	45500	700	68250
800	48000	800	74858
900	49500	900	80679
1000	50000	1000	85715

The concept of marginal productivity is central to economists' underst anding of efficient allocation of resources. For an illustrative example, consider a farmer who has two fields to plant. He can grow a crop of corn (let's say) on each of them, but has a limited amount of labour to allocate between them. Let us say that the farmer can spend 1000 hours of labour, total, on the two fields. If he spends one more hour of labour on the north field, that means he has one hour less to spend on the south field.

Production Functions for the Two Fields

We can visualize the production functions for the two fields. The production function for the relatively fertile south field with a vertically dashed purple curve and the less fertile north field with a solid green curve. As we see, the south field can always produce more, with the same amount of labour, as the north field can.

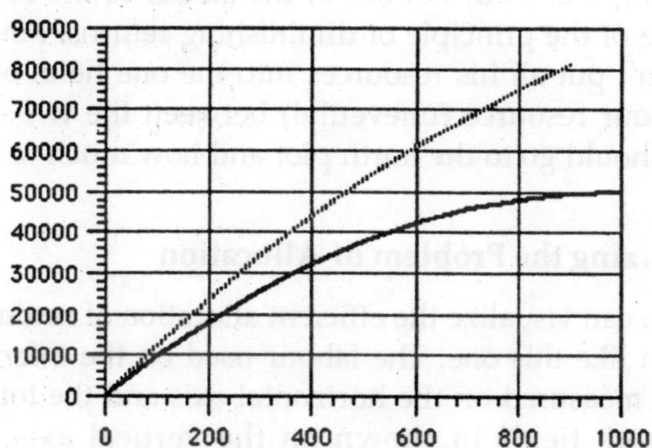

Fig: Production Functions for Two Fields

THE PROBLEM OF ALLOCATION

The farmer's "allocation problem" is: How much labour to commit to the north field and how much to the south field? One "common sense" approach might be to ab andon the infertile north field and allocate the whole 1000 hours of labour to the south field. But a little arithmetic shows that this won't work. Here is a table that shows the correlated quantities of labour on the two fields and the total output of corn from both fields taken together.

Table: Allocation of Labour and Total Output on Two Fields

Labor on North Field	Labor on South Field	Total output in bushels of corn
0	1000	85000
100	900	89600
200	800	92400
300	700	93400
400	600	92600
500	500	90000
600	400	85600
700	300	79400
800	200	71400
900	100	61600
1000	0	50000

We see that the farmer gets his largest output by allocating most, but not all, of his labour to the south field. Because of the principle of diminishing returns, however, he shouldn't put all his resources into the one field, but divide the labour resource (unevenly!) between the two. But how much should go to the north plot and how much to the south plot?

Visualizing the Problem of Allocation

We can visualize the efficient allocation of resources with a graph like this one. The labour used on the infertile north field is measured on the horizontal axis and the total output from both fields in shown on the vertical axis. (We are assuming, of course, that all labour not used on the North field is used on the South field).

The dark green curve shows how total output changes as we shift labour from the north field to the south field. Thus, the top of the curve is the interesting spot—that's where we get the most output. In this example, that's the efficient allocation of resources between the two fields.

It's easy to see that we should put some labour to work on the north field—but not too much. The vertical orange line shows that the maximum output—the top of the dark green curve—comes when about 300 labour days are allocated to the north field and the rest, 700 labour days, to the south field. and that's exactly right.

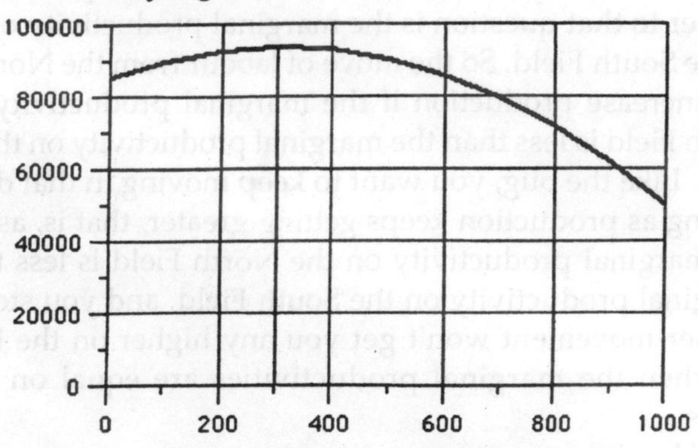

Fig: Maximum Production

It's pretty easy to see where the maximum is in this simple example. But in a more realistic example, in which there could be many more than just two dimensions, it's harder to visualize. We need a rule that we can apply in more complex, realistic examples, a rule that will tell us if we have or don't have an efficient allocation of resources.

That's where the economist's "marginal approach" comes in. The objective is to get to the top of the hill. You could call "the marginal approach" the "bug's-eye view." Think of yourself as a bug climbing up that production hill in the picture. How will you know when you are at the top?

If you were a bug, you couldn't see much. Perhaps you couldn't see to the top of the hill. But you would be able to tell if you were going up, or down, or neither. So you would just keep going as long as you were going up and stop when you were neither going up nor down. That's the way a bug gets to the top of a hill.

If you were a farmer with two fields, it's a little more complicated, but the same principles apply: take it step by step. However much you may be producing, ask yourself "What would happen if I were to take one worker away from the

North Field and put her to work on the South Field? How much less will the North Field produce? The answer to that question is the marginal productivity of labour on the North Field. How much more will the South Field produce? The answer to that question is the marginal productivity of labour on the South Field. So the move of labour from the North Field will increase production if the marginal productivity on the North Field is less than the marginal productivity on the South Field. Like the bug, you want to keep moving in that direction as long as production keeps getting greater, that is, as long as the marginal productivity on the North Field is less than the marginal productivity on the South Field. and you stop when further movement won't get you any higher on the hill, that is, when the marginal productivities are equal on the two fields.

Here it is:

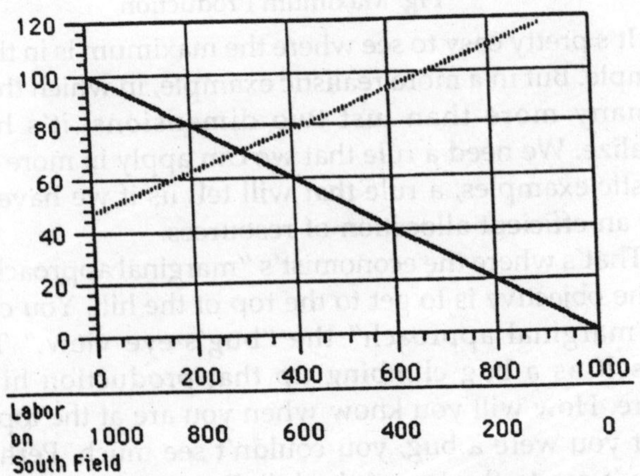

Fig: Marginal Productivity and Efficient Allocation

So now, let's visualize the marginal productivities for these two fields. But this time we will do it a slightly different way. We will measure the labour used on the infertile north field from left to right on the horizontal axis. Then, what's left is what's available for the north field, so we will measure the labour used on the south field from left to right—from 1000 hours down to zero. The marginal product on the north field is shown with the green line and the marginal product on the south field with the vertical-dashed purple line. (Remember, the marginal productivity on the south field decreases as the labour input on the south field gets bigger, so the marginal productivity on that field increases as labour used on the field gets smaller, as it does here)

MARGINAL PRODUCTIVITY

Figure shows the most efficient allocation of resources in this case. It is to allocate 300 hours of labour to the north field and 700 hours to the south field, as shown by the vertical red-orange line. For maximum output, labour is allocated so that the marginal productivity of labour on the north field is equal to the marginal productivity of labour on the south field.

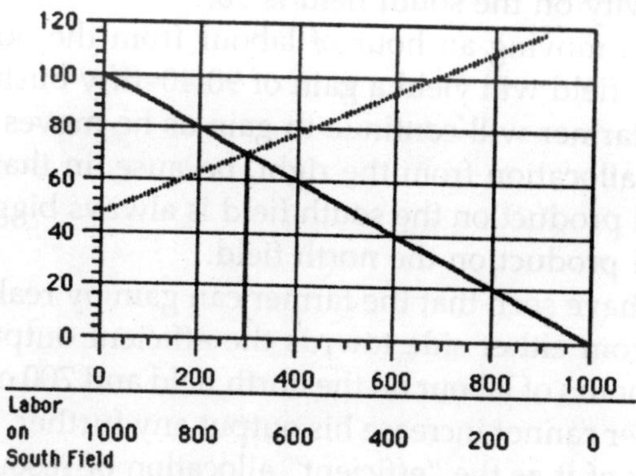

Fig: Efficient Allocation

To see why this works, think it through in reverse: what happens if the allocation of labour is not 300 to the north field and 700 to the south field? For example, suppose 200 hours are allocated to the south field and 800 to the north field. This puts us to the left of the orange line—and we read off the diagram that the marginal productivity of labour on the north field is 80 bushels of corn, while the marginal productivity on the south field is about 62. Remembering the definition of marginal productivity, that means: if the farmer spends one additional hour on the north field, he will gain 80 bushels, while spending one less on the south field will cost him 62 bushels, leaving a net gain of 18 bushels. What has happened is that spending 800 hours of labour on the south field has pushed the "diminishing returns" on that field so far that it is less productive at the margin than the north field. and that will be true anywhere to the left of the orange line, since, in that range, the marginal productivity on the north field is always greater than the marginal productivity on the south field.

Now let's see what happens if the allocation is to the right of the most efficient one—for example, suppose the farmer were to allocate 600 hours to the north field and 400 to the south field. Looking at the diagram, we see that the marginal productivity on the north field is 40 while the marginal productivity on the south field is 90.

Thus, moving an hour of labour from the north field to the south field will yield a gain of 90-40=fifty bushels of corn. and the farmer will continue to gain as he moves towrds the efficient allocation from the right, because, in that range, the marginal product on the south field is always bigger than the marginal product on the north field.

We have seen that the farmer can gain by reallocating his labour from either side towrds the efficient output. Once he has 300 hours of labour on the north field and 700 on the south, the farmer cannot increase his output any further. That is why we think of it as the "efficient" allocation of resources.

The efficient allocation of labour between the two fields. Try typing in a number between zero and one thous and in the "Labour on North Field" blank and see if you can't find the maximum total production by trial and error and notice how the marginal productivities are closer together when total production is higher.

MARGINAL PRODUCTIVITY AND THE EQUIMARGINAL PRINCIPLE

This is a quite general principle, which we may state as follows.

Rule: When the same product or service is being produced in two or more units of production, in order to get the maximum total output, resources should be allocated among the units of production in such a way that the marginal productivity of each resource is the same in each unit of production.

This example may also be a little clearer example of what we mean by "efficient allocation of resources." In the example, we have a tiny economy, consisting of one farmer and two plots of l and. When the marginal productivities on the two plots are equal, this tiny economy has an "efficient allocation of resources." Of course, real economies are more complex, but the principles governing the efficient allocation of resources are the same.

This rule has a name: it is the Equimarginal Principle. The idea is to make two things equal "at the margin"—in this case, to make the marginal productivity of labour equal on the two fields. As we will see, it has many applications in economics. In more complicated cases, we will have to generalize the rule carefully.

In this example, for instance, we are allocating resources between two fields that produce the same output. When the different areas of production are producing different kinds of goods and services, it will be more complicated. But a version of the Equimarginal Principle will still apply.

THEORY OF THE FIRM

In developing the supply and demand approach to economics, economists first worked out the basis of the demand curve. By treating the demand for a product or service as a rational decision by a (primarily) self-interested individual or family, economists were able to underst and the relation of the demand for one product or service to the dem ands for other products and services and to many other forms of economic activity. It was natural to apply the same approach to supply.

As a first step, we need to think about the decision-makers in supplying goods and services and what a "rational decision" to supply goods and services would mean. In economics, this is often called the "Theory of the Firm."

In the remainder of this chapter we will apply the concepts of marginal productivity and diminishing returns to the theory of the firm. First we will talk a bit about business firms and their role in a market economy, then we will return to the marginal productivity approach.

About Firms

A firm is a unit that does business on it's own account. (Firm is from the Italian, "firma, " a signature and the idea is that a firm can commit itself to a contract). Thus, the firm is the decision-maker in supplying goods and services. There are three main kinds of firms in modern market economies:

Proprietorships

A proprietorship (or proprietary business) is a business owned by an individual, the "proprietor." Many "Mom and Pop stores"—and other "Mom and Pop" businesses—are proprietorships. Some proprietorships are too small even to employ one person full time.

Craftsmen, such as plumbers and painters, may have "day jobs" and work as self-employed proprietors part time after hours. Computer programmers and others may also do that. At the other extreme, some proprietary businesses employ many hundreds of workers in a wide range of specializations. In a proprietorship, the proprietor is almost always the decision-maker for the business.

Partnerships

A partnership is a business jointly owned by two or more persons. In most partnerships, each partner is legal liable for debts and agreements made by any partner. Of course, this requires a great deal of trust and thus partners generally know one another well enough to have that sort of trust. Family partnerships are very common for that very reason. (There are now a few "limited partnerships" in which some partners are protected from legal liability for the agreements made by others, beyond some limits). In many cases, one partner is designated as the managing partner and is the main decision-maker for the business.

Corporations

A corporation has two characteristics that distinguish it from most proprietorships and partnerships:

- Limited liability
- Anonymous ownership

Limited liability means that the owner of shares in a corporation cannot lose more than a certain amount if the company fails. Usually the amount is the money paid to buy the shares. Anonymous ownership means that the owner of the shares can sell them without getting the permission of anyone other than the buyer. By contrast, in most partnerships, no one partner can sell out without getting the agreement of the other partners. In such a case the continuing partners will, of course, want to know about the new partner—he will not be an "anonymous owner." In a typical corporation, the shareholders formally elect a board of directors, who in turn select the officers of the company. One of these officers, often called the "president, " will be the principle decision-maker for the firm, but he will be expected to make decisions in the interest of the shareholders.

While there are millions of proprietorships, typically very small, the biggest businesses are corporate and corporations are particularly important because of their size.

OBJECTIVES

As we recall, Malthus did not have firms in mind when he formulated the Law of Diminishing Returns. But this law has applications Malthus did not envision and we will see how to apply the law to a business firm. In the Reasonable Dialog of economics in the nineteenth century, the development of these ideas was a bit indirect. In about the eighteen-seventies, economists were rethinking the theory of consumer demand. They applied a version of "diminishing returns" and the Equimarginal Principle to determine how a consumer would divide up her spending among different consumer goods. That worked pretty well and so some other economists, especially the American economist John Bates Clark, tried using the same approach in the theory of the firm. These innovations were the beginning of Neoclassical Economics. Following the Neoclassical approach, we will interpret "rational decisions to supply goods and services" to mean decisions that maximize—something! What does a supplier maximize? The operations of the firm will, of course, depend on its objectives. One objective that all three kinds of firms share is profits and it seems that profits are the primary objective in most cases. We will follow the neoclassical tradition by assuming that firms aim at maximizing their profits.

There are two reasons for this assumption. First, despite the growing importance of nonprofit organizations and the frequent calls for corporate social responsibility, profits still seem to be the most important single objective of producers in our market economy. Thus it is the right place to start. Second, a good deal of the controversy in the reasonable dialog of economics has centred on the implications of profit motivation. Is it true, as Adam Smith held, that the "invisible h and" leads profit-seeking businessmen to promote the general good? To assess that question, we need to underst and the implications of profit maximization.

PROFIT

Profit is defined as revenue minus cost, that is, as the price of output times the quantity sold (revenue) minus the cost of producing that quantity of output.

However, we need to be a little careful in interpreting that. Remember, economists underst and cost as opportunity cost—the value of the opportunity given up. Thus, when we say that businesses maximize profit, it is important to include all costs—whether they are expressed in money terms or not.

For example, a cab-driver—the self-employed proprietor of an independent cab service—says: "I'm making a 'profit,' but I can't take home enough to support my family, so I'm going to have to close down and get a job." The proprietor is ignoring the opportunity cost of her own labour. When those opportunity costs are taken into account, we will find that he is not really making a profit after all. Let's say that the cab-driver makes $500 a week driving his cab, after all expenses (gasoline, maintenance, etc.) have been taken out. Suppose he can get wages (including tips!) of $800 driving for someone else, with hours no longer and about the same conditions otherwise. Then $800 is the opportunity cost of his labour and after we deduct the opportunity cost from his $500 net as an independent cabbie, he is actually losing $300 per week.

This is one of the most important reasons for using the opportunity cost concept: it helps us to underst and the circumstances that will lead people to get into and out of business. Because accountants traditionally considered only money costs, the net of money revenue minus money cost is called "accounting profit." (Actually, modern accountants are well aware of opportunity cost and use the concept for special purposes). The economist's concept is sometimes called "economic profit." If there will be some doubt as to which concept of profit we mean, we will sometimes use the terms "economic profit" or "accounting profit" to make it clear which is intended.

THE JOHN BATES CLARK MODEL

Like any other unit, a firm is limited by the technology available. Thus, it can increase its outputs only by increasing its inputs. As usual, this will be expressed by a production function. The output the firm can produce will depend on the l and, labour and capital the firm puts to work.

In formulating the Neoclassical theory of the firm, John Bates Clark took over the classical categories of l and, labour and capital and simplified them in two ways. First, he assumed that all labour is homogenous—one labour hour is a perfect substitute for any other labour hour. Second, he ignored the distinction between l and and capital, grouping together both kinds of nonhuman inputs under the general term "capital." and he assumed that this broadened "capital" is homogenous.

Of course, the simplifying assumptions aren't true—John Bates' Clark's conception of the firm is highly simplified, like a map at a very large scale.

In more advanced economics, we can get rid of the simplifying assumptions and deal with a much more realistic "map" of the business firm. But for most of this book, we'll take that on faith and stick to the simplified version Clark gave us. That will make it simpler and the principles we will discover are sound and applicable to the real world in all its complexity. In the John Bates Clark model, there are some important differences between labour and capital and they relate to the long and short run.

SHORT AND LONG RUN

A key distinction here is between the short and long run.

Some inputs can be varied flexibly in a relatively short period of time. We conventionally think of labour and raw materials as "variable inputs" in this sense. Other inputs require a commitment over a longer period of time. Capital goods are thought of as "fixed inputs" in this sense.

A capital good represents a relatively large expenditure at a particular time, with the expectation that the investment will be repaid—and any profit paid—by producing goods and services for sale over the useful life of the capital good. In this sense, a capital investment is a long-term commitment. So capital is thought of as being variable only in the long run, but fixed in the short run.

Thus, we distinguish between the short run and the long run as follows: In the perspective of the short run, the number and equipment of firms operating in each industry is fixed. In the perspective of the long run, all inputs are variable and firms can come into existence or cease to exist, so the number of firms is also variable.

MORE SIMPLIFYING ASSUMPTIONS

The John Bates Clark model of the firm is already pretty simple. We are thinking of a business that just uses two inputs, homogenous labour and homogenous capital and produces a single homogenous kind of output.

The output could be a product or service, but in any case it is measured in physical (not money) units such as bushels of wheat, tons of steel or minutes of local telephone calls. In the short run, in addition, the capital input is treated as a given "fixed input." Also, we can identify the price of labour with the wage in the John Bates Clark model. (In a modern business firm, we have to include benefits as well as take-home wages. The technical term for the total, wages and benefits, is "employee compensation.")

We will add two more simplifying assumptions. The new simplifying assumptions are:

- The price of output is a given constant.
- The wage (the price of labour per labour hour) is a given constant.

Putting them all together—just two kinds of input and one kind of output, one kind of output fixed in the short run and given output price and wage—it seems to be a lot of simplifying assumptions and it is. They are the assumptions that fit best into many applications and the starting point for still others. Once we have simplified our conception of the firm to this extent, what is left for the director of the firm to decide.

THE FIRM'S DECISION

In the short run, then, there are only two things that are not given in the John Bates Clark model of the firm. They are the output produced and the labour (variable) input. and that is not actually two decisions, but just one, since labour input and output are linked by the "production function." Either

- The output is decided and the labour input will have to be just enough to produce that outputor
- The labour input is decided and the output is whatever that quantity of labour can produce.

Thus, the firm's objective is to choose the labour input and corresponding output that will maximize profit. Let's continue with the numerical example in the first part of the chapter. Suppose a firm is producing with the production function shown there, in the short run. Suppose also that the price of the output is $100 and the wage per labour-week is $500.

Then let's see how much labour the firm would use and how much output it would produce, in order to maximize profits. The relationship between labour input and profits will look something like this:

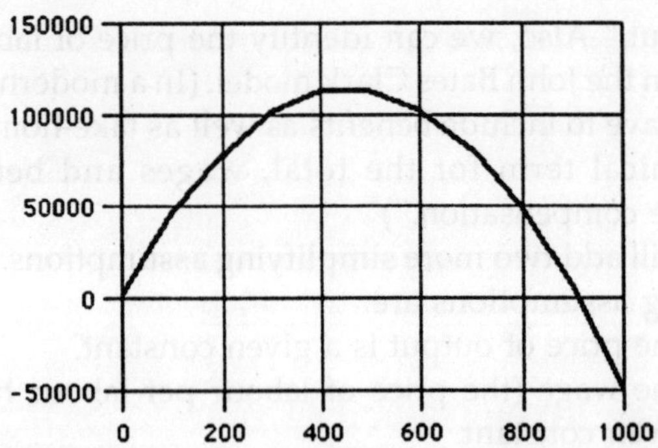

Fig: Labour Input and Profits in the Numerical Example

In the figure, the green curve shows the profits rising and then falling and the labour input increases. Of course, the eventual fall-off of profits is a result of "diminishing returns, " and the problem the firm faces is to balance "diminishing returns" against the demand for the product.

The objective is to get to the top of the profit hill. We can see that this means hiring something in the range of four to five hundred workers for the week. But just how many?

The way to approach this problem is to take a bug's-eye view. Think of yourself as a bug climbing up that profit hill. How will you know when you are at the top?

THE MARGINAL APPROACH

The bug's-eye view is the marginal approach. However much labour is being employed at any given time, the really relevant question is, supposing one more unit of labour is hired, will profits be increased or decreased? If one unit of labour is eliminated, will profits increase or decrease? In other words, what does one additional labour unit add to profits? What would elimination of one labour unit subtract from profits? We can break that question down. Profit is the difference of revenue minus cost. Ask, "What does one additional labour unit add to cost? What does one additional labour unit add to revenue? The first question is relatively easy. What one additional labour unit will add to cost is the wage paid to recruit the one additional unit.

The second question is a little trickier. It's easier to answer a related question: "What does one additional labour unit add to production?" By definition, that's the marginal product—the marginal product of labour is defined as the additional output as a result of increasing the labour input by one unit. But we need a measurement that is comparable with revenues and profits, that is, a measurement in money terms. Since the price is given, the measurement we need is the Value of the Marginal Product:

Value of the Marginal Product

The Value of the Marginal Product is the product of the marginal product times the price of output. It is abbreviated VMP. To review, we have made some progress towrds answering the original question.

Adding one more unit to the labour input, we have:

Increase in revenue = Value of marginal product

Increase in cost = Wage

So the answer to "What will one additional labour unit add to profits?" is "the difference of the Value of the Marginal Product Minus the wage." Conversely, the answer to "What will the elimination of one labour unit add to profits?" is "the wage minus the Value of Marginal Product of Labour." and in either case the "addition to profits" may be a negative number: either building up the work force or cutting it down can drag down profits rather than increasing them.

So, again taking the bug's-eye view, we ask "Is the Value of the Marginal Product greater than the wage, or less?" If greater, we increase the labour input, knowing that by doing so we increase profits by the difference, VMP-wage. If less, we cut the labour input, knowing that by doing so we increase profits by the difference, wage-VMP. and we continue doing this until the answer is "Neither.

" Then we know there is no further scope to increase profits by changing the labour input—we have arrived at maximum profits. Let's see how that works. Let's go back to the numerical example from earlier in the chapter and assume that the price of output is $100 per unit and the wage is $500.

The value of the marginal product, $100*MP and the wage for that example.

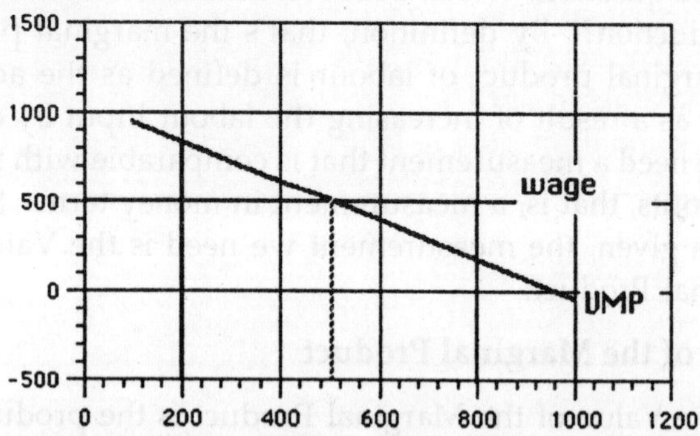

Now suppose that the firm begins by using just 200 units of labour, as shown by the orange line. The manager asks herself, "If I were to increase the labour input to 201, that would increase both costs and revenues.

By how much? Let's see: the VMP is 850, so the additional worker will add $850 to revenues. Since the wage is $500, the additional worker will add just $500 to cost, for a net gain of $350. It's a good idea to "upsize" and add one more worker.

On the other h and, suppose that the firm is using 800 units of labour, as shown by the other orange line. The manager asks herself, "If I were to cut the labour input to 799, that would cut both costs and revenues. By how much? Let's see: the VMP is 200, so the additional worker will add just $200 to revenues. Since the wage is $500, the additional worker will add just $500 to cost, for a net loss of $300. It's time to "downsize" and cut the labour force. In each case, there is an unrealised potential and the amount of unrealised potential is the difference between the VMP and the wage. The firm's profit potential will not be 100% realised until the VMP is equal to the wage. That's the "equimarginal principle" again.

THE EQUIMARGINAL PRINCIPLE

By taking the marginal approach—the bug's-eye view—we have discovered the diagnostic rule for maximum profits. The way to maximize profits then is to hire enough labour so that,

VMP=wage

where p is the price of output and VMP = p*MP the marginal productivity of labour in money terms. This is another instance of the Equimarginal Principle. The rule tells us that profits are not maximized until we have adjusted the labour input so that the marginal product in labour, in dollar terms, is equal to the wage. Since the wage is the amount that the additional (marginal) unit of labour adds to cost, we could think of the wage as the "marginal cost" of labour and express the rule as "value of marginal product of labour equal to marginal cost." But we will give a more compete and careful definition of marginal cost (of output).

Table

Labor	Marginal Productivity	p*MP	Wage	Accounting Profit
0			500	0
	9.45	945		
100			500	44500
	8.35	835		
200			500	78000
	7.25	725		
300			500	100500
	6.15	615		
400			500	112000
	5.05	505		
500			500	112500
	3.95	395		
600			500	102000
	2.85	285		
700			500	80500
	1.75	175		
800			500	48000
	0.65	65		
900			500	4500
	-0.45	-55		
1000			500	-50000

Profit Maximization

The maximization of profits in the example. Remember, the wage is $500 per labour week. The theory tells us that profits will be biggest when the value of the marginal product is exactly equal to the wage, that is, $500.

Try adjusting the number of labour weeks input and see how profits increase as the value of the marginal product gets closer to $500.

Profit Maximization: In our numerical example, suppose that the price of output is $100 per unit and the wage is $500 per worker per period. Then the p*MP, wage and profits will be something like this.

VISUALIZING PROFIT MAXIMIZATION

What we see in the table is that the transition from 400 to 500 units of labour gives p*MP=505, very nearly VMP=wage. and that is the highest profit. So the profit-maximizing labour force is about 500 units.

We can get a more exact answer by looking at a picture or tinkering with the programme example a bit. Here is a picture of the profit-maximizing hiring in this example:

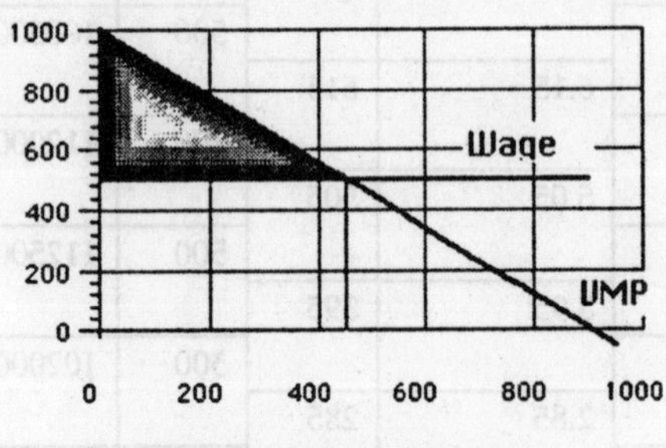

Fig: Maximizing Profit

The picture suggests that the exact amount is a bit less than 500 units of labour. If you tinker with the programme example enough, you will see that the exact profit maximizing labour input is 454.54545454545... units of labour—a repeating decimal fraction.

Notice the shaded area between the VMP curve and the price (wage) line. n the picture, the area of the shaded triangle is the total amount of payments for profits, interest and rent—in other words, everything the firm pays out for factors of production other than labour.

The rectangular area below the wage line and left of the labour=454 line is shows the wage bill. Thus, the John Bates Clark model provides us with a visualization of the division of income between labour and property. We'll make use of this fact in exploring the economics of income distribution in the last Part of this chapter.

PROFIT MAXIMIZATION

We can use the diagram also to underst and why VMP=wage is the diagnostic that tells us the profit is at a maximum. Suppose the labour input is less than 500—for example, suppose labour input is 200. Than an additional labour-day of labour will add about 7.8 units to output and about $780 to the firm's sales revenue, but only $500 to the firm's costs, adding roughly $220 to profits. So it is profitable to increase the labour input from 200, or, by the same reasoning, from any labour input less than $500.

This difference between the VMP and the wage is the increase or decrease in profits from adding or subtracting one unit of labour. It is sometimes called the marginal profit and (as we observed in studying consumers' marginal benefits) the absolute value of the marginal profits is a measure of unrealised potential profits. That's why the businessman wants to adjust the labour input so that VMP-wage=0.

Let's try one more example. Suppose the labour input is 800 labour-days per week. If the firm "downsizes" to 799 labour-days, it reduces its output by just about 1.2 units and its sales revenue by about $120, but it reduces its labour cost by $500, increasing profits by about $380. Thus a movement towrds the VMP=wage again increases profits by realizing some unrealised potential profit.

The formula VMP=wage is a diagnostic for maximum profits because it tells us that there is no further potential to increase the profits by adjusting the labour input—marginal profit is zero. The marginal productivity rule is the key to maximization of profits in the short run. But now let's take a look at the long run perspective.

Increasing Returns to Scale and the Long Run

In microeconomics, we think of diminishing returns as a short run thing. In the long run, all inputs can be increased or decreased in proportion. Reductions in the marginal productivity of labour, due to increasing the labour input, can be offset by increasing the tools and equipment the workers have to work with. How will that come out, on net? The answer is—"it all depends!" In the long run we define three possible cases:

Decreasing Returns to Scale

If an increase in all inputs in the same proportion k leads to an increase of output of a proportion less than k, we have decreasing returns to scale. Example: If we increase the inputs to a dairy farm (cows, l and, barns, feed, labour, everything) by 50% and milk output increases by only 40%, we have decreasing returns to scale in dairy farming. This is also known as "diseconomies of scale, " since production is less cheap when the scale is larger.

Constant Returns to Scale

If an increase in all inputs in the same proportion k leads to an increase of output in the same proportion k, we have constant returns to scale. Example: If we increase the number of machinists and machine tools each by 50% and the number of st andard pieces produced increases also by 50%, then we have constant returns in machinery production.

Increasing Returns to Scale

If an increase in all inputs in the same proportion k leads to an increase of output of a proportion greater than k, we have increasing returns to scale. Example: If we increase the inputs to a software engineering firm by 50% output and increases by 60%, we have increasing returns to scale in software engineering. (This might occur because in the larger work force, some programmers can concentrate more on particular kinds of programming and get better at them). This is also known as "economies of scale, " since production is cheaper when the scale is larger.

In introductory economics, we usually discuss these long run tendencies in the context of cost analysis, rather than marginal productivity analysis. However, increasing returns to scale, in particular, creates some complications for the application of marginal productivity thinking. Thus, I think there may be something to gain by exploring how increasing returns to scale goes together with marginal productivity. To keep it as simple as possible, we will look at a numerical example of a two-person labour market and a fictitious product that is produced with increasing returns to scale. Economists often like to talk about the production of "widgets, " so our fictitious industry is the widget-tying industry.

EXAMPLE OF PRODUCTION WITH INCREASING RETURNS TO SCALE

- Since this is a long run analysis, there is no fixed input. Indeed, for simplicity, there is only one input. Labour is the only input and is variable.
- Our small economy is populated by three people: Bob and John, workers and Gordon, an entrepreneur (that is, a person who will organize a business if and only if it is profitable to do so).
  - Bob, working alone, can produce output worth 2000 per week.
  - Bob's opportunity cost is 2100 per week. (That means Bob can earn 2100 in producing some other good or service).
  - John, working alone, can produce 2000 per week.
  - John's opportunity cost is 2800 per week.
- If Bob and John work together, thanks to division of labour, they can produce 5500 per week. Suppose, for example, that Gordon sets up a Widget-Tying business and hires Bob and, later, John to do the work. This is an example of "increasing returns to scale" since input increases by 100% when the second

worker is hired and output increases by 175% as a result.

Why would output increase more than in proportion to inputs? First, simply having four h ands may increase productivity as the two men can simultaneously do different parts of the job. Second, each may concentrate on some part of the work, getting better at it with more practice, but leaving the other part to the other worker who also gains practice and skill in that part. (These were the kinds of advantages Adam Smith particularly stressed). Finally, each may concentrate on the tasks for which he has a greater inborn talent.

Notice that the two-person widget-tying operation uses resources with an opportunity cost of 2800+2100=4900 and produces output worth 5500, for a net increase in production of 600. Evidently, it is a good thing that such a team be organized.

MARGINAL PRODUCTIVITY AND INCREASING RETURNS TO SCALE

Now, what is the marginal productivity of labour with two persons employed? With one worker, output was 2000; with two, 5500, for a difference of 3500. If either Bob or John quits, reducing the firm to 1 worker, the firm loses 3500—so 3500 is the marginal productivity of both Bob and John. That is, 3500 is the marginal productivity of labour, between 1 and 2 units of labour, not the marginal product of some specific worker who happens last. Here is the marginal productivity of labour in the form of a table. Remember, the law of diminishing marginal productivity does not apply in this long run perspective, since there is no fixed input.

Labour	Output	MP
0	0	
1	2000	2000
2	5500	3500

But see what this means. If both Bob and John are paid their marginal productivity, the wage bill is 2*3500=7000. But the product of the firm is only 5500, so Gordon ends up losing 1500. Clearly, it will not be possible to pay the marginal productivity wage. Suppose both are paid a wage less than marginal productivity. Will they continue to work for Gordon if they are paid less than marginal productivity? Yes, up to a point.

The Supply of Labour from Bob and John

How much does Gordon have to pay? Suppose Gordon starts cutting the wage. When the wage drops below 2800, John will resign and then the firm produces only 2000, not enough to pay Bob his 2100 opportunity cost, so Bob resigns too. Evidently 2800 is the least wage Gordon can pay and keep his work force. However, at a wage of 2800 per worker, Gordon's wage bill is 5600 and with an output of 5500, he is still losing 100. Not as much as before, but a loss is a loss and Gordon will choose not to set up a widget-tying enterprise.

THE DARK SIDE OF THE FORCE

Increasing returns to scale are a powerful force for increasing productivity, but the problem of organizing them efficiently is "the dark side of the force." We have seen that an enterprise that yields a net gain of 600 to society cannot be organized, in this example, without producing a loss. The market system cannot take advantage of the potentiality for gain through division of labour and increasing returns to scale in this case. This possibility was discovered by an early 20th Century British economist named Arthur Charles Pigou, but despite 80 years of discussion, this analysis is not at all widely understood, even among professional economists. Pigou thought it might be a good idea for the government to subsidize enterprises with increasing returns to scale. In this case a subsidy of 150 would make the widget-tying enterprise profitable and produce a gain of 600 in national product.

There may be another solution. Since the widget-tying enterprise adds 600 to national output but loses at least 100, we might ask, what happens to the difference of 700? The answer is that Bob gets it. Bob is paid at least 2800 but his opportunity cost is only 2100, accounting for the difference of 700. Suppose that Bob and John were not paid the same wage, but, instead, each was paid his opportunity cost plus 100. The wage bill would then be 2200+3000=5200 and Gordon would finish with a profit of 300.

Thus, wage discrimination may make it possible for the widget-tying enterprise to exist when it cannot exist so long as each worker is paid the same wage for the same work.

The conclusions are surprising and underst andably, controversial—yet the numbers support them, both in this and more complicated and abstract examples.

- Some people believe it is just that each person be paid according to her or his contribution and interpret "marginal productivity" as the person's contribution. However, this may impossible when there are increasing returns to scale, as there may not be enough output to pay everyone on that basis.
- Compromising, some would say that each person ought to be paid in proportion to her or his contribution, so that people are paid equally for the same work. That, too, may be impossible.
- Discrimination or subsidy may be necessary to allow some socially useful activities to exist.
- There may be no simple system of payment (such as supply and demand or equal pay for equal work) that will allow a socially useful enterprise with increasing returns to scale to exist.

REFLECTIONS

We think this is the reason we have organizations. If there were no increasing returns to scale, there would be little reason for any business to employ more than one person. We would instead have an economy consisting of self-employed individuals, like a yeoman agricultural system. Instead we see an economic system consisting in part of large, complicated organizations with internal arrangements and payments systems that have little to do with contributions or marginal productivity and may be discriminatory. From an abstract point of view, they may waste resources by not paying at the marginal productivity; but the benefits of increasing returns to scale are so great that, even falling far short of potential efficiency, they can still be very productive.

This is sometimes lost sight of by the organizations themselves. People naturally avoid complexity and organizations sometimes try to set up simple, market-like internal payment and fund transfer systems, hoping that this will increase efficiency. But, as we have seen, this can fail badly in the context of increasing returns to scale (and that is the context of any large productive organization).

We have recently been through such an experience at Drexel. A few years ago we went over to "revenue centred budgeting." The idea was to let the colleges retain a high proportion of the revenues they produce, through tuition, grants, contracts and so on. This would (it was felt) give the deans and college faculties more "incentive" to set up popular new programmes and initiatives.

However, it wasn't possible to let the colleges keep 100%, since some money is needed to run shared services like the computer centre, student-life activities and the library, not to mention the salaries of high administrators (and we wouldn't think of mentioning that). But it couldn't be made to work. If the proportion kept by the colleges was high enough to make it profitable for them to set up new programmes and initiatives, there was not enough for the purposes of the central administration; while if the proportion taken by the central administration was enough to do its job, then the colleges were losing money on their new programmes and initiatives—no incentive!

So Drexel has moved away from "revenue centred budgeting" in practice, although there is still some work being done to try to work out a "revenue centred budgeting" system that will work. Here's a prediction based on the theory of increasing returns to scale: a revenue-centred budgeting system probably can be made to work, but it will be just as complex and frustrating than the centralized budgeting traditionally has been. That complexity and frustration (and large organizations) are the price we pay for the benefits of increasing returns to scale.

9

Externality

In managerial economics, an *externality* is a cost or benefit from an economic transaction that parties "external" to the transaction bear. An externality rises when one party directly conveys a benefit or cost to others. A network externality arises when a benefit or cost directly conveyed to others depends on the total number of other users. An item is a public good if one person's increase in consumption does not reduce the quantity available to others. Equivalently, a public good provides nonrival consumption.

The benchmark for externalities and public goods is economic efficiency. At that point, all parties maximize their net benefits. Externalities can be resolved through unilateral or joint action, but resolution may be hampered by differences in information and free riding. Similarly, the commercial provision of a public good depends on being able to exclude free riders. Excludability depends on law and technology.

Markets with network externalities differ from conventional markets in several ways. Demand is insignificant until a critical mass of users is established. Expectations of potential users help to determine the attainment of critical mass. Externalities can be either positive, when an external benefit is generated, or negative, when an external cost is imposed upon others. In the case of "public goods," it is practically impossible to charge people for the benefits they get from the "public good," and that creates a problem.

Since the beneficiaries of the public good do not pay for the benefits they get, a profit-oriented market economy will not supply the public good, and that is inefficient. That point can be generalized somewhat. In general, when there are goods, services, and resources that people can get without paying for them at a market equilibrium price, inefficiency will be the result. The term for this in economics is "externality."

An externality occurs when a decision causes costs or benefits to third parties (stakeholders), often, though not necessarily, from the use of a public good (for example, production which causes pollution may impose costs on others). In other words, the participants do not bear all of the costs or reap all of the gains from the transaction. As a result, in a competitive market too much or too little of the good may be produced and consumed from the point of view of society, depending on incentives at the margin and strategic behaviour.

If third parties benefit substantially, such as in areas of education or safety, then the good will be under-provided (or under-consumed); if costs to "the public" exceed costs to the individual(s) making the choice in areas such as pollution then the good will be over-provided, from society's point of view. The "point of view" is specified as the greatest collective economic utility for society.

This should be contrasted with purely private economic agreements that do not affect third parties, where the assumption may be made that, if each party is acting in his or her own interests (as defined by utility) and there are no other major market failures, the agreement or exchange improves overall utility for society.

Put more simply, if an economic transfer between two parties enhances the utility of both without negatively affecting the utility of any third party, the well being (collective utility) of society is improved; if the utility of others is harmed, it is no longer unambiguously clear that society's collective utility has increased, and may have decreased.

A situation in which the private costs or benefits to the producers or purchasers of a good or service differs from the total social costs or benefits entailed in its production and consumption. An externality exists whenever one individual's actions affect the well-being of another individual — whether for the better or for the worse — in ways that need not be paid for according to the existing definition of property rights in the society.

An "external diseconomy," "external cost" or "negative externality" results when part of the cost of producing a good or service is born by a firm or household other than the producer or purchaser. An "external economy," "external benefit," or "positive externality" results when part of the benefit of producing or consuming a good or service accrues to a firm or household other than that which produces or purchases it.

Example. If one neighbour decides to repaint his house and spruce up his yard so he can get a better price when selling it, he also at the same time is slightly improving the market value of other houses in the neighbourhood, creating a "positive externality" benefitting his neighbours. On the other hand, another neighbour who is a grade-A slob and lets the external appearance of his house run down creates a "negative externality" by depressing the attractiveness and thus the market value of the whole neighbourhood.

Externalities of either the "positive" or the "negative" sort create a problem for the effective functioning of the market to maximize the total utility of the society. The "external" portions of the costs and benefits of producing a good will not be factored into its supply and demand functions because rational profit-maximizing buyers and sellers do not take into account costs and benefits they do not have to bear.

Hence a portion of the costs or benefits will not be reflected in determining the market equilibrium prices and quantities of the good involved. The price of the good or service producing the externality will tend towrds equality with the marginal personal cost to the producer and the marginal personal utility to the purchaser, rather than towrds equality with the marginal social cost of production and the marginal social utility of consumption. Thus, normal market incentives for the buyer and seller to maximize their personal utilities will lead to the over- or under-production of the commodity in question from the point of view of society as a whole, not the socially optimal level of production.

Goods involving a positive externality will be "underproduced" from the point of view of society as a whole, while goods involving a negative externality will be "overproduced" from the point of view of society as a whole. In our example above, the individual homeowner pays all the cost of sprucing up his home but realises only part of the benefits created — so consequently each homeowner will probably not keep his house up as well as he otherwise might if his neighbours could somehow be induced or required to pay him something for their share of the benefits from his labours.

Contracts often can be worked out as a means to "internalize" potential externalities because the existence of the externality implies there is at least the potential opportunity for mutual gains if the "third party" by-standers affected can offer compensation to the buyers or sellers in exchange for adjusting production or consumption levels of the good to a more acceptable level. For example: If each homeowner in the neighbourhood will agree to be legally responsible for maintaining a high common standard of upkeep in exchange for everyone else in the neighbourhood also guaranteeing to do the same, then everyone can be financially better off than they would be without the agreement — which is precisely why we observe such phenomena as homeowners associations and restrictive deed covenants.

Or other homeowners in the neighbourhood might even band together and agree to finance jointly the entire cost of purchasing, fixing-up, and reselling some particularly run-down homestead in the neighbourhood if the expected increase in their individual property values would be greater than their share of the cost of buying out their slovenly neighbour. Unfortunately, where externalities affect very large numbers of third parties (but only to a relatively minor degree in each case), the transaction costs of negotiating such many-sided contracts among them all may often be so large as to make this contractual solution impractical.

Where the transaction costs to arrive at contractual solutions to "externality" problems are prohibitively high, complex modern societies normally provide "second best" remedies to private persons through the courts. Nearly the whole area of "tort" law (including especially law suits for "nuisance" and for "negligence") deals with externality problems in one way or another.

People adversely affected by other people's activities may go to court and sue them in an effort to obtain an award of financial compensation for the damages and/or a court injunction requiring their obnoxious neighbours to change their ways in the future. (Of course, filing and prosecuting a law suit is itself a costly procedure, both for the individuals involved and for the taxpayers — more transactions costs.)

Government regulations or tax policies are often justified to the public as a means of "correcting" the outcome of the market for goods involving especially sizable externalities, especially negative externalities. The government might, for example, place a special tax or licensing fee on the production (or purchase) of a good or service believed to involve significant negative externalities, with the size of the tax or fee to be determined by some estimate of the total costs being imposed on third parties.

The government charges would force the sellers (or the buyers) of the good or service to begin to start taking into account these external costs along with their own and would effectively shift the supply curve (or the demand curve) to the left, resulting in somewhat smaller quantities of the good being sold at a somewhat higher price in the new equilibrium after inauguration of the tax — and thus, somewhat fewer costs will be imposed on third parties. (But note that it is the government that gets to keep the money, not the unfortunate bystanders still suffering the damage!)

In the case of a good or service involving a positive externality, government might cope in an analogous fashion by offering to pay subsidies to the producers or consumers of the good or service in question in order to encourage an appropriate expansion of production, or by using government's power to compel obedience without first negotiating mutually agreeable terms of cooperation among the affected parties, government might avoid the sizable transaction costs that would be involved in achieving a contractual solution to the problem by using its law-making or regulatory powers — for example, a city ordinance requiring all householders to keep their lawns mowed and their houses painted and forbidding them to allow trash or old automobile hulks to litter their front yards.

An important problem with the tax/subsidy approach to remedying externalities problems is, of course, that it may well be impossible or prohibitively expensive for the government to determine the size of the external costs or benefits involved and hence to determine even approximately what an appropriate tax or subsidy rate would be.

More generally, there are bound to be transaction costs for all forms of government action, including regulatory or legal strategies for correcting externalities — costs of gathering information, costs of debating and making policy decisions, and costs of administration or policing once the policy has been made. It will often be the case that the costs imposed on society by government taking corrective action would be larger than the decrease in welfare to society from the externalities that the government action is supposedly designed to cure.

In any given case of externality, society may well be better off by simply leaving the externality in place, unless the third-party effects of the externality are truly massive. More precisely, government policy-makers need to devote their attention to the problem of lowering total transaction costs, rather than simply focussing on "fixing" this or that externality problem regardless of costs, if their intention is to maximize social welfare.

One area in which government has a great deal of control over the size of transactions costs throughout the economy is in the design and construction of the legal system. The costs to private firms and individuals of enforcing their contracts and protecting their other property rights are largely determined by the government's arrangements for the legal system. If the legal system is costly and cumbersome and unpredictable, mutually beneficial trades may often not take place because of potentially high transactions costs involved in protecting and enforcing complex property rights and contracts once made.

Moreover, negative externalities often arise because certain third party property rights have not been clearly defined or effectively enforced in some aspect of social life, and the law has mandated that social or common ownership will be imposed instead of conventional private ownership and control. Excessive air and water pollution problems are often examples of such negative externalities from flaws in property law.

For example, factory owners nearly always refrain from dumping waste products on neighbouring privately-owned property for fear of the massive lawsuits they would surely lose — but they can often get by with dumping noxious waste products into "the public's air" or "the public's river" or "the public's ocean" without having to pay to secure the consent of those who later will be breathing or drinking or eating these poisons (or paying extra to remove them) precisely because the victims often have had no practical legal way of purchasing or selling a fully recognized exclusive property right in the portion of the air or rivers or the oceans (and their wildlife) on which they nevertheless depend.

Implications

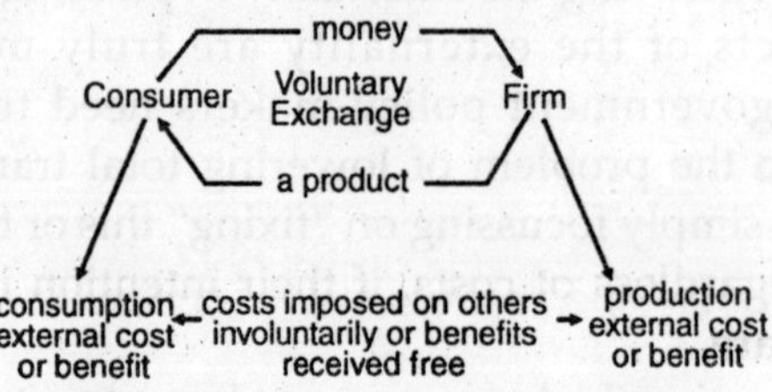

Fig. External Costs and Benefits

To most economists, the problem of an externality usually concerns the results of market activity. Economists see voluntary exchange as mutually beneficial to both parties in an exchange. On the other hand, either the consumption of a product such as perfume or other luxuries or its production may have external effects — as in the diagram. Those who suffer from external costs do so involuntarily, while those who enjoy external benefits do so at no cost. The left-hand-side of the diagram shows consumption externalities, such as those of perfume, while the right-hand-side shows production externalities, such as those produced by a perfume factory.

From the perspective of a social planner or welfare economist, this will result in an outcome that is not socially optimal. From the perspective of anybody affected by the externality, it is either a negative factor in their lives, as with pollution by the factory (or the wearer), or a boon, such as the pleasant smell of those wearing the perfume (in the opinion of some). In the first case, the person who is affected by the negative externality in the case of air pollution will see it as lowered utility: either subjective displeasure or potentially explicit costs, such as higher medical expenses. The externality even be seen as trespassing on their lungs, violating their property rights.

Thus, an external cost may often pose an ethical or political problem. Alternatively, it might be seen as a case of poorly-defined property rights, as with, for example, pollution of bodies of water that may belong to no-one (either figuratively, in the case of publicly-owned, or literally, in some countries and/or legal traditions).

An external *benefit*, on the other hand, may increase the utility of third parties at no cost to them. In effect, it can be called a "free lunch" for them. Since the collective utility of society is improved but the direct participants have no way of monetizing the benefit, there is the likelihood that less of the good will be produced or consumed than would be optimal for society as a whole. Typical examples of goods with positive externalities include education (which is believed to increase overall productivity and therefore well-being) and health care (which may reduce the health risks and costs for third parties).

Positive externalities are frequently associated with the free rider problem. For example, individuals who are vaccinated reduce the risk of contracting the relevant disease for all others around them, and at high levels of vaccination, society may receive large health and welfare benefits; but any one individual may receive most of the benefits at no expense by "free riding" on the costs borne by others.

There are a number of potential means of improving overall social utility when externalities are involved. The most efficient means of correcting for externalities is to "*internalize*" the costs and benefits, for example, by requiring a polluter to repair any damage caused. In many cases, however, internalizing costs or benefits is not feasible or the costs uncertain.

The value of the effects of the externality may be difficult to calculate in a technocratic way by economists or social planners, since they reflect the ethical views and preferences of the entire population: it may not be clear whose preferences are most important; interests may conflict; the "value" of the externalities may be difficult to determine; and all parties involved may attempt to influence the policy responses to their own benefit (particularly if "others" can be made to pay for the proposed solutions). Because it may not be feasible to monetize the costs and benefits, some method is (arguably) needed to either impose solutions or aggregate the choices of society. This may be through some form of representative democracy or other means. Political economy is, in broad terms, the study of the means and results of aggregating those choices and benefits that are not limited to purely private transactions.

Sometimes, *laissez-faire* economists such as Friedrich Hayek and Milton Friedman refer to externalities as "neighbourhood effects" or "spillovers". Externalities may, however, be neither small nor localized.

Going outside the broadly-defined liberal political tradition, Marxists see externalities of all sorts, including pecuniary ones, as ubiquitous, being the rule rather than the exception. Production is socialized or totally interdependent. On the other hand, under capitalism, property rights, the appropriation of income, and the making of economic decisions are largely individualized.

In order to solve this contradiction between socialized production and individual decision-making, Marxists often call for democratic economic planning, as a key part of socialism.(cf. Frederick Engels, "Socialism: Utopian and Scientific")

Types of Externalities

Examples of negative externalities (external cost or external diseconomy) include:

- Pollution by a firm in the course of its production which causes nuisance or harm to others.
- The harvesting by one fishing company in the ocean depletes the stock of available fish for the other companies and overfishing may result. This is an example of a common property resource, sometimes referred to as the *Tragedy of the commons*.
- Individuals collectively choose to use a public transportation resource (such as roads), imposing congestion costs on all other users.
- A business, like an airline company or software company, may purposely underfund one part of their business, such as their pension funds, in order to push the costs onto someone else, creating an externality. Here, the "cost" is that of providing minimum social welfare or retirement income; economists may more frequently attribute this problem to the category of moral hazards.
- A property tycoon buying up a large number of houses in a town, causing prices to rise and therefore making other people who want to buy the houses worse off, perhaps by excluding them from the housing market. These effects are sometimes called "pecuniary externalities"; many economists do not accept the concept of pecuniary externalities, attributing such problems to anti-competitive behaviour, monopoly power, or other definitions of market failures.

Many of the most important negative externalities in the economy are concerned with pollution and the environment.

Examples of positive externalities (beneficial externality, external benefit, external economy, or Merit goods) include:

- A beekeeper keeps the bees for their honey. A side effect or externality associated with his activity is the pollination of surrounding crops by the bees. The value generated by the pollination may be more important than the value of the harvested honey.
- An individual planting an attractive garden in front of his house may provide benefits to others living in the area, and even financial benefits in the form of increased property values for all property owners.
- An individual buying a picture-phone for the first time will increase the usefulness of such phones to people who might want to call him or her. When each new user of a product increases the value of the same product owned by others, the phenomenon is called a network externality or a network effect. Network externalities often have "tipping points" where, quite suddenly, the product reaches general acceptance and near-universal usage.
- Inventions and information - once an invention (or most other forms of practical information) is discovered or made more easily accessible, others benefit by exploiting the invention or information. Copyright and intellectual property law are mechanisms to allow the inventor or creator to benefit from a temporary, state-protected monopoly in return for "sharing" the information through publication or other means.
- Education leads to a more civically-minded citizenry with a greater sense of altruism, and leads to a work force that can create more wealth.
- Flu vaccinations of school children - the children themselves are unlikely to be greatly harmed by the flu, but vaccination of school children may often be the most efficient way to protect the vulnerable elderly.

As noted, externalities (or proposed solutions to

externalities) may also imply political conflicts, rancorous lawsuits, and the like. This may make the problem of externalities too complex for the concept of Pareto optimality to handle. Similarly, if too many positive externalities fall outside the participants in a transaction, there will be too little incentive on parties to participate in activities that lead to the positive externalities.

Externalities in Supply and Demand

The usual economic analysis of externalities can be illustrated using a standard supply and demand diagram if the externality can be monetized and valued in terms of money. An extra supply or demand curve is added, as in the diagrams below.

One of the curves is the *private cost* that consumers pay as individuals for additional quantities of the good, which in competitive markets, is the marginal private cost. The other curve is the *true* cost that society as a whole pays for production and consumption of increased production the good, or the marginal social cost.

Similarly there might be two curves for the demand or benefit of the good. The social demand curve would reflect the benefit to society as a whole, while the normal demand curve reflects the benefit to consumers as individuals and is reflected as effective demand in the market.

Negative Externalities

The graph below shows the effects of a negative externality.

For example, the steel industry is assumed to be selling in a competitive market – before pollution-control laws were imposed and enforced (e.g. under laissez-faire). The marginal private cost is less than the marginal social or public cost by the amount of the external cost, i.e., the cost of air pollution and water pollution. This is represented by the vertical distance between the two supply curves. It is assumed that there are no external benefits, so that social benefit *equals* individual benefit.

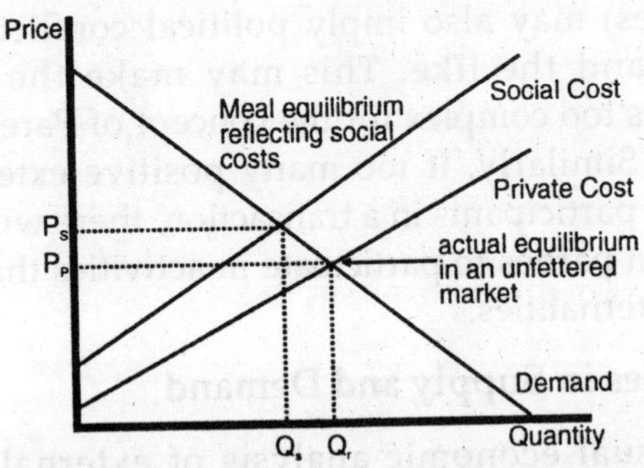

Fig. Supply and Demand with External Costs

If the consumers only take into account their own private cost, they will end up at price P_p and quantity Q_p, instead of the more efficient price P_s and quantity Q_s. These later reflect the idea that the marginal social benefit should equal the marginal social cost, that is that production should be increased *only* as long as the marginal social benefit exceeds the marginal social cost. The result is that a free market is *inefficient* since at the quantity Q_p, the social benefit is less than the societal cost, so society as a whole would be better off if the goods between Q_p and Q_s had not been produced. The problem is that people are buying and consuming *too much* steel.

This discussion implies that pollution is *more than* merely an ethical problem; it is more than just "greedy" and profit-maximizing firms. The problem is one of the disjuncture between marginal and social costs that is not solved by the free market. There is a problem of societal communication and coordination to balance benefits and costs. This discussion also implies that pollution is not something solved by competitive markets. In fact, a monopoly might be able to use some of its excess profits to be benevolent and *internalize the externality* (pay the cost of the pollution).

More likely, a monopoly would artificially restrict the quantity supplied in order to maximize profits. This would actually benefit society in this situation because it would mean less pollution than in the competitive case. Perfectly competitive firms have no choice but to produce according to market incentives or private costs: if one decides to internalize external costs, it implies that this producer would incur higher costs than those of its competitors and likely be forced to exit from the market. So some *collective* solution is needed, such as, government intervention banning or discouraging pollution, by means of economic incentives such as taxes, or an alternative economy such as participatory economics.

Beneficial Externalities

The graph below shows the effects of a positive or beneficial externality. For example, the industry supplying smallpox vaccinations is assumed to be selling in a competitive market. The marginal private benefit of getting the vaccination is less than the marginal social or public benefit by the amount of the external benefit, i.e., the fact that if one person gets the vaccination, others are less likely to get the smallpox even if they themselves are not vaccinated. This marginal external benefit of getting a smallpox shot is represented by the vertical distance between the two demand curves. Assume that there are no external costs, so that social cost *equals* individual cost.

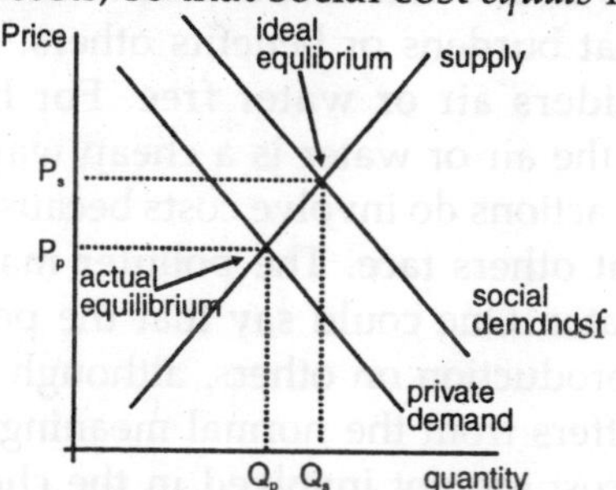

Fig. Supply and Demand with External Benefits

If consumers only take into account their own private benefits from getting vaccinations, the market will end up at price P_p and quantity Q_p as before, instead of the more efficient price P_s and quantity Q_s. These latter again reflect the idea that the marginal social benefit should equal the marginal social cost, i.e., that production should be increased as long as the marginal social benefit exceeds the marginal social cost. The result in an unfettered market is *inefficient* since at the quantity Q_p, the social benefit is greater than the societal cost, so society as a whole would be better off if more goods had been produced. The problem is that people are buying *too few* vaccinations.

The issue of external benefits is related to that of public goods, which are goods where it is difficult if not impossible to exclude people from benefits. The production of a public good has beneficial externalities for all, or almost all, of the public. As with external costs, there is a problem here of societal communication and coordination to balance benefits and costs. This also implies that pollution is not something solved by competitive markets. The government may have to step in with a collective solution, such as subsidizing or legally requiring vaccine use. If the government does this, the good is called a merit good.

The second problem when resources are "free" is that the wrong mix of goods and services will be produced. In terms of efficiency, the marginal rate of transformation will not equal the marginal rate of substitution. This is a common result when decision-makers do not take into account some by-product of their actions that burdens or benefits others. A polluter, for example, considers air or water free. For him, dumping pollutants into the air or water is a cheap way to dispose of wastes. Yet, his actions do involve costs because he affects the alternatives that others face. The polluter may make others forego clean water. One could say that the polluter imposes some costs of production on others, although this use of the word "cost" differs from the normal meaning of cost. Those who bear this cost are not involved in the choice, and in its pure meaning cost is an alternative foregone in a choice.

It is easy to show that when a decision-maker ignores some costs of his decision, his decision may be economically inefficient. The graph below assumes that the market can be represented by supply and demand curves. The demand curve represents the marginal benefit to consumers (and to firms because they are price takers). The supply curve represents the marginal cost to sellers, and because producing the product requires resources that could be used elsewhere, it also represents a cost to buyers. But the production of the product also generates an unwanted by-product that sellers ignore. The marginal cost from the point of view of society as a whole includes this by-product and is thus higher than it seems to the firm. The economically efficient amount to produce in this illustration is q0, but the forces of the market will tend to result in the production of q1.

With externalities, some effects of decisions are ignored by those making decisions, so results are not optimal

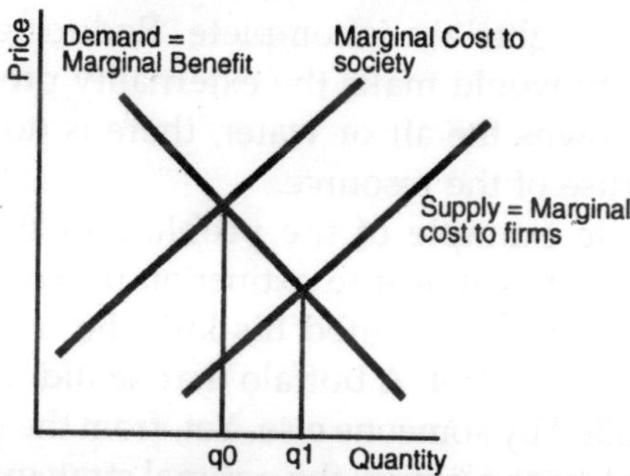

If negative externalities cause too much of a product to be produced, positive externalities should cause too little to be produced. When a person improves his house, his neighbours benefit. Because the decision-maker will not generally consider these spillover advantages to others, less than the efficient amount of the activity will take place. In terms of a supply-and-demand diagram, the marginal benefit curve as perceived by the decision-maker will be to the left of the marginal benefit curve of society as a whole, and thus too little of the activity will take place.

When scarce resources are perceived as "free", there will be potential value that a market will not capture. Is it possible for a society to capture this value, and if so, how?

A common "solution" to this problem has been to assume it away. This solution is especially common in plans for utopias, and writers in the Marxian tradition frequently illustrate it. In some of these arguments, pollution exists because capitalistic man is greedy, but when the new socialist man comes into existence, the problem will cease. Solution by assumption has at times crept into mainstream economic thinking as well.

A more practical solution is to increase private ownership in the system of property rights. This is an ironic solution in a way, because many environmentalists and ecologists have argued that the existence of externalities proves that a market system is seriously flawed and should be scrapped for an alternative, generally with greater state ownership and control. Economic analysis, however, shows that externalities exist when property rights are incomplete. Reducing the role of private property would make the externality problem worse. When no one owns the air or water, there is no incentive to avoid an overuse of the resource.

In a classic example of the problem of the commons, buffalo were hunted almost to extinction in the 19th century. If an individual hunter limited his kills, he was unlikely to benefit from his restraint. A buffalo that he did not kill would probably be killed by someone else. Yet, from the point of view of buffalo hunters as a group, the optimal strategy would have been to limit killing so that the industry could maintain itself indefinitely.

In contrast with the buffalo, the number of cattle in the American West increased during the 19th century. The key difference between the different fates of buffalo and cattle was not that buffalo hunters were greedy and cattle raisers were not. It was that cattle were privately owned and buffalo were "free." Private-property rights force people to take into account all costs and benefits of their actions. A cattleman's decision to kill or not kill his cattle did not affect other cattlemen in the way that a buffalo hunter's decision to kill or not kill buffalo affected other buffalo hunters. When a resource is owned by all, when it is "free," there is a strong tendency for individuals to misuse that resource.

The existence of private property rights allows the law to deal with externality problems. A person who is harmed by someone's actions can ask the courts to decide about compensation. The court's decision will depend on whether or not he has a right to some good or service. Courts have established property rights for clean air, clean water, scenic views, sunshine, and quiet. If a person is not due compensation, then he does not have the property rights but the other party may have them. In this case he can pay the party harming him to stop the offending activity.

Victims of pollution seldom band together and sue the polluter, nor do they band together and pay him not to pollute. The difficulty with legal action is that there are serious problems (and thus large costs) in contracting and organizing large groups for legal action.

One of these problems is the free-rider problem. Ronald Coase pointed out that pollution problems would not exist if there were no difficulties and expenses in making contracts between polluter and victim. The implication of Coase's work is that externalities should not be a serious small-group problem because if only a very few people are involved they can usually organize and seek legal remedies. On the other hand, the costs of organizing and negotiating when large groups are involved make non-governmental solutions very difficult. Coase shows that private-property rights are not always a feasible way to solve the externality problem of "free" resources. Another solution is for the government to act as if it were the owner of these resources. The government does this when it regulates the number of ducks that hunters can kill. It says in effect that the government owns the ducks, and people cannot kill them without the permission of the government.

Government can charge for the use of its resources. It could, for example, charge polluters for the use of clean water and air. This charge would make polluters take into account the side effects of their activities (or in the jargon of economists, they would internalize the externalities), and would move the marginal cost curve in the graph upward. There is some user fee (pollution tax) that would make the decision-makers' marginal cost curves coincide with the marginal-cost-to-society curve, and thus correct the efficiency problem.

Government policy dealing with pollution and negative externalities has largely been one of regulation. Most economists believe that this is a less-desirable (efficient) method of dealing with the problem than a policy of a pollution tax.

Finally, there may not be a good solution to the problem of "free" resources for two reasons. First, the cost of a solution may be greater than the benefits of the solution. Most economists believe that there is some "optimal level" of pollution. Many productive processes produce waste products. These waste products, when considered damaging to people, are pollution. To remove them or to transform them into a form that no one considers damaging requires resources, and the use of those resources means that fewer other products can be produced.

Thus the reduction of pollution involves the weighing of costs and benefits as does virtually all other activity that economists discuss. The optimal level of pollution becomes that level at which the marginal benefit of any more reduction just equals the marginal cost of any more reduction. If removing pollution that causes $1.00 worth of harm costs $10.00, it is economically inefficient to remove it. It is extremely unlikely that the optimal (economic efficient) level will ever be zero.

Second, there may be externality problems within the government just as there can be externality problems in the market. When there are externality problems in the market, we can call on the government as an outside agent to solve them. But if these problems exist in the government, there is no one to turn to.

For example, suppose that the citizens of a country are split into fifty special interest groups, and each group gets special benefits from the government. To pay for those benefits, the government must tax the citizens. The citizens end up paying a dollar in taxes to get eighty cents of special benefits. (Bureaucracy eats up the other 20%.) Though all would be better off getting rid of all special benefits, no one group will want to give up its special benefits, and the costs of organizing the fifty different groups to come up with an agreement may be very large. There may be no solution to this problem of the commons.

Resolving an Externality

Involves deliberate action, not accomplished through the market. Merger of the source and recipient of an externality. Once the source and recipient of the externality are combined, no matter who acquires whom, the single entity will take account of all benefits and costs of its investments and invest up to the economically efficient level (group marginal benefits equal group marginal costs).

Joint Action

Where merger is not feasible:

- The source and recipient of the externality could negotiate and resolve the externality (while remaining separate entities). They collect information on the benefits and costs to the various parties and plan the level of activity that generates the externality.
  E.g., in the case of a positive externality, the recipient will pay the source (a contribution equal to the recipient's marginal benefit from the activity generating the externality) to increase the source's investment. The source will maximize profit by choosing the level of activity where marginal benefits equal marginal costs.
- Then, they must enforce the agreed plan: monitoring the source and applying incentives to ensure that the source complies with the planned level of activity.

Coase Theorem

In law and economics, the Coase theorem, attributed to Ronald Coase, relates to the economic efficiency of a government's allocation of property rights. In essence, the theorem states that in the absence of transaction costs, all government allocations of property rights are equally efficient, because interested parties will bargain privately to correct any externality. This theorem, along with his 1937 paper on the nature of the firm which also emphasises the role of transaction costs, earned Coase the 1991 Nobel Prize in Economics. The

Coase theorem is an important basis for most modern economic analyses of government regulation, especially in the case of externalities.

George Stigler summarised the resolution of the externality problem in the absence of transaction costs in a 1966 economics textbook in terms of private and social cost, and for the first time called it a "theorem". Since the 1960s, a voluminous literature on the Coase theorem and its various interpretations, proofs, and criticism has developed and continues to grow.

The Theory

What Coase originally proposed in 1959 in the context of the regulation of radio frequencies was that as long as property rights in these frequencies were well defined, it ultimately did not matter if adjacent radio stations would initially interfere with each other by broadcasting in the same frequency band. The station able to reap the higher economic gain of the two from broadcasting would in this case have an incentive to pay the other station not to interfere. In the absence of transaction costs, both stations would strike a mutually advantageous deal. Put differently, it would not matter whether one or the other station had the initial right to broadcast; eventually, the right to broadcast would end up with the party that was able to put it to the most highly valued use.

Coase's main point, clarified in an article published in 1960 (Coase 1960) and cited when he was awarded the Nobel Prize in 1991, was that transaction costs, however, could not be neglected, and therefore, the initial allocation of property rights mattered in the presence of side effects (externalities). In essence, the normative conclusion most often drawn from the Coase theorem is that the property rights should initially be assigned to the actors gaining the most utility from them. Thus allocation is optimal, and even in cases where bargaining would correct the misallocation, economic resources won't have to be spent on transaction costs. The problem in real life is that governments most often do not know ex ante the most valued use of a resource.

Another, more refined normative conclusion also often discussed in law and economics is that government should create institutions which minimize transaction costs, so as to allow misallocations of resources to be corrected for as cheaply as possible.

Criticism

The main criticism often targeted at the Coase theorem is to say that transaction costs are almost always too high for efficient bargaining to happen. For instance, economist James Meade argued that even in a simple case of a beekeeper's bees dusting a nearby farmer's crops, a coasean bargaining is inefficient.

However, such criticism often comes from economists such as Meade, who often analyse economic situations from a non-coasean, traditional neoclassical point of view, with exogenous transaction costs. However, coasean economic analysis, or new institutional economics also often looks at the dynamics of the institutions that create the transaction costs.

As it turns out, new institutional economists more sympathetic to Coase's point of view researched the empirical evidence, and found out coasean agreements between beekeepers and nearby farmers had been common practice for nearly a century.

The other strain of criticism often points out other problems often associated with public goods which manifest in coasean bargainings. In many cases of externalities, the bargaining doesn't happen between two economic actors, but instead the parties might be a single large factory versus a thousand landowners nearby. In such situations, say the critics, not only do transaction costs rise extraordinarily high, but bargaining is hindered by basic prisoner's dilemma problems. For instance property rights might say the landowners must pay the factory to stop polluting, certain landowners might downplay the harm of pollution on them, trying to free ride on the other landowners' wallets.

Again, new institutional economics and coasean insights into the dynamics of institutions often taken exogenous in neoclassical analysis provides quite a different point of view into how public goods are created. As a counterexample against the neoclassical models' pessimistic views on public goods and collective action, Coase investigated the empirical evidence on lighthouses, perhaps the most common textbook example a public good. In the article *The lighthouse in economics,* Coase pointed that *"contrary to the belief of many economists, a lighthouse service can be provided by private enterprise... [Before the 20th century] The lighthouses were built, operated, financed and owned by private individuals, who could sell a lighthouse or dispose of it by bequest."*

Externalities and the Coase Theorem

Ronald Coase argued that individuals could organize bargains so as to bring about an efficient outcome and eliminate externalities without government intervention. The government should restrict its role to facilitating bargaining among the affected groups or individuals and to enforcing any contracts that result. This result, often known as the "Coase Theorem," requires that

- Property rights are well defined;
- People act rationally
- Transaction costs are minimal

Only if all three of these apply, will individual bargaining solve the problem of externalities.

Thus, this theorem does not apply to the steel industry case discussed above. For example, with a steel factory that trespasses on the lungs of a large number of individuals with pollution, it is difficult if not impossible for any one person to negotiate with the producer, and there are large transaction costs. Hence the most common approach may be to regulate the firm (by imposing limits on the amount of pollution considered "acceptable") while paying for the regulation and enforcement with taxes.

The case of the vaccinations also does not fit with the Coase Theorem. The firms of the vaccination industry would have to get together to bribe large numbers of people to have their shots. Individual firms would be tempted to "free ride" and not pay the cost of these bribes. The property rights involved are not well defined.

This does not say that the Coase theorem is irrelevant. For example, if a logger is planning to clear-cut a forest in a way that has a negative impact on a nearby resort, it is quite possible that the resort-owner and the logger could get together to agree to a deal. For example, the resort-owner could pay the logger not to clear-cut – or could buy the forest. The most problematic situation, from Coase's perspective, occurs when the forest literally does not belong to anyone; the question of "who" owns the forest is not important, as any specific owner will have an interest in coming to an agreement with the resort owner (if such an agreement is mutually beneficial).

Also, the central government may not be needed. Traditional ways of life may have evolved as ways to deal with external costs and benefits. Alternatively, democratically-run communities can agree to deal with these costs and benefits in an amicable way.

Network Externalities

Network externality has been defined as a change in the benefit, or surplus, that an agent derives from a good when the number of other agents consuming the same kind of good changes. As fax machines increase in popularity, for example, your fax machine becomes increasingly valuable since you will have greater use for it. This allows, in principle, the value received by consumers to be separated into two distinct parts. One component, which in our writings we have labeled the autarky value, is the value generated by the product even if there are no other users. The second component, which we have called synchronization value, is the additional value derived from being able to interact with other users of the product, and it is this latter value that is the essence of network effects.

An illustration: As this article was being written, commentators are speculating on whether Apple computer will survive, since its network (base of users) is shrinking, some think, below a minimum acceptable level. Since the actual quantity of Apple computers sold is still among the very largest of personal computer manufacturers which should allow Apple to take advantage of economies of scale in production, and the computers are not thought to be deficient in terms of quality, any lack of viability must be due to the fact that the network of Apple computer users is small. In other words, the synchronization value of Apple computers is thought to be too low.

First a definitional concern: Network effects should not properly be called network externalities unless the participants in the market fail to internalize these effects. After all, it would not be useful to have the term 'externality' mean something different in this literature than it does in the rest of economics. Unfortunately, the term externality has been used somewhat carelessly in this literature. Although the individual consumers of a product are not likely to internalize the effect of their joining a network on other members of a network, the owner of a network may very well internalize such effects. When the owner of a network (or technology) is able to internalize such network effects, they are no longer externalities. This distinction, first discussed in Liebowitz and Margolis (1994) now seems to be adopted by some authors but has not been universally adopted.

Putting aside definitional concerns, the import of network effects comes largely from the belief that they are endemic to new, high-tech industries, and that such industries experience problems that are different in character from the problems that have, for more ordinary commodities, been solved by markets. The purported problems due to network effects are several, but the most arresting is a claim that markets may adopt an inferior product or network in the place of some superior alternative. Thus if network effects are a typical characteristic of modern technologies, the theory suggests that markets may be inadequate for managing the fruits of such technologies.

The concept of network externality has been applied in the literature of standards, where a primary concern is the choice of a correct standard. The concept has also played a role in the literature of path dependence. The literature has identified two types of network effects. Direct network effects have been defined as those generated through a direct physical effect of the number of purchasers on the value of a product (e.g. fax machines). Indirect network effects are "market mediated effects" such as cases where complementary goods (e.g. toner cartridges) are more readily available or lower in price as the number of users of a good (printers) increases.

In early writing, however, this distinction was not carried into models of network effects. Once network effects were embodied in payoff functions, any distinction between direct and indirect effects was ignored in developing models and drawing conclusions. However, our 1994 paper demonstrates that the two types of effects will typically have different economic implications. It is now generally agreed that the consequences of internalizing direct and indirect network effects are quite different.

Indirect network effects generally are pecuniary in nature and therefore should not be internalized. Pecuniary externalities do not impose deadweight losses if left uninternalized, whereas they do impose (monopoly or monopsony) losses if internalized. An interesting aspect of the network externalities literature is that it seemed to ignore, and thus repeat, earlier mistakes regarding pecuniary externalities. Concern about marginal adjustment of the level of network activity has not been the primary focus of the network externality literature. Instead, this literature has focused primarily on selection among competing networks.

Levels of Network Related Activities

Harvey Liebenstein's work on bandwagon and snob effects (1950) anticipates much of the argument regarding network effects. His main result is that demand curves are more elastic when consumers derive positive value from increases in the size of the market. One branch of the modern network literature would easily fit in the Liebenstein framework. Such research has reexamined various economic models with network effects introduced. For example, an analysis of the impacts of unauthorized software copying will change when network effects are introduced. Copying increases the size of a network, increasing the value to authorized users, so that any harm from unauthorized copying will likely be mitigated.

The difference between a network effect and a network externality lies in whether the impact of an additional user on other users is somehow internalized. Since the synchronization effect is almost always assumed to be positive in this literature, the social value from another network user will always be greater than the private value. If network effects are not internalized, the equilibrium network size may be smaller than is efficient. For example, if the network of telephone users were not owned, it would likely be smaller than optimal since no agent would capture the benefits that an additional member of the network would impose on other members. (Alternatively, if the network effects were negative, a congestion externality might mean that networks tend to be larger than optimal.) Where networks are owned, this effect is internalized and under certain conditions the profit maximizing network size will also be socially optimal.

Perhaps surprisingly, the problem of internalizing the network externality is largely unrelated to the problem of choice between competing networks that is taken up in the next section. In the case of positive network effects, all networks are too small. Therefore, it is not the *relative* market shares of two competing formats, but rather, the overall level of network activity that will be affected by this difference between private and social values. This is completely compatible with the literature on conventional externalities. For reasons that we will expand on below, this is a far more likely consequence of uninternalized network effects than the more exotic cases of incorrect choices of networks, standards or technologies.

Network size is a real and significant issue that is raised by network effects. Nevertheless, this issue has received fairly little attention in the contemporary literature of network externality, perhaps because it is well handled by more conventional economic models.

Competing Networks Under Increasing Returns

The literature on network externalities challenges economists' traditional use of decreasing returns and grants primacy to economies to scale. Positive network effects, which raise the value received by consumers as markets get larger, have impacts that are very similar to conventional firm-level economies of scale. If we start an analysis with the assumption that firms produce similar but incompatible products (networks), and that the network effects operate only within the class of compatible products, then competitors (networks) with larger market shares will have an advantage over smaller competitors, *ceteris paribus*. If larger competitors have a forever widening advantage over smaller firms, we have entered the realm of natural monopoly, which is exactly where most models that address network and standards choices find themselves.

It is critical to note, however, that network effects are not in general *sufficient* for natural-monopoly-type results. In cases where average production costs are falling, constant, or nonexistent, network effects would be sufficient for a result of natural monopoly. Many, if not most, models in this literature ignore production costs and thus with any assumption of positive network effects are unavoidably constructed as instances of natural monopoly. But notice that if production costs exhibit decreasing returns, and if these decreasing returns overwhelm the network effects, then natural monopoly is not implied, and competing incompatible networks (standards) will be possible.

Though economists have long accepted the possibility of increasing returns, they have generally judged that except in fairly rare instances, the economy operates in a range of decreasing returns. Some proponents of network externalities models predict that as newer technologies take over a larger share of the economy, the share of the economy described by increasing returns will increase. Brian Arthur has emphasized these points to a general audience: "Roughly speaking, diminishing returns hold sway in the traditional part of the economy – the processing industries. Increasing returns reign in the newer part – the knowledge-based industries. They call for different management techniques, strategies, and codes of government regulation. They call for different understandings".

If the choice of a standard or network is dominated by natural monopoly elements, then only one standard will survive in the market. It thus is of great importance that the standard that comes to dominate the market also be the best of the alternative standards available. Traditionally it has been assumed that the natural monopolist who comes to dominate a market will be at least as efficient as any other producer, but this assumption is specifically questioned in the newer literature. Specifics differ across the many versions of this problem that appear in the literature. The recurring issue, however, is that we lose the usual assurances that the products that prevail in markets are the ones that yield the greatest surpluses.

The mere existence of network effects and increasing returns is not sufficient to lead to the choice of an inferior technology. For that, some additional assumptions are needed. One common assumption that can generate a prediction of inefficient network choice is that the network effect differs across the alternative networks. In particular, it is sometimes assumed that the network type that offers the greatest surplus when network participation is large is the one that offers the smallest surplus when participation is small. This condition, however, is not likely to be satisfied, since synchronization effects are likely to be uniform. For example, if there is value in a cellular telephone network becoming larger, this should be equally true whether the network is digital or analog.

Similarly, the network value of an additional user of a particular video recorder format is purported to be the benefits accrued by having more opportiunities to exchange video tapes. But this extra value does not depend on the particular format of video recorder chosen. If network effects are the same for all versions of a given product, it is very unlikely that the wrong format would be chosen if both are available at the same time.

10

Regulation

A regulation is a legal restriction promulgated by government administrative agencies through rulemaking supported by a threat of sanction or a fine. This administrative law or regulatory law is in contrast to statutory or case law. Regulation mandated by the government or state attempts to produce outcomes which might not otherwise occur, produce or prevent outcomes in different places to what might otherwise occur, or produce or prevent outcomes in different timescales than would otherwise occur. Common examples of regulation include attempts to control market entries, prices, wages, pollution effects, employment for certain people in certain industries, standards of production for certain goods and services. The economics of imposing or removing regulations relating to markets is analysed in regulatory economics.

The marginal benefit of an item may diverge from the marginal cost for three basic reasons: market power, asymmetric information, and externalities and public goods. This divergence results in economic efficiency. Government regulation may help where private action fails to resolve the economic inefficiency.

Generally, the government can regulate the conduct, information, and structure of an industry. Specifically, the conduct of a franchised monopoly may be regulated directly through price or indirectly through the rate of return. Competition law regulates the conduct and structure of businesses in general. In situations of asymmetric information, mandatory disclosure is one form of regulation.

Externalities may be regulated through fees or standards. The efficient degree of an externality depends on location and time. The government can help to resolve inefficiency in accidents and public goods by providing an appropriate legal framework. The laws regarding copyrights and patents must balance the incentive for new research against inefficient use of existing knowledge.

Regulation as a Legal Term

A *regulation* as a legal term is a rule created by an administration or administrative agency or body that interprets the statutes setting out the agency's purpose and powers, or the circumstances of applying the statute.

A *regulation* is a form of secondary legislation which is used to implement a primary piece of legislation appropriately, or to take account of particular circumstances or factors emerging during the gradual implementation of, or during the period of, a primary piece of legislation.

Other forms of secondary legislation are *statutory instruments, statutory orders, by-laws* and *rules*. Some of these (but not all of them) need to be referred back before being implemented, to the primary legislative process.

Type of Regulation

Regulations, like any other coercive action, have costs for some and benefits for others. Efficient regulations may only be said to exist where the total benefits to some people exceed the total costs to others.

Regulation are justified using various reasons and therefore can be classified in several broad categories:

- *Market failures:* Regulation due to inefficiency. Intervention due to a classical economics argument to market failure.
- Risk of monopoly
- Collective action, or public good
- Inadequate information
- Unseen externalities
- *Collective desires:* Regulation about collective desires

or considered judgements on the part of a significant segments of society

- *Diverse experiences:* Regulation with a view of eliminating or enhancing opportunities for the formation of diverse preferences and beliefs
- *Social subordination:* Regulation aimed to increase or reduce social subordination of various social groups
- *Endogenous preferences:* Regulation's purpose is to affect the development of certain preferences on an aggregate level
- *Irreversibility:* Regulation that deals with the problem of irreversibility – the problem in which a certain type of conduct from current generations results in outcomes from which future generations may not recover from at all.
- *Interest group transfers:* Regulation that results from efforts by self-interest groups to redistribute wealth in their favour, which may disguise itself as one or more of the justifications above.

Regulatory Economics

Regulatory economics is the economics of regulation, in the sense of the application of law by government that is used for various purposes, such as centrally-planning an economy, remedying market failure, enriching well-connected firms, or benefiting politicians. It is not considered to include voluntary regulation that may be accomplished in the private sphere.

Regulation as a Process

Public services can encounter conflict between commercial procedures (e.g. maximising profit), and the interests of the people using these services. Most governments therefore have some form of control or regulation to manage this possible conflict. This regulation ensures that a safe and appropriate service is delivered, while not discouraging the effective functioning and development of businesses.

For example, the sale and consumption of alcohol and prescription drugs are controlled by regulation in most countries, as are the food business, provision of personal or residential care, public transport, construction, film and TV, etc. Monopolies are often regulated, especially those which are difficult to abolish (natural monopoly). The financial sector is also highly regulated.

Regulation can have several elements:

- Public statutes, standards or statements of expectations.
- A process of registration or licensing to approve and to permit the operation of a service usually by a named organisation or person.
- A process of inspection or other form of ensuring standard compliance, or reporting and management of non-compliance with these standards: where there is continued non-compliance, then:
- A process of de-licensing whereby that organisation or person is judged to be operating unsafely, and is ordered to stop operating at the expense of acting unlawfully.

This differs profoundly from regulation in any voluntary sphere of activity. For example, when a broker purchases a seat on the New York Stock Exchange, there are explicit rules of conduct to which the broker must conform as contractual and agreed-upon conditions governing participation. Contrast this with the coercive regulations of the U.S. Securities and Exchange Commission, which are imposed without regard for any individual's consent or dissent. Other examples of voluntary compliance in structured settings include the activities of Major League Baseball, FIFA (the international governing body for professional soccer), and the Royal Yachting Association (the UK's recognised national association for sailing). Regulation in this sense approaches the ideal of an accepted standard of ethics for a given activity, to promote the best interests of the people participating as well as the acceptable continuation of the activity itself within specified limits.

In the United States, throughout the 18th and 19th centuries, the government engaged in substantial regulation of the economy. For example, in the 18th century, with mercantilism production and distribution of goods were regulated by government ministries. Subsidies were granted to agriculture and tariffs were imposed. This type of intervention continued throughout the 19th century. From the time of the administration of President Franklin D. Roosevelt until the late 1970s, the regulation of infrastructure was considered necessary from the standpoint of national security: whether in war or peace, a nation without adequate and reliable transport, telecommunications, public health, banking, and public utilities was considered insecure, and the government assumed the responsibility to ensure that this infrastructure was adequate.

It was considered imprudent to give this responsibility over to private hands. In 1946, the U.S. Congress enacted the Administrative Procedure Act, which established some means to oversee the expansion of federal regulation. The APA established uniform procedures for a federal agency's promulgation of regulations, and adjudication of claims. The APA also sets forth the process for judicial review of agency action.

Regulation as Red Tape

The World Bank's *Doing Business* database collects data from nearly 150 countries on the costs of regulation in certain areas, such as starting a business. For example, it takes a minimum of 19 working days to start a business in the OECD, compared to 60 in Sub-Saharan Africa; the cost as a percentage of GNP (not including bribes) is 8% in the OECD, and 225% in Africa.

Deregulation

During the late 1970s and 1980s, regulation was seen as imposing unnecessary 'red tape' and other restrictions on businesses. This in turn was interpreted as hurting economic efficiency. Further, regulatory agencies were often seen as having been captured by the regulated industries and so not serving the public interest. As a result, there has been a movement towards deregulation in recent years. One example is the international monetary system: it is now much easier to transfer capital between countries. As a result, the globalisation of markets has increased.

Privatisation of industries which had been under previous government control was a wide form of deregulation in Britain throughout the later years of the last century. Some argue that although this has increased choice in services, their standards have declined and wages and employment have been reduced.

Some, particularly libertarians, feel that there has been little progress on deregulation, and that controls on small businesses are greater than ever. They feel that deregulation is an aspirational rather than a real intention. Others, usually those on the Left, have argued that deregulation has gone too far, and given too much power to corporations and special interests, while removing the power of the people's elected representatives. Therefore they support a process of re-regulation. Many criticize the influence of Intellectual Property Rights and other sorts of national regulations on the internet and IT business (software patents, DRM, trusted computing).

Criticism of Economic Regulation

Some economists, such as Nobel prize-winning economist Milton Friedman as well as those of the Austrian School, oppose economic regulation. They argue that government should limit its involvement in economies to protecting negative individual rights (life, liberty, property) rather than diminishing individual autonomy and responsibility for the sake of remedying any sort of putative "market failure." They tend to regard the notion of market failure as a misguided contrivance wrongly used to justify coercive government action to further various political agendas, such as mercantilistic or egalitarian goals. These economists believe that government intervention creates more problems than it is supposed to solve — as well-meaning as some of these interventions may be — chiefly because government officers are incapable of accurate economic calculation, lacking any reliable ability (or true incentive) to gather, integrate, or honestly evaluate the vast amounts of information that guide the "Invisible Hand" of a free market.

The Austrian School economists, beginning with Ludwig von Mises, see regulations as problematic not only because they disrupt market processes, but also because they tend only to bring about more regulations. According to Austrian theory, every regulation has some consequences besides those originally intended when the regulation was implemented.

If the unintended consequences are undesirable to those with the power to regulate, there exist two alternative possibilities: do away with the existing regulation, or keep the existing regulation and institute a new one as well to treat the unintended consequence of the old one. In practice, regulators very seldom even consider that the problems they detect may actually be the consequence of prior regulation, so the second option is preferred far more often than the first. The new regulation, however, has unintended consequences of its own which bring about this cycle anew. If unchecked, the result over time is regulation so extensive as to amount to a state run economy.

Laissez-faire advocates do not oppose monopolies unless they maintain their existence through coercion to prevent competition, and often assert that monopolies have historically developed only *because* of government intervention rather than due to a lack of intervention. Specifically, every regulation has some associated cost of compliance. If these costs increase the total cost of operation enough to make new entry into a market prohibitive but allow existing firms to continue to generate a profit, the regulation effectively cartellizes or monopolizes the industry. When existing firms are able to lobby for regulation, this effectively becomes an opportunity to do away with competitive rivals.

Some economists argue that minimum wage laws cause unnecessary unemployment, for the same reason that a minimum price on anything will decrease the quantity of it that people purchase. If a minimum wage law is passed that makes it illegal to pay less than M per hour, employers will continue to keep on payroll only those workers whose hourly work brings in more than M in revenues. Consequently, those workers who are least productive, and therefore are likely to be paid the least before a minimum wage, are also the ones most likely to become unemployed after a minimum wage is implemented.

Another argument against regulation is that laws against insider trading reduce market efficiency and transparency. If a firm is "cooking the books," insiders, without restraint on insider trading, will take short positions and lower the share price to a level that aggregates both insider and outsider knowledge.

If insiders are restrained from using their knowledge to make transactions, the share price will not reflect their insider information. If outsider investors (those whom such laws are supposed to protect) buy shares, their purchase price won't reflect the insider knowledge and will be high by comparison to the price after the insider information becomes public. The outsider wind up taking an avoidable loss. If insiders were allowed to trade freely, the price would never get as high to begin with, and outsiders would lose less money.

Another position held by most economists is that government-enforced price-ceilings cause shortages. If the public is willing to buy Q units of some good at price P, and the sellers of that good are willing to sell Q units at P, then in the absence of regulation, the market for that good will clear. That is, everyone who wants to buy or sell at price P will be able to do so. If a regulation imposes a price ceiling below P, sellers will be willing to sell some lesser quantity, Q – a, and buyers will be willing to buy some greater quantity, Q + b, at the new price. In addition to a shortage of a + b units, there is also the matter of deciding who should get the units offered, since at the regulation price, demand will exceed supply.

Economic Analysis

Primary Characteristics of a Monopoly

- *Single seller:* A *pure* monopoly is an industry in which a single firm is the sole producer of a good or the sole provider of a service. This is usually caused by barriers to entry.

- *No close substitutes:* The product or service is unique in ways which go beyond brand identity, and cannot be easily replaced (a monopoly on water from a certain spring, sold under a certain brand name, is not a true monopoly; neither is Coca-Cola, even though it is differentiated from its competition in flavour).
- *Price maker:* In a pure monopoly a single firm controls the total supply of the whole industry and is able to exert a significant degree of control over the price, by changing the quantity supplied (an example of this would be the situation of Viagra before competing drugs emerged). In subtotal monopolies (for example diamonds or petroleum at present) a single organization controls enough of the supply that even if it limits the quantity, or raises prices, the other suppliers will be unable to make up the difference and take significant amounts of market share.
- *Blocked entry:* The reason a *pure* monopolist has no competitors is that certain barriers keep would-be competitors from entering the market. Depending upon the form of the monopoly these barriers can be economic, technological, legal (e.g. copyrights, patents), violent (competing businesses are shut down by force), or of some other type of barrier that completely prevents other firms from entering the market.

Price Setting for Unregulated Monopolies

In economics a firm is said to have monopoly power if it faces a downward sloping demand curve. This is in contrast to a price taker that faces a horizontal demand curve. A price taker cannot choose the price that they sell at, since if they set it above the equilibrium price, they will sell none, and if they set it below the equilibrium price, they will have an infinite number of buyers (and be making less money than they could if they sold at the equilibrium price). In contrast, a business with monopoly power can choose the price they want to sell at. If they set it higher, they sell less. If they set it lower, they sell more.

In most real markets with claims, falling demand associated with a price increase is due partly to losing customers to other sellers and partly to customers who are no longer willing or able to buy the product. In a pure monopoly market, only the latter effect is at work, and so, particularly for inflexible commodities such as medical care, the drop in units sold as prices rise may be much less dramatic than one might expect.

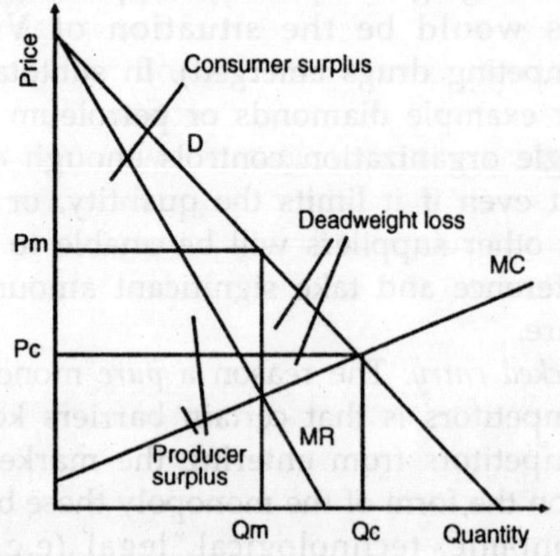

Fig. Surpluses and Deadweight loss Created by Monopoly price setting

If a monopoly can only set one price it will set it where marginal cost (MC) equals marginal revenue (MR) as seen on the diagram on the right. This can be seen on a big supply and demand diagram for many criticism of monopoly. This will be at the quantity Qm; and at the price Pm;. This is above the competitive price of Pc and with a smaller quantity than the competitive quantity of Qc. The offensive monopoly gains is the shaded in area labeled profit (note that this diagram looks only at the case where there is no fixed cost. If there were a fixed cost, the average cost curve should be used instead).

As long as the price elasticity of demand (in absolute

value) for most customer is less than one, it is very advantageous to increase the price: the seller gets more money for less goods. With an increase of the price, the price elasticity tends to rise, and in the optimum mentioned above it will be above one for most customers. A formula gives the relation between price, marginal cost of production and demand elasticity which maximizes a monopoly profit:

$$\frac{P}{MC} = \frac{1}{1+1/e}$$

(known as Lerner index). The monopolist's monopoly power is given by the vertical distance between the point where the marginal cost curve (MC) intersects with the marginal revenue curve (MR) and the demand curve. The longer the vertical distance, (the more inelastic the demand curve) the bigger the monopoly power, and thus larger profits.

The economy as a whole loses out when monopoly power is used in this way, since the extra profit earned by the firm will be smaller than the loss in consumer surplus. This difference is known as a deadweight loss.

Calculating Monopoly Output

The single price monopoly profit maximization problem is as follows: The monopoly's profit is its total revenue less its total cost. Let the price it sets as a market response be a function of the quantity it produces (Q) $P(Q)$ and let its cost function be as a function of quantity $C(Q)$. The monopoly's revenue is the product of the price and the quantity it produces. Hence its profit is:

$$\Pi = P(Q)\bullet Q - C(Q)$$

Taking the first order derivative with respect to quantity yields:

$$\frac{d\Pi}{dQ} = P'(Q)\bullet Q + P(Q) - C'(Q)$$

Setting this equal to zero for maximization:

$$\frac{d\Pi}{dQ} = P'(Q)\bullet Q + P(Q) - C'(Q) = 0$$

$$\frac{d\Pi}{dQ} + C'(Q) = P'(Q)\bullet Q + P(Q) = C'(Q)$$

i.e. marginal revenue = marginal cost, provided,

$$\frac{d^2\Pi}{dQ^2} = P''(Q)\cdot Q + 2\cdot P'(Q) - C''(Q) < 0$$

(the *rate* of marginal revenue is less than the *rate* of marginal cost, for maximization). This procedure assumes that the monopolist knows exactly the demand function.

Monopoly and Efficiency

In standard economic theory, a monopoly will sell a lower quantity of goods at a higher price than firms would in a purely competitive market. In this way the monopoly will secure monopoly profits by appropriating some or all of the consumer surplus, as although the higher price deters some consumers from purchasing, most are willing to pay the higher price. Assuming that costs stay the same, this does not lead to an outcome which is inefficient in the sense of Pareto efficiency; no-one could be made better off by shifting resources without making someone else worse off. However, total social welfare declines compared with perfect competition, because some consumers must choose second-best products.

It is also often argued that monopolies tend to become less efficient and innovative over time, becoming "complacent giants", because they don't have to be efficient or innovative to compete in the marketplace. Sometimes this very loss of efficiency can raise the potential value of a competitor enough to overcome market entry barriers, or provide incentive for research and investment into new alternatives.

The theory of contestable markets argues that in some circumstances (private) monopolies are forced to behave *as if* there were competition, because of the risk of losing that monopoly to new entrants. This is likely to happen where a market's barriers to entry are low. It might also be because of the availability in the longer-term of substitutes in other markets. For example, a canal monopoly in the late eighteenth century United Kingdom was worth a lot more than in the late nineteenth century, because of the introduction of railways as a substitute.

Some argue that it can be good to allow a firm to attempt to monopolize a market, since practices such as dumping can benefit consumers in the short term; and once the firm grows too big, it can then be dealt with via regulation. (This is a rather optimistic view of how effectively regulation can substitute for competition.) When monopolies are not broken through the open market, often a government will step in to either regulate the monopoly, turn it into a publicly owned monopoly, or forcibly break it up. Public utilities, often being natural monopolies and less susceptible to efficient breakup, are often strongly regulated or publicly owned. AT&T and Standard Oil are debatable examples of the breakup of a private monopoly. When AT&T was broken up into the "Baby Bell" components, MCI, Sprint, and other companies were able to compete effectively in the long-distance phone market and started to take phone traffic from the less efficient AT&T.

Monopsony

In economics, a monopsony is a market form with only one buyer, called "monopsonist," facing many sellers. It is an instance of imperfect competition, symmetrical to the case of a monopoly, in which there is only one *seller* facing many buyers. The term "monopsony" was first introduced by Joan Robinson (1933). The term "monopsony power", in a manner similar to "monopoly power" is used by economists as a short hand reference to buyers who face an upwardly sloping supply curve but that are not the only buyer; better, but more cumbersome terms may be oligopsony or monopsonistic competition. A monopsonist may be at the same time a monopolist.

Overview

A monopsonist has market power, due to the fact that he/she can affect the market price of the purchased good by varying the quantity bought. Formally, this is so because a monopsonist faces a supply curve with a *finite* (and generally positive) price elasticity. However, one can find this condition – and hence monopsony power – also in markets with more than one buyer. In all such cases the resulting market form is called an oligopsony.

For most practical purposes, what matters is monopsony power as such, whether it is exercised by one or more subjects. In standard microeconomics, where monopsonists or oligopsonists are assumed to be profit-maximizing firms, monopsony power leads to a market failure, due to a *restriction of the quantity purchased* relative to the (Pareto-) optimal competitive outcome. Moreover, markets with monopsony power are predicted to react differently to public price regulations. Monopsony power is thus relevant from both the normative and positive points of view. The practical importance of its effects depends however on its actual *intensity*, measured by the size of the deviation from competitive outcomes.

Traditional microeconomics tended to assume that in most modern cases such intensity was small enough to be ignored, justifying as an acceptable approximation the general use of much simpler competitive models. The only and oft-quoted exception to this principle was assumed to be the labour markets of the nineteenth-century "company towns", which were isolated mining centres with only one employer (the mining company) for almost everybody. This view has however been variously questioned by the more recent literature devoted to the actual *measurement* of monopsony power in observed markets.

On the one hand, econometric exercises on the available data have apparently ruled out significant labour monopsony for the typical West Virginia "company towns" of the early twentieth century. On the other hand, many observations appear to suggest significant monopsony power in various *contemporary* labour markets, from baseball players to nurses, college professors and many others. There have also been attempts to measure possible monopsony power in some non-labour markets as well.

Reasoning *a priori*, the specific dynamics of labour markets – and particularly search behaviour by workers – may indeed formally produce upward-sloping labour supply curves faced by most individual firms *in the short run*: see Mortensen (1970). On the longer-run supply behaviour of dynamic models, however, it is much more difficult to get simple general results on purely theoretical grounds, so that any firm conclusion must come from case-by-case empirical analysis.

Static Monopsony in a Labour Market

A monopsonist employer maximises profits with employment L, that equates demand, given by the *MRP* curve, to marginal cost *MC* at point *A*.

The wage is then determined on the supply curve, at point *M*, and is equal to w. By contrast, a competitive labour market would reach equilibrium at point *C*, where supply *S* equals demand. This would lead to employment L' and wage w'.

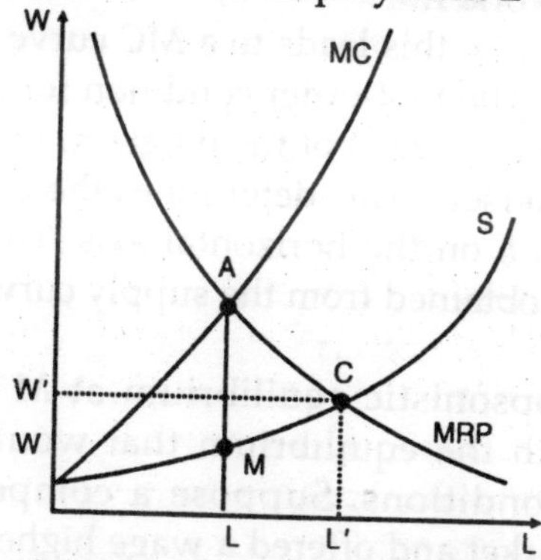

The standard textbook monopsony model refers to static partial equilibrium in a labour market with just one employer who pays the same wage to all its workers. In this model, the employer is assumed to be a firm facing an upward-sloping *labour supply curve,* represented by the *S* blue curve in the diagram on the right.

This curve relates the wage paid, w, to the level of employment, L, and is denoted as the increasing function $w(L)$. Total labour costs are then given by $w(L)L$. Assume now that the firm has a total revenue R, which increases with L according to the concave function $R(L)$. It wants to choose L to maximise profits, which are given by:

$$R(L) - w(L)L$$

This leads to the first-order condition:

$$R'(L) = w(L) + w'(L)L$$

The left-hand side of this expression is the *marginal revenue product* of labour (roughly, the extra revenue produced by an extra worker) and is represented by the red *MRP* curve in the diagram. The right-hand side is the *marginal cost* of labour (roughly, the extra cost due to an extra worker) and is represented by the green *MC* curve in the diagram. It should be noticed that this marginal cost is *higher* than the wage $w(L)$ paid to the new worker by the amount

$$w'(L)L$$

This is due to the fact that the firm has to increase the wage paid to all the workers it already employs whenever it hires an extra worker.

In the diagram, this leads to a *MC* curve that is *above* the supply curve *S*. The first-order condition for maximum profit is then satisfied at point *A* of the diagram, where the *MC* and *MRP* curves intersect. This determines the profit-maximising employment as *L* on the horizontal axis. The corresponding wage *w* is then obtained from the supply curve, through point *M*.

The monopsonistic equilibrium at *M* should now be contrasted with the equilibrium that would obtain under competitive conditions. Suppose a competitor employer entered the market and offered a wage higher than that at *M*. Then every employee of the first employer would choose instead to work for the competitor.

Moreover, the competitor would gain all the former profits of the first employer, minus a less-than-offsetting amount from the wage increase of the first employer's employees, plus profits arising from additional employees who decided to work in the market because of the wage increase.

But the first employer would respond by offering an even higher wage, poaching the new rival's employees, and so forth. In other words, a group of perfectly competitive firms would be forced, through competition, to intersection *C* rather than *M*. Just as a monopoly is thwarted by the competition to win sales, minimizing prices and maximizing output, competition for employees between the employers in this case would maximize both wages and employment, as shown in the graph.

Welfare Implications

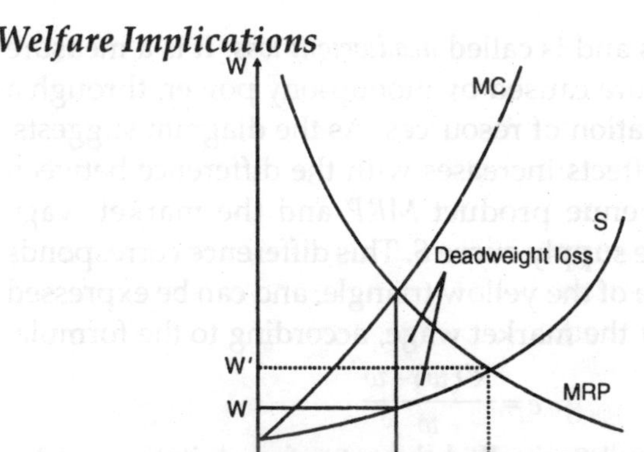

The grey rectangle is a measure of the amount of economic welfare transferred from the workers to their employer(s) by monopsony power. The yellow triangle shows the *overall deadweight loss* inflicted on both groups by the monopsonistic restriction of employment. It is thus a measure of the *market failure* caused by monopsony. The lower employment and wage caused by monopsony power has two distinct effects on the economic welfare of the people involved. First, it redistributes welfare away from workers and to their employer(s). Secondly, it reduces the aggregate (or social) welfare enjoyed by both groups taken together, as the employers' net gain is smaller than the loss inflicted on workers. The diagram on the right illustrates both effects, using the standard approach based on the notion of *economic surplus*. According to this notion, the workers' economic surplus (or net gain from the exchange) is given by the area between the *S* curve and the horizontal line corresponding to the wage, up to the employment level. Similarly, the employers' surplus is the area between the horizontal line corresponding to the wage and the *MRP* curve, up to the employment level. The *social* surplus is then the sum of these two areas.

Following such definitions, the grey rectangle in the diagram is the part of the competitive social surplus that has been redistributed from the workers to their employer(s) under monopsony. By contrast, the yellow triangle is the part of the competitive social surplus that has been lost by *both* parties, as a result of the monopsonistic restriction of employment. This is a net social loss and is called *deadweight loss*. It is a measure of the market failure caused by monopsony power, through a wasteful misallocation of resources. As the diagram suggests, the size of both effects increases with the difference between the marginal revenue product *MRP* and the market wage determined on the supply curve *S*. This difference corresponds to the vertical side of the yellow triangle, and can be expressed as a proportion of the market wage, according to the formula:

$$e = \frac{R'(w) - w}{w}$$

The ratio *e* has been called the rate of exploitation, and it can be easily shown that it equals the reciprocal of the elasticity of the labour supply curve faced by the firm. Thus the rate of exploitation is zero under competitive conditions, when this elasticity tends to infinity. Empirical estimates of *e* by various means are a common feature of the applied literature devoted to the measurement of observed monopsony power.

Finally, it is important to notice that, while the grey-area redistribution effect could be reversed by fiscal policy (i.e., taxing employers and transferring the tax revenue to the workers), this is not so for the yellow-area deadweight loss. The market failure can only be addressed in one of two ways: either by breaking up the monopsony through anti-trust intervention, or by regulating the wage policy of firms. The most common kind of regulation is a binding minimum wage higher than the monopsonistic wage.

Minimum Wage

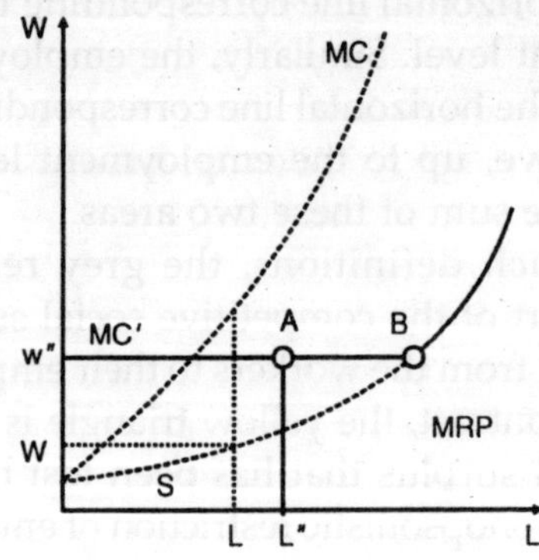

With a binding minimum wage of w'' the marginal cost to the firm becomes the horizontal black MC' line, and the firm maximises profits at A with a higher employment L''. However in this example the minimum wage is higher than the competitive one, leading to *involuntary unemployment* equal to the segment AB.

A binding minimum wage can be introduced either by law or through collective bargaining, and its possible effects in a special case are shown in the diagram on the right. Here the minimum wage is w'', higher than the monopsonistic w. At this given wage the firm can now hire all the workers it wants, up to the supply curve, so that in the relevant employment range its marginal cost of labour becomes effectively constant and equal to w'', as shown by the new black horizontal line MC'. Hence the firm maximises profits at the new intersection point A, choosing the employment level L'', which is higher than the monopsonistic level L. As the reader can check, the rate of exploitation has been reduced to zero.

More generally, a binding minimum wage modifies the form of the supply curve faced by the firm, which becomes:

$$w = \begin{cases} w_{\min}, & \text{if } w_{\min} \geq w(L) \\ w(L), & \text{if } w_{\min} \leq w(L) \end{cases}$$

where $w(L)$ is the original supply curve and w_{min} is the minimum wage. The new curve has thus a horizontal first branch and a kink at the point

$$w(L) = w_{min}$$

as is shown in the diagram by the kinked black curve MC' S. The resulting equilibria can then fall into one of three classes or regimes, according to the value taken by the minimum wage, as is seen by the following table:

Table. Minimum-wage Regimes in Monopsonistic Labour Markets

	Minimum wage	*Resulting equilibrium*
First regime	not higher than monopsony wage	unchanged from monopsony
Second regime	higher than monopsony wagebutnot	at kink of

	higher than competitive wage	supply curve
Third regime	higher than competitive wage	at intersection where minimum wage equals *MRP*

As it is now seen, the example illustrated by the diagram belongs to the third regime. As a result, there is an excess supply of labour – i.e. *involuntary unemployment* – equal to the segment *AB*. So, although the exploitation rate has vanished, there is still a deadweight loss to society. This illustrates the problems that may arise when the proper level of the binding minimum wage is not exactly known, or cannot be enforced for political reasons.

Yet, even when it is sub-optimal, a minimum wage higher than the market rate raises the level of employment anyway. This is a highly remarkable result, because it only follows under monopsony. Indeed, under competitive conditions any minimum wage higher than the market rate would actually *reduce* employment. Thus, spotting the effects on employment of newly introduced minimum wage regulations is among the indirect ways economists use to pin down monopsony power in selected labour markets.

Wage Discrimination

Just like a monopolist, a monopsonistic employer may find that its profits are maximised if it *discriminates* prices. In this case this means paying different wages to different groups of workers even if their MRP is the same, with lower wages paid to the workers who have a lower elasticity of supply of their labour to the firm. Some researchers have tried to use this fact to explain at least part of the observed wage differentials whereby women earn often less than men, even after controlling for observed productivity differentials. However, all such attempts have had to contend with the statistical fact that in most cases women actually display a *higher* labour supply elasticity than men.

Some authors have argued informally that, while this is so for *market* supply, the reverse may somehow be true of the supply to individual firms. In particular, Manning and others have shown that, in the case of the UK Equal Pay Act, implementation has led to higher employment of women. Since the Act was effectively minimum wage legislation for women, this might perhaps be interpreted as a symptom of monopsonistic discrimination.

Dynamic Problems

In many real-world situations a monopsonist firm will have to maximise its profits *through time*, rather than instantaneously as in the previous static model. In all such cases, any short-run outcomes will have to be balanced against longer-run ones, and the resulting equilibrium may differ.

The simplest dynamic model to bring out this idea, used in Boal and Ransom (1997), is one where the supply of labour to the firm reacts to wage changes with a lag, due for instance to information costs and search behaviour. Assume hence that the supply function has a distributed-lag specification, leading to:

$$L_t = L(w_t, L_{t-1}),$$

where the subscript refers to the time period and L is increasing in both arguments. Inverting this function gives:

$$w_t = w_t(Lt, L_{t-1}),$$

with $\frac{\partial w_t}{\partial L_t} \geq 0$

and $\frac{\partial w_t}{\partial L_{t-1}} \leq 0$.

If the firm has a time-discount rate r, the present value of profits is now given by:

$$\sum_{t=1}^{\infty}\left[R_t(L_t) - w_t(L_t, L_{t-1})L_t\right]\left(\frac{1}{1+r}\right)^{t-1}$$

The tth first-order condition to maximise this present value is:

$$\frac{dR_t}{dL_t} - w_t - \frac{\partial w_t}{\partial L_t}L_t - \frac{\partial w_{t+1}}{\partial L_t}\frac{L_{t+1}}{1+r} = 0$$

Define next the short-run simultaneous and lagged inverse supply elasticities respectively as:

$$\in_{SR}^{-1} \underline{\underline{\text{def}}} \frac{\partial w_t L_t}{\partial L_t w_t}, \quad \in_{SRL}^{-1} \underline{\underline{\text{def}}} \frac{\partial w_{t+1}}{\partial L_t}\frac{L_t}{w_{t+1}}$$

Now, assume these elasticities to be constant over time.

Assume further a steady state, with $L_t = L_{t+1}$ and $w_t = w_{t+1}$. Then the first-order condition gives the exploitation rate as:

$$e_t \underline{\underline{\text{def}}} \frac{MRP_t - w_t}{w_t} = \epsilon_{SR}^{-1} + \frac{\epsilon_{SRL}^{-1}}{1+r}$$

Finally, the steady-state long-run inverse elasticity, ϵ_{LR}^{-1}, is given by the sum of the two short-run inverse elasticities defined above, and so one has:

$$e_t = \epsilon_{SR}^{-1}\left(\frac{r}{1+r}\right) + \epsilon_{LR}^{-1}\left(\frac{1}{1+r}\right)$$

The exploitation rate is thus a weighted average of the short- and long-run inverse supply elasticities, where the weight of the long-run one is much bigger, because r is much smaller than unity even when the discounting period is one year. It follows that, as the long-run (direct) supply elasticity of labour tends to be much higher than the short-run one, this very simple dynamic model predicts an exploitation rate which is much smaller than the one produced by static analysis.

However, less simplified dynamic models tell less simple stories. Even the employment effect of minimum wages is not as clear cut as static models would have.

Empirical Problems

The simplified dynamics sketched above suggests that the frequent observation of short-run relative inelasticity of labour supply to individual firms may not be very relevant to the diagnosis of significant monopsony power. Efforts to measure the size of the exploitation rate in specific labour markets have hence taken various forms:

- Direct measurement of wage and MRP
- Estimates of the long-run supply elasticity of labour to firms
- Cross-sectional comparisons of wages and employer concentration
- Correlations between wages and workers' mobility
- Structural estimation of equilibrium search models
- Employment effects of minimum wages

The results of these empirical works are rarely unambiguous.

However, even in cases such as coal miners or nurses, most US studies suggest rates of exploitation probably lower than marginal tax rates on workers' incomes, or union relative wage effects. The better documented instances of significant exploitation are found in the probably rare cases of explicit collusion, such as US baseball before the reserve clause.

Sources of Labour Monopsony Power

The simpler explanation of monopsony power in labour markets is barriers to entry on the *demand* side. In all such cases, oligopsony would result from oligopoly in the product markets of the industries that use that type of labour as input. If the hypothesis was generally true, one would then find a positive statistical correlation between exploitation, on one side, and industry concentration and firm size on the other. However, numerous statistical studies document significant positive correlations between firm or establishment size and *wages*. These results, by themselves inconsistent with the oligopoly-oligopsony hypothesis, may be due to the prevalence of other factors, such as efficiency wages.

However, monopsony power might also be due to circumstances affecting entry of workers on the *supply* side, directly reducing the elasticity of labour supply to firms. Paramount among these are moving costs for workers, which are also a cause of differentiation among potential employees, possibly leading to discrimination. But a similar effect might also be produced by all the institutional factors that limit labour mobility between firms, including job protection legislation.

Finally, as already noticed, a significant reduction in the short-run elasticity of supply may come from information costs and search behaviour. An alternative that has been suggested as a source of monopsony power is worker preferences over job characteristics. Such job characteristics can include distance from work, type of work, location, the social environment at work, etc. If different workers have different preferences, employers have local monopsony power over workers that strongly prefer working for them.

Monopsony in Product Markets

The same or similar empirical difficulties dog the attempts to identify significant monopsony in non-labour markets, and specifically in markets for intermediate goods bought as inputs by very large firms. Among the most likely US candidates, one finds in the literature:

- *Trade in technological knowledge*: Rodriguez (1975)
- *Tomatoes for tomato processing*: Just and Chern (1980)
- *Beef for the beef packing industry*: Schroeter (1988)
- *Western coal for electric utilities*: Atkinson and Kerkvliet (1989)
- *Pulpwood and sawlogs*: Murray (1995)
- Sophisticated weaponry (i.e. jet fighters, tanks, artillery, etc.)

A related issue is the role of monopsony power from the point of view of anti-trust policy affecting vertical integrations. It has been argued that vertical integration by a monopsony – whereby the production of the previously bought input becomes an in-house operation – may reduce or eliminate the inefficiencies due to monopsonistic restriction of purchases.

In Australia, the Pharmaceutical Industry can be viewed as a kind of monopsony, as the Commonwealth government is the principle buyer of products through the Pharmaceutical Benefits Scheme (PBS) In the US, several, including *Harper's* and the PBS Programmeme *Frontline,* have made the case case is that Wal-Mart is a monopsonist, dictating terms to suppliers, whilst at the same time a monopolist dictating terms to consumers - at least in certain market segments.

Asymmetry Information

Asymmetric Information: is where one person has economically relevant information that another person does not have. In economics, information asymmetry occurs when one party to a transaction has more or better information than the other party. (It has also been called asymmetrical information). Typically it is the seller that knows more about the product than the buyer, however, it is possible for the reverse to be true: for the buyer to know more than the seller.

In situations of asymmetric information, the allocation of resources will not be economically efficient. The asymmetry can be resolved directly through appraisal or indirectly through screening, signaling, or contingent payments. The indirect methods depend on inducing self-selection among parties with different characteristics. Screening is an initiative of the party with less information, while signaling is an initiative of the party with better information.

A key business application of screening is indirect segment discrimination in pricing. A related application is auctions, which exploit strategic interaction among competing bidders to force bidders with higher values to pay higher prices. When the distribution of information is asymmetric, one or more parties will have imperfect information and hence bear risk. The distribution of risk may conflict with the self-selection needed to resolve the asymmetric information.

Information asymmetry models assume that at least one party to a transaction has relevant information whereas the other(s) do not. Some asymmetric information models can also be used in situations where at least one party can enforce, or effectively retaliate for breaches of, certain parts of an agreement whereas the other(s) cannot. In adverse selection models the ignorant party lacks information while negotiating an agreed understanding of or contract to the transaction, whereas in moral hazard the ignorant party lacks information about performance of the agreed-upon transaction or lacks the ability to retaliate for a breach of the agreement.

An example of moral hazard is when people are more likely to behave recklessly if insured, either because the insurer cannot observe this behaviour or cannot effectively retaliate against it, for example by failing to renew the insurance. An example of adverse selection is when people who are high risk are more likely to buy insurance, because the insurance company cannot effectively discriminate against them, usually due to lack of information about the particular individual's risk but also sometimes by force of law or other constraints.

Imperfect information: the absence of certain knowledge by a single person or by more than one party. Risk (uncertainty about benefits or costs) arises whenever there is imperfect information about something that affects benefits or costs.

Note: a person can have imperfect information about something, but if that thing does not affect her/his benefits or costs, it does not impose any risk on her/him.

A risk averse person is one who prefers a certain amount to risky amounts with the same expected value. A risk-neutral person is indifferent. Insurance is the business of taking certain payments in exchange for eliminating risk. A market could be perfectly competitive even when buyers and sellers have imperfect information, as long as they all have the same imperfect information.

Asymmetric information: one party has better information than another, e.g., antiques, insurance, and lending markets. When the distribution of information is asymmetric, one or more parties will have imperfect information and hence bear risk. Cannot be a perfectly competitive market. In an imperfectly competitively market, if buyers and sellers can resolve the information asymmetries, they can increase benefits by more than their costs

Index